Also by Vladimir Pericliev

MACHINE-AIDED LINGUISTIC DISCOVERY: An Introduction and Some Examples

PROFILING LANGUAGE FAMILIES BY THEIR KIN TERM PATTERNS: A Computational Approach

Componential Analysis of Kinship Terminology

Componential Analysis of Kinship Terminology

A Computational Perspective

Vladimir Pericliev

Bulgarian Academy of Sciences, Sofia

First published 2013 by
PALGRAVE MACMILLAN

Palgrave Macmillan in the UK is an imprint of Macmillan Publishers Limited, registered in England, company number 785998, of Houndmills, Basingstoke, Hampshire RG21 6XS.

Palgrave Macmillan in the US is a division of St Martin's Press LLC, 175 Fifth Avenue, New York, NY 10010.

Palgrave Macmillan is the global academic imprint of the above companies and has companies and representatives throughout the world.

Palgrave® and Macmillan® are registered trademarks in the United States, the United Kingdom, Europe and other countries.

ISBN 978–1–137–03117–4

Contents

List of tables in the Appendix

Preface

The notion of 'system' is central in all post-Saussurean linguistics, and componential analysis is the method for exposing the systems of linguistic entities. In componential analysis, the meaning (or value) of the entities forming a system is described as a conjunction of smaller components that are necessary and jointly sufficient to distinguish each entity in the system from all others. Componential analysis originated in phonology, but the approach was naturally extended also to the other levels of linguistic analysis: grammar and semantics. Componential analysis of kinship terminology, which lies at the crossroads of linguistics and anthropology, is the prototype example from semantics.

The early influential work on kinship semantics by Lounsbury, Goodenough and others laid the foundations of the field and was followed by numerous attempts to reveal the semantic structure of kin terms in various 'exotic' languages, hoping to understand the meaning and use of the terms, and more optimistically, to highlight the categorization and world view of native speakers. The topic flourished for several decades, but as happens all too often in science, after this peak the method became somewhat less visible in published work. Nevertheless the approach was not abandoned altogether: in linguistics, it continued to be quite regularly used in semantic analyses of various theoretical persuasions, and in anthropology, 'formal analysis' (as the componential method is usually referred to in anthropology) continued to be an indispensable part of kin term studies. This persistence in methodology is understandable insofar as rejecting the method basically implies rejecting the fundamental idea of system in linguistics. Additionally, the semantic structure arrived at by componential analysis, as is well known, is important for constructing dictionary definitions, for translation purposes, and for historical reconstruction.

A major goal of the present book is to critically review previous conceptions of the method and improve on previous practice of componential analysis of kin terms by setting the problem in a computational perspective. Two basic problems are isolated in previous work: the consistency of componential models, and their indeterminacy. Regarding the first problem, I will try to show, with examples

ix

from the literature, that not infrequently proposed models are inconsistent in that they do not provide definitions of kin terms with necessary and sufficient conditions. Thus, some definitions of kin terms fail to discriminate them from the rest of the terms (failing sufficiency), whereas others contain redundant components (failing necessity). This problem has evaded previous analysts, which is no surprise, given that componential analysis is a computationally complex task (strictly speaking, NP-complete), and there existed no computational means at the time of testing proposed models. The second problem, indeterminacy, in contrast, attracted much attention owing to Robbins Burling, who warned against the existence of multiple models of the same data set and the difficulty (or even impossibility) of choosing among equally 'valid' alternatives, this circumstance putting the method in jeopardy. Dell Hymes and others objected to this view, suggesting that further constraints from the studied culture, simplicity, etc. would normally constrain the choices, but as a result of this debate no consensus was arrived at, except that what was needed were concrete empirical tests of complete kinship vocabularies rather than simplified examples and programmatic and theoretical arguments. No such empirical evidence or explicit formulation of constraints were presented to support either view, and again, the reason was the absence of computational aids to process reliably large terminological data sets.

This book describes a computer program, called KINSHIP, developed by Dr Raúl Valdés Pérez (Carnegie Mellon University) and the present author. The program is designed to resolve the above problems and, more generally, to serve as a computational tool for conducting componential analysis of kin terms. The program accepts as input the standard linguistic data, viz. the kin terms of a language with their attendant kin types (=relatives), and can generate all consistent alternative analyses (thus providing the empirical bases for evaluating the degree of indeterminacy). Additionally, the program introduces intuitive simplicity constraints on dimensions and components in kin term definitions in order to diminish, or even eliminate, multiple solutions (thus attempting to resolve the indeterminacy problem). In the book, I apply this computational machinery to complete kinship vocabularies of particular languages. The results show, first, that completely unconstrained analyses, targeting only necessary and sufficient conditions, yield an astronomical number of componential models (in accord with Burling's warning), but second, that the introduction of our natural simplicity constraints reduces this number significantly, even to unique models (tipping the balance in the direction of the opposing camp). In effect, the operation of the KINSHIP program on concrete data from a sizable number of languages (from Indo-European and other language families) presents strong support for the power and usefulness of the method.

Our system is a sophisticated general tool for multiple-concept discrimination and therefore can be used for componential analysis of other than the kinship domain (for instance, in phonological distinctive feature analysis). Thus, for the first time after almost a century following the introduction of the concept of system and structuralism in general, linguists are capable of handling adequately the task of componential analysis, generally recognized as creative and difficult. Revealing the distinctive features of phonological and kinship systems are tasks of well-known complexity; regarding the latter, Leech (1974) for instance writes that 'kinship analyses have a mind-teasing quality of mathematical puzzles. The only cure for bafflement is to think hard and hope that the light will dawn!'

Acknowledgments

This book would have hardly been possible without the efforts of my friend and collaborator computer scientist Raúl Valdés Pérez. It was he who implemented the first version of KINSHIP, which allowed me to implement my own versions of the system (in another programming language) and continue with the linguistic investigations reported here, for which I am much indebted to him. I also gratefully acknowledge financial support for my studies on kinship terminology over the years from the International Program of the US National Science Foundation, as well as from the Bulgarian Ministry of Education and Science. Last but not least, acknowledgement is due to the Institute for Mathematics and Informatics of the Bulgarian Academy of Sciences, where I conducted much of the reported work.

1
Introduction: the historical background

This chapter looks at componential analysis of kinship terminologies from a historical perspective. The underlying ideas and the basic notions of componential analysis are introduced, as described by the pioneers of the field, and some alternative approaches to describing the semantics of kinship terms are briefly sketched.

1.1 General

Every known human language has a kinship terminological system, but different languages have different organizations of these terminological systems; hence the interest of linguists and anthropologists in studying these systems. In his pioneering book *Systems of Consanguinity and Affinity of the Human Family* Henry Lewis Morgan (1871) made extensive studies of kinship terminologies of the world languages and their reflection in the social structure of society, and this work was extended and enriched by other scholars, notably anthropologist George Peter Murdock (1949). In this tradition, the meaning of kin terms in foreign languages is represented by a primitive English term (for instance 'mother, 'father', etc.), a relative product of two or more primitive terms (for instance 'mother's father') or a collection of primitive and/or relative product terms, where each primitive term and each relative product denotes a 'kin type'. This type of notation alone, useful as it is for constructing typologies of kinship terms (such as Hawaiian, Eskimo, Crow, etc. already discovered by Morgan), poses certain difficulties to the analyst regarding the important question of what the common pieces of meaning of all the kin types are that allow them to be covered by a single kin term, or what the principles of classification are of kinship in the society the anthropologist/linguist is studying. This question is

1

addressed by 'componential analysis', a formal procedure developed in linguistics for other purposes, and based on the Saussurian idea of 'linguistic system'.

In his *Course in General Linguistics* (*Cours de linguistique générale*, 1916), Ferdinand de Saussure created a general linguistic theory at the heart of which lay the notion of 'linguistic system' (see the brief review in Pericliev 2010: 2–3). Language (*langue*), according to Saussure, is a system in the sense that the meaning or value (*valeur*) of all linguistic entities can only be determined by their contrasts, or distinctions, from all other entities in the same system. '*In the language itself, there are only differences*', wrote Saussure (1996[1916]: 118; italics in original), 'A linguistic system is a series of phonetic differences matched with a series of conceptual differences' (p. 118). The basic task of linguistics, then, is to reveal the structure of linguistic systems by applying the structural method of contrasts and oppositions.

Saussure's idea of language as a system broke a long tradition in Western thought dominant from Plato on, of viewing language as just an inventory of names (whatever they stood for, ideas or things in the external world), and the goal of language science as relating these names (whether derived from the true nature of things or by convention) to ready-made ideas and things given in advance of language. Saussure, in contrast to this view, conceived language not as a mere collection of discrete items, but as a highly organized totality (or, a *Gestalt*), in which the items are interrelated and derive their meaning from the system as a whole. Thus, he writes:

> In all these cases, what we find, instead of *ideas* given in advance, are *values* emanating from the linguistic system. If we say that these values correspond to certain concepts, it must be understood that the concepts in question are purely differential. That is to say they are concepts defined not positively, in terms of their content, but negatively by contrast with other items in the same system. What characterises each most exactly is being whatever the others are not. [Saussure 1996[1916]: 115; italics in original]

The importance of the idea of language as a system, and structuralism in general, cannot be overstated. It influenced researchers both in linguistics and outside of linguistics. Within linguistics, the structural method came to be recognized as an indispensable tool at all levels of linguistic analysis: phonology ('distinctive feature analysis'), semantics ('structural semantics'), morphology, etc. Transformationalists (especially Chomsky) emphasized that formal, generative grammar as a whole is a 'systemic notion' in that a simplification in some component leads to more complexities in another component. Also, the idea gave rise to different linguistic trends like the Prague school (Trubetzkoy, Jakobson), the Copenhagen school (Hjelmslev) and American structuralism (Bloomfield, Bloch, Harris, etc.). Outside of linguistics, the principles and methods of structuralism were adopted by scholars of such diverse areas as anthropology (Claude Lévi-Strauss), psychoanalysis (Lacan) and literary criticism (Barthes) and were implemented in their respective areas of study. According to Assiter (1984), there are four common ideas regarding structuralism that form an 'intellectual trend'. First, the structure is what determines the position of each element of a whole. Second, structuralists believe that every system has a structure. Third, structuralists are interested in 'structural' laws that deal with coexistence rather than changes. And, finally, structures are the 'real things' that lie beneath the surface or the appearance of meaning.

The Saussurian idea of system, and the related formal procedures developed in linguistics for discovering oppositions in phonological and semantic systems, were transferred by direct analogy to componential analysis of kinship terminologies. The pioneers in the field, Floyd Lounsbury and Ward Goodenough, readily acknowledge this. Thus, in a seminal article in *Language*, Lounsbury states that 'The aim of this paper is to point out a relatively simple problem in semantics which can be analysed by means of techniques analogous to those already developed in linguistics [...]' (Lounsbury 1956: 158–9). Goodenough, analogously, refers to the utility and rigour of the procedures already developed in linguistics:

Inspiration [...] has come largely from accomplishments of linguistic science. Linguists are able to produce elegant and accurate representations of what one has to know in phonology and grammar if one is to speak particular languages acceptably by native standards. Their procedures enable them to replicate one another's work readily. Application of the basic strategies of descriptive linguistics to the problem of describing other facets of culture is helping to raise the standards of rigor in ethnographic description. These strategies include what is best described as contrastive analysis. Its use for describing how people classify phenomena, insofar as their classifications are reflected in the vocabulary of their language, has led to the analytic method described here. (Goodenough 1967: 1203)

The following section describes the method of componential analysis of kinship vocabularies in more detail.

1.2   Componential analysis of kinship terminological systems: the basic notions

The method of componential analysis was introduced into kinship semantics basically through the work of anthropologists Lounsbury and Goodenough (Goodenough 1956, 1964, 1967; Lounsbury 1956, 1964, 1965; but see also Greenberg 1949; Wallace and Atkins 1960; Hammel 1965; Leech 1974, and more recently, Geeraerts 2010; Bernard 2011).

1.2.1   Kin terms and kin types

The *kin terms* of a language, such as English *mother, aunt, son-in-law,* etc., are linguistic labels for a range of *kin types* (= denotata), which specify the genealogical position of one's kin with respect to oneself. In the following, we shall use the following standard abbreviations (Murdock 1949) of atomic genealogical relationships in terms of which the kin types are expressed:

Fa = 'father', Mo = 'mother', Br = 'brother', Si = 'sister',

So = 'son', Da = 'daughter', Hu = 'husband', and Wi = 'wife'.

(Another common notation for the atomic relationships is: F = father, M = mother, B = brother, Z = sister, S = son, D = daughter, H = husband, W = wife.)

Additional symbols may be used to specify relative age or sex of the speaker, for instance:

y = younger, e = elder; m = male ego, f = female ego

These atomic relationships are juxtaposed to express more distant kin types (relatives), as for example, MoBr 'mother's brother', MoSi 'mother's sister', MoSiHu 'mother's sister's husband', MoBre 'mother's elder brother', etc.

The meaning of kin terms is represented by all kin types, or relatives, covered by the term. For example, the (simplified) meaning of the English term *uncle* is FaBr and MoBr. The set of all kin terms in a language is the *kinship vocabulary* of the language.

In the terminology of Charles Morris, used by Lounsbury and Goodenough, the kin types are known as the *denotata* of a kin term, and the range of meaning, or the class of all denotata of a kin term, are known as the *designatum* of the term. The (componential) definition of a kin term, in this terminology, is often referred to as the *significatum* of the term, and I turn to this notion in the next subsection.

1.2.2 Componential definitions of kin terms

A kin term may be viewed as a class and the kin types, covered by the term, as elements of this class. In principle, there are two ways to define a class: either by enumerating the elements of the class, or by giving the 'defining features' of the class, that is to say, the necessary and sufficient conditions for membership in the class. This is analogous to the procedures in phonology, where a given phoneme is defined either by listing the allophonic types which belong to it (in which case we are defining it by enumeration), or by a specific bundle of distinctive phonetic features (in which case we are defining it in the second way). The first mode of definition reveals one aspect of the structure of the system, viz. how the kinship semantic field is segmented by the kin types. This definition, however, does not exhibit the underlying principles of organization. This underlying structure can only be revealed if we can proceed by definitions in terms of distinctive semantic features and each kin term is assigned a bundle of features, demarcating each kin term from all remaining kin terms in the kinship vocabulary of a language. Componential analysis is concerned with definitions in terms of distinctive semantic features (or with the significatum of the terms). These are the necessary and sufficient conditions for discrimination.

There is general consensus on this point – for example, Lounsbury writes '[the] bundle of features states the necessary and sufficient conditions which an object must satisfy if it is to be a *denotatum* of the term so defined' (1964: 1074); see also 'A significatum is a statement of various necessary and sufficient conditions for a kin type to belong to the class of kin types denoted by a term' (Wallace and Atkins 1960: 67).

Another essential feature of componential definitions is their *conjunctiveness*. Such a definition is a Boolean class product, which is a conjunctive (or 'unitary') definition. It is assumed in the field that kin terms are susceptible to such representations. Componential analysis is performed starting with definitions of kin terms by their attendant kin types (extensional definitions) and aims to arrive at definitions by distinctive semantic features (intensional definitions). We note that disjunctive definitions would generally be conceived as a major short-coming by kinship analysts, Lounsbury for example writing on this topic:

> We feel that we have failed if we cannot achieve conjunctive def-initions for every terminological class in the system. Were we to compromise on this point and admit disjunctive definitions (class sums, alternative criteria for membership) as on a par with conjunc-tive definitions (class products, uniform criteria for membership), there would be no motivation for analysis in the first place, for def-initions of kin classes by summing of discrete members. [...] . are disjunctive definitions par excellence. (Lounsbury 1964: 1074)

There is also empirical evidence that kin terms are actually con-junctive notions, coming from typological studies. Thus, in a study of grandparent terminology (Greenberg 1966), involving the four kin types FaFa, MoFa, FaMo, and MoMo, fifteen grandparental kin terms are pos-sible, resulting from the different groupings of the kin types. Of these fifteen possible kin terms, it was found, inspecting about one hundred languages, that four did not actually occur in the sample, and these were exactly the kin terms that involved logically disjunctive defini-tions. Impressive results in this vein were found for sibling terminology as well (Nerlove and Romney 1967; Kronenfeld 1974; Epling, Kirk and Boyd 1973).

1.2.3   Dimensions, or features of contrast

What are the dimensions, or features of contrast, serving to demarcate the kin terms in a kinship vocabulary? There is great diversity in struc-turing human societies and kinship terminology is, accordingly, diverse. In a widely known paper 'Classificatory systems of relationship', Alfred Kroeber (1909) writes: 'It is apparent that what we should try to deal with is not the hundreds or thousands of slightly varying relationships that are expressed or can be expressed by the various languages of man, but the principles or categories of relationship which underlie these. Eight such categories are discernible.' He then describes and explains a set of contrasts, or oppositions, existing between kin terms of the languages of the world: (1) differences of generation; (2) the difference between lineal and collateral kinsmen, and different degrees of collater-ality; (3) differences of age within one generation; (4) sex of kinsman; (5) sex of ego; (6) sex of linking kinsman; (7) the difference between consanguineal and affinal relationships; and (8) the condition, living or deceased, of the linking kinsman.

It was found by some of the later researchers in the field that Kroeber's features generally suffice for analyses of a range of very diverse languages. Thus, for instance, Lounsbury (1956) writes that although some of these have been found to require modification or further elaboration in specific instances, this list is still a good guide and he used it in his analysis of the Pawnee data he examined. Other analysts assume a wider range of dimensions, or features, than those envisioned by Kroeber as constituting a standard for anthropological work. Goodenough (1967), for example, notes that although all kinship terminology, by definition, must employ features that reflect properties of the genealogical space (like sex, generation, etc.), the particular terminologies he had investigated required additional features reflecting the social life of the studied communities (like clan, kin group membership, etc.). The first type of dimensions are universal, while the second are specific to the culture, so one cannot avoid using relevant cultural information.

1.2.4 Meaning

There are many facets to the 'meaning' of a word, a well-known dichotomy being that between referential (definitional) and connotational meaning. The aspect of meaning that componential analysis deals with is reference as distinct from connotation. What is meant by these terms is explained for instance by Goodenough (1956) in the following fashion:

> [...] the significatum [referential meaning] of a linguistic form is composed of those abstracted contextual elements with which it is in perfect association, without which it cannot properly occur. Its connotata are the contextual elements with which it is frequently but less than perfectly associated. Significata are prerequisites while connotata are probabilities and possibilities. Only the former have definitive value. (Goodenough 1956: 195)

Within referential meaning of kin terms, additionally, the difference between 'terms of reference' and 'address (or, vocative) terms' is recognized, both modes legitimately being subjected to componential analysis.

Non-kin uses of words, such as 'priest' for the term *father*, are excluded from consideration (this meaning of *father* cannot be represented in terms of the primitives Fa, Mo, etc.). Synonymous terms like *father, dad, daddy, pop, old man,* etc. normally receive identical componential definition in practical exercises of the method, although they may have different colloquial uses (i.e. such meaning nuances are ignored).

A more complex situation is provided by *homonymy* or *polysemy* of kin terms. Most kin terms are usually defined (extensionally) by a set of two or more kin types, or denotata, as for instance *uncle* as FaBr, MoBr etc. However, kinship analysts do not regard this fact a priori as homonymy/polysemy – such an analysis would require giving two or more componential definitions to the kin term. Rather, the very idea of componential analysis is to uncover the commonalities of meaning of all attendant kin types of a kin term, so that in this case, for example, all users of the language classify all these kin types under the single label *uncle.* On some occasions, viz. when finding such commonalities of meaning shared by all kin types of a kin term is possible within the framework of the set of dimensions, or contrasting features, employed in the analysis, the preferred move is to have just one rather than more than one componential definition. On other occasions, when this is not possible, analysts (reluctantly) either recourse to disjunctive componential definitions or alternatively split the kin term into several 'homonymous' lexemes, and give each a separate (conjunctive) componential definition.

1.2.5 Steps in componential analysis

The task of the linguist is to determine the relevant conditions for distinguishing the meaning of any of the kin terms within the semantic field from any other. Componential analysis, as commonly conceived, consists of the following steps:

(1) The linguist isolates the kin terms of a language, and identifies the range of reference of each by a list of kin types (denotata), expressed in terms of the above primary relationships symbols. Thus the range of the kin term *uncle* (somewhat narrowly conceived) can be specified as the disjunction: FaBr 'father's brother' or MoBr 'mother's brother' or FaSiHu 'father's sister's husband' or MoSiHu 'mother's sister's husband'.

(2) The significant dimensions of contrast, or the overall 'contrasting features', are found, which are sufficient to describe the kinship vocabulary.

(3) Finally, a 'conjunctive definition' of each kin term in the kinship vocabulary is produced, in which the meaning of any one term is distinguished from the meaning of every other term by at least one

contrasting feature. (Notice again that, in contrast, the definition of kin terms in terms of their denotata is a *disjunctive* one, for example *uncle* is FaBr *or* MoBr *or* FaSiHu, etc.)

As a simple illustration of the method, we may consider a set of English consanguineals (i.e. terms for blood relatives) in their referential sense, and perform a componential analysis of their meanings, following in broad outline Wallace and Atkins (1960). At Step 1, the selection of the terms *grandfather, grandmother, father, mother, brother, sister, son, daughter, grandson, granddaughter, uncle, aunt, cousin, nephew, niece* is made, which are commonly used in English to refer to consanguineal kinsmen. These kin terms are associated with a list of kin types (denotata), expressed in terms of the above primary relationships symbols Fa, Mo, Br, Si, So, Da, resulting in:

grandfather: FaFa ∨ MoFa
grandmother: FaMo ∨ MoMo
father: Fa
mother: Mo
brother: Br
sister: Si
son: So
daughter: Da
grandson: SoSo ∨ DaSo
granddaughter: SoDa ∨ DaDa
uncle: FaBr ∨ MoBr
aunt: FaSi ∨ MoSi
cousin: FaBrSo ∨ FaBrDa ∨ MoBrSo ∨ MoBrDa ∨ FaSiSo ∨ FaSiDa ∨ MoSiSo ∨ MoSiDa ∨ FaFaBrSo ∨ FaMoBrSo ∨ MoFaSiDa
nephew: BrSo ∨ SiSo ∨ BrSoSo ∨ SiSoSo
niece: BrDa ∨ SiDa ∨ BrDaDa ∨ SiDaDa

We note again that the above set is incomplete not only in leaving out affinal kin terms, but also in assigning kin types to some kin terms (for instance, kin types denoting relatives two or more generations above ego to *uncle* and *aunt*, which are sometimes referred to as *great/grand uncle* and *great/grand aunt*). At Step 2, the most challenging aspect of analysis, the dimensions, or features of contasts, must be uncovered. It can be observed in the data that the feature of sex is relevant for the demarcation of the kin terms, as it is shared by all kin types of each kin term, with the exception of *cousin*, which includes kin types of both sexes (for example FaBrSo (male) vs. FaBrDa (female)). Another contrasting feature, evident from the data, is generation, partitioning the English kinship vocabulary into groups of two generations above ego (*grandmother, grandfather*), one generation above ego (*mother, father, uncle, aunt*), ego's generation (*brother, sister*), and one generation below ego (*son, daughter, nephew, niece*), etc. A third relevant contrasting feature to be observed in the data is lineality, as all kin terms specify whether the relative is lineally or non-lineally related to ego. (Here, Wallace and Atkins use Goodenough's definition of the values on this feature of lineality: lineals are persons who are ancestors or descendants of ego; co-lineals are non-lineals all of whose ancestors include, or are included in, all the ancestors of ego; ablineals are consanguineal relatives who are neither lineals nor co-lineal.) Based on these observations, one may conjecture that three dimensions will be sufficient to define all the terms:

(1) Sex of relative, with two values
     m – male
     f – female
(2) Generation of relative, with five values
     2 – two generations above ego
     1 – one generation above ego
     0 – ego's own generation
     −1 – one generation below ego
     −2 – two generations below ego
(3) Lineality, with three values
     lin – lineal
     colin – co-lineal
     ablin – ablineal

At Step 4, the terms are defined by a conjunction of feature-value components (see Table 1.1. *Note: all tables are collected in the Appendix*).

In the resultant componential analysis, each kin term is given a conjunctive definition in terms of components (or, feature values) such that at least one component discriminates a term from any other term. Each definition of a kin term is 'consistent' in that it contains the necessary and jointly sufficient components for the demarcation. Thus, for instance, in the definition of *grandfather* the component generation $= 2$ distinguishes the term from all terms with different generation (viz. *father, mother, brother, sister, son, daughter, grandson, granddaughter, uncle, aunt, nephew* and *niece*), the component lineality $=$ lin distinguishes it from all non-lineals (in particular, *cousin*), and sex = m, from all terms that are female (in particular, *grandmother*); in effect, these three components are sufficient to set apart *grandfather* from all kin terms in the inspected vocabulary. The components used are also necessary for the demarcation in that none of them can be removed without failing a discrimination with some other kin term. Thus, removing sex = m will fail the discrimination with *aunt*, removing generation = 2 will fail the discrimination with *father*, and lineality = lin that with *cousin*.

1.2.6 Adequacy criteria

The structural linguistic goal of componential analysis is to determine the relevant conditions for distinguishing the meaning of any of the kin terms within the kinship vocabulary from any other. Put differently, componential analysis should find, for any kin term, the common features for all its attendant kin types, such that these common features demarcate this term from all other kin terms in the kinship vocabulary. As in other grammatical tasks, a general common *adequacy requirement* to componential analysis would be to discover, for any data set, *all and only* the componential paradigms that describe the structure of the domain (but see below our constraints pertaining to simplicity).

1.2.7 Uses of componential analysis

The semantic structure revealed by componential analysis may be useful for a number of purposes, the most important perhaps being translation and historical semantic reconstruction.

In translation studies, it has been stressed by many that the new developments in linguistics, like componential analysis (and transformational analysis), may provide far more satisfactory bases for translation than have existed in the past. In an article in *Language*, Eugene Nida (1969), for instance, states the connection in vivid terms and so deserves to be quoted at length:

> In transferring the referential content of the message, one is not concerned primarily with the precise words or exocentric units (i.e. the idioms), but with the sets of components. In fact, one does not really translate words but bundles of componential features. The words may be regarded essentially as vehicles for carrying the components of meaning. In fact the words may be likened to suitcases used for carrying various articles of clothing. It really does not make much difference which articles are packed in which suitcase. What

counts is that the clothes arrive at the destination in the best pos-sible condition, i.e. with the least damage. The same is true in the communication of referential structures. What counts is not the par-ticular words which carry the componential features, but the fact that the correct componential features are lexically transported. (Nida 1969: 492)

Componential analysis may be crucial in historical semantic recon-struction insofar as the meanings of the words in the semantic domain are strongly interdependent, each of them being restricted by the mean-ings of the other words in the field. In kinship vocabularies, this tenet is particularly conspicuous and has been exploited by various scholars. Frisch and Schutz (1967), for instance, analyse along these lines the Proto Central Yuman kinship system, while more recently Fox (1994) and Blust (1994) in the same volume elegantly employ the method to Malayo-Polynesian/Austronesian sibling terminology.

1.3   Goals of componential analysis: 'psychological validity' vs. 'social-structural reality'

Analysts, advocating the use of componential (or, formal) analysis, seem to have had two different, but not unrelated, objectives in mind. The first objective was to specify the necessary and sufficient conditions under which each term is used. The problem here is to determine the minimal information one needs to know in order to be capable of deter-mining whether two persons are kinfolk or not and what term to apply. The second objective was to detect the criteria by which speakers of the language themselves decide what term to apply to two persons that are kinfolk. The latter far more ambitious goal presupposes some under-standing of the internal mental processes of classification of the native speakers of the language. The first approach is usually known as one describing 'social-structural reality', and the second as one describing 'psychological reality'.

From the very introduction of the componential method in kin-ship studies, theorists claimed that the method reveals the criteria by which native speakers themselves classify phenomena (for example Frake 1962; Goodenough 1956; Lounsbury 1956). The type of mean-ing they intended to reveal was not only the referential, or definitional, meaning of kin terms, but above all, the internal meanings of terms for their native users (Wallace 1965: 229). In general, it was assumed that such an approach would improve the explanatory power of the analysis.

The methodological promises of componential analysis, and to a great extent the reason for its popularity, lay precisely in its claim to be a systematic and trustworthy procedure for discovering what words mean to the people of the community studied, for penetrating into people's minds. The goal was to understand native mental processes, to grasp the native world view and inner thoughts.

Thus, for instance, in his pioneering work on Trukese kin terms, Goodenough (1956) repeatedly states that the goal of the componential analysis of kinship terms is to uncover psychologically real definitions of kin terms. He says that the method 'can [...] tell us much about human cognitive processes' (p. 195). In his earlier book on the Trukese he justifies the choice of features by characterizing them as 'criteria' or 'rules', which are valid in 'Trukese thinking', and by which a native 'appraise[s] his relationship with another individual'. Goodenough produces three different componential analyses of Trukese kin terms, all of which correctly describe the data set, and seems to assume that all of these extensionally equivalent paradigms are equally psychologically valid, writing: 'Since we can reproduce Trukese kinship usage equally well from any one of these three paradigms, we cannot eliminate from the Trukese cognitive world any one of the alternative conceptual variables [he uses in the analyses]'.

The problem of psychological validity became particularly acute after the appearance in 1964 of the paper 'Cognition and componential analysis: God's truth or hocus-pocus' by Robbins Burling. Burling showed that, logically, in a set consisting of three kin terms, the possible componential analyses number 6, in a set of four terms their number is 24, and so on, the indeterminacy increasing steeply with the number of kin terms. Additional factors, such as homonymy, empty semantic spaces, non-binary components, parallel components and redundancy complicate the analysis further, so that '[i]n principle, the number of possible analyses becomes infinite' (Burling 1964: 21). So, Burling's basic conclusion is obvious: one has to abandon the goal of psychological reality.

Burling's position was questioned by several scholars. Dell Hymes (1964), for instance, noted that not all logically possible componential models would be arrived at by an analyst in field work, since the natives' behaviours and culture would significantly limit the possibilities. Hammel (1964) argued that 'simplicity' and 'formal elegance', in addition to natives' behaviours, would lead to psychologically valid analyses. In his procedure, Hammel, first, constructs his own set on the bases of observation and analysis of native sets, choosing the one which most closely fits to the biggest number of native sets (or to their central tendency in sorting). Then, he applies his simplicity criteria, pertaining to replicability, internal consistency, correspondence with observation, and economy of statement. Other scholars who seem to equate simplicity with cognitive validity are Sheffler and Lounsbury (1971), Noricks (1987) and others.

However, general psychological arguments to the effect that simplicity is not a necessary ingredient of cognitive systems, which may actually be very complex and unorganized (for instance, Neisser 1967), and, additionally, that it is sometimes difficult to assess which model is 'simpler' from a set of alternatives (for example, Burling 1965), led Hammel to retreat to the position of the proponents of social-structural reality, as did some of the pioneers of the field, Lounsbury and Goodenough.

In his treatment of the problem of psychological validity of componential models, Wallace (1965) insists that conducting componential analysis on the one hand and determining the cognitive credibility of componential models on the other, are two distinct tasks: one should first find the models and subsequently test them for psychological validity. Wallace writes in this connection:

> From this point of view the dispute over whether properly conducted componential analysis yields only one true analysis ("god's truth") or a multitude of equally true analyses ("hocus pocus") is [...] beside the point. One or many, their psychological validity [...] must be established by means independent of the mechanics internal to componential analysis itself. [...] The publications on componential analysis to date [...] suggest that the application of its procedures to lexical and denotative data does not automatically yield a unique description of a native cognitive (or semantic) system. (Wallace 1965: 231)

Various procedures were suggested in the literature for testing psychological validity. A widely known approach is the triad test of Romney and D'Andrade (1964), in which native speakers make similarity judgments. From three terms, all their pair-wise combinations are constructed and opposed to the remaining term in the triplet, and the subjects are asked which two terms are most similar or which one is most different. With a similar procedure, Romney and D'Andrade (1964) attempted to compare the model they arrived at with the one proposed by Wallace and Atkins (1960), which we discussed briefly above. In a triad test, they presented all possible triads of a set of eight male kin terms to 116 high school students, asking which term in the triad was most different from the other two. Their finding was that the reciprocal terms (as for example, *grandfather* and *grandson*) were judged as more similar than those terms that are closer in absolute number of generations (for instance, *grandfather* and *father*). This was in agreement with their own model but not with that of Wallace and Atkins (1960). Additionally, the dimensions used in their analysis, viz. reciprocity, generational difference and lineality, fitted with the three dimensions of a multidimensional scaling of the similarity judgments. Thus, Romney and D'Andrade concluded that their model was psychologically more valid than the model proposed by Wallace and Atkins and that in the cognitive space of native speakers of English there must exist only two degrees of lineality (direct and collateral) rather than three (lineal, co-lineal and ablineal, as previously suggested). In addition, they concluded that generational terms that are reciprocals of one another (as, for instance, *grandmother, granddaughter; mother, daughter*) must be viewed as sharing the feature value of being one or two generations away from ego, rather than demarcating kin terms by their absolute generation values. (Further important works on using psychological tests are Wexler and Romney 1972, Rose and Romney 1979 and Nakao and Romney 1984.)

The work of Romney and D'Andrade on evaluating the psychological validity of componential models led to two developments. Some scholars abandoned the basically linguistic methods of componential analysis and turned to statistics. The followers of this line of research began eliciting similarity judgments in order to build directly their models of kinship semantics, without recourse to componential analysis and related methods. In effect, multidimensional scalings and cluster diagrams of similarity judgments replaced the previous tables, taxonomies and paradigms as illustrations in the ethnosemantic literature. A second group of scholars, however, continued to expand the field and in the next section I turn to these developments.

1.4 Componential analysis and alternative approaches

Componential analysis is not the only method for describing the semantic structure of kinship terminology. Some of the basic alternative approaches are briefly mentioned below.

Floyd Lounsbury has developed an influential early alternative to componential analysis, called the 'extensionist model'. In this approach, one, or sometimes a couple, of the kin types of a kin term are considered as primary or focal, and the definition of the kin term is fitted to these. The other kin types of the kin term are then treated as 'extensions', which are accounted for by rules. The rules may be formulated either as expansions, in which case the distant members of the class are derived from the focal members, or alternatively, as reductions, in which case the distant members are reduced to the focal types. The meaning of the focal kin types themselves are described in traditional componential analysis terms.

The basic underlying idea of the extensionist hypothesis is that classificatory kin terms are polysemous (rather than monosemous, as assumed by traditional componential analysis). One of these multiple meanings, which refers to the closest relative, is primary, while the others are secondary and derived by narrowing or broadening of the meaning of the primary one. This idea goes back to Bronisław Malinowski's (1929: 525–6) discussion of classificatory kinship, describing how a child first acquires the terms for the elementary relationships (like *mother*, *sister*, etc.) and is then taught to extend the terms to more distant kin, the latter always remaining 'an extension or metaphor' for the prototypical relationship. Another, formal, source of inspiration for the extensionist approach was transformational grammar, which was popular in linguistics in the 1960s, and which assumed some basic sentence types and derived more complex sentence types via re-write rules. It is not accidental, then, that the extensionist method is also called the 're-write rules' or 'production rules' method.

Lounsbury described the extensionist method on a number of data sets. Here I will give as an illustration his brief and simplified treatment of the Choctaw sub-type (a variety of the Crow type) in regards to the two cousin kin types: father's sister's son (FaSiSo), which goes by the 'father' kin term in these systems and father's sister's daughter (FaSiDa), which goes by the 'grandmother' kin term. Lounsbury formulates these as reduction rules, reducing the more remote kin types to the focal types. The formulated rules, given below, account for the whole Choctaw system (Lounsbury 1964: 1089–90).

(1) Skewing rule (equating kin types of different generations). 'Let any woman's brother, whenever it occurs as a link between ego and any other relative, be regarded as structurally equivalent to that woman's son, as linking relative'.

female Br . . . → female So . . .

The rule implies a corollary for the consequent relationship for the reciprocals, viz. 'Any male linking relative's sister will then be equivalent to that male linking relative's mother'.

$$\ldots \text{male Si} \rightarrow \text{male Mo}$$

(2) Merging rule (equating siblings of the same sex). 'Let any person's sibling of the same sex as himself (or herself), when a link to some other relative, be regarded as equivalent of that person himself (or herself) directly linked to said relative'.

$$\text{male Br} \ldots \rightarrow \text{male} \ldots; \text{female Si} \ldots \rightarrow \text{female} \ldots$$

This implies the corollary for reciprocals, viz. 'Any linking relative's sibling of the same sex as himself/herself will then be equivalent to that relative himself/herself as the object of reference'.

$$\ldots \text{male Br} \rightarrow \ldots \text{male}; \ldots \text{female Si} \rightarrow \ldots \text{female}$$

(3) Half-sibling rule (equating one's parents' child with one's sibling). 'Let any child of one of one's own parents be regarded as one's sibling'.

$$\text{FaSo} \rightarrow \text{Br; FaDa} \rightarrow \text{Si; MoSo} \rightarrow \text{Br; MoDa} \rightarrow \text{Si}$$

The rule contains its own reciprocal corollary.

Two remarks regarding the nature of the rules. First, some of the rules in an extensionist analysis are universal, while others are language-specific. In the above illustration, only the third rule seems universal, whereas the other two are specific to Crow systems, even if encountered in other unrelated kinship systems. Secondly, the rules form an unordered set, meaning that they can be applied in any order.

Applying the reduction rules to the two kin types FaSiSo and FaSiDa, results in:

FaSiSo → FaMoSo (by skewing rule corollary)
      → FaBr   (by half-sibling rule)
      → F   (by merging rule
      → 'father'   (by definition)

FaSiDa   →   FaMoDa   (by skewing rule corollary)
         →   FaSi   (by half-sibling rule)
         →   FaMo   (by skewing rule corollary)
         →   'grandmother'   (by definition)

Lounsbury's account gives the logical explanation of why a Crow might call his father's sister's son 'father', and his father's sister's daughter 'grandmother'.

Goodenough (1967) observes that Lounsbury's approach can be usefully combined with 'traditional' componential analysis, and he has found similar structural equivalence rules helpful in the analysis of Trukese. Goodenough also uses similar procedures in his analysis of Yankee English (Goodenough 1965). Lounsbury himself uses componential analysis to describe the meaning of his primary kin types, so the two approaches are complementary rather than contradictory.

A number of papers have been produced using the extensionist approach; for instance, Bhargava and Lambek (1992) treating Sanskrit, Bhargava and Lambek (1995) treating Western Pacific systems, etc. Noricks (1987) is an attempt to evaluate the psychological validity of analyses conducted in traditional componential analysis as opposed to those conducted in terms of the extensionist approach. Some work has been done on automating the kinship analysis task within the framework of the extensionist approach (see Kronenfeld 1976).

Wallace (1970) proposes a 'relational approach' to analysis of the semantics of English kinship terms, based on the logic of relations rather than on the logic of classes, employed in traditional componential analysis. The essential idea of this approach is that most speakers of English reckon kinship by relational phrases.

The English system, according to this view, may be conceived as a set of transformations on a basic sentence that states the relation between a specific X (the relative) and a specific Y (the ego):

X is a | member of the family of | Y (or X is Y's | |)

In English, there are precisely fourteen male/female pairs of terms that may be substituted for the core term, namely:

Consanguineals:
        cousin/cousin
        uncle/aunt
        nephew/niece

brother/sister
father/mother
son/daughter
Affinals:
son-in-law/daughter-in-law
brother-in-law/sister-in-law
uncle/aunt
father-in-law/mother-in-law
Steps:
step-brother/step-sister
step-father/step-mother
step-son/step-daughter
Spouses:
husband/wife

For each of these terms, a reckoning phrase (which is also the defining phrase) may be substituted consisting of a subset of no more than three of the following four relational phrases: child of, sibling of, parent of, and spouse of. Child of, parent of, and spouse of may be taken as primitives; but sibling must be further defined as 'child of a parent of'.

The elementary reckoning and some of the defining sentences are shown in Table 1.2; for more details, see Wallace (1970: 843). The relational analysis, according to Wallace, has the following virtues: it is simple, psychologically plausible (as it mimics actual reckoning of kinship) and unique. The careful reader, however, may notice some problems in this analysis, as for instance, the failure to give a unitary definition of the pair *uncle/aunt*, as well as the failure to discriminate the sex of all male-female kin terms pairs.

Another attempt at handling the semantics of kin terms is that of Ellen Woolford (1984), who proposed a generative framework, synthesizing aspects of the previous approaches of traditional componential analysis, extension rule analysis and relational analysis. This framework allows one to predict a number of implicational universals (for example, 'if you refer to the same sex siblings of your parents with the same terms you use for your parents, you will refer to their children with the same terms you use for your siblings').

Yet another important approach has emerged, the 'algebraic' one, which takes as primary data not the genealogies, but the kin terms themselves, defining an algebra of these terms (e.g., Read 1984; cf. Boyd, Haehl and Seiler 1972). A computer implementation, KAES (Kinship Analysis Expert System), following the algebraic paradigm, may be found in Read and Behrens (1990b; for a general discussion of these, and various other computational aids in kinship studies, see Read and Behrens 1990a). In the models produced by the KAES system, one still has to apply psychological tests of the sort suggested by Romney and D'Andrade (1964) in order to decide whether KAES produces psychologically real outcomes (for a more recent treatment, see Read 2000).

Finally, some other approaches need only be mentioned here, as Wierzbicka's theory of semantic primitives (Wierzbicka 1991, 1992), which supposedly eliminates alternative solutions, and that of Kay (1974, 1975), which emphasizes the role of morphological rules in kinship semantics.

Concluding this section, it should be emphasized that the alternative approaches to the study of kinship semantics I sketched above have by no means replaced 'traditional' componential analysis. The field is indeed somewhat less active at present, but this is quite understandable after its boom for several decades. At present, 'formal analysis', as the method is sometimes referred to in anthropological work, is not infrequently regarded as a necessary ingredient of kinship studies in the discipline, and, in linguistics, not only the kinship domain, but also other lexical fields, are subject to componential analysis (see, for instance, Geeraerts 2010, Bernard 2011, and others). Perhaps the basic reason for this is that componential analysis is the sole method for uncovering the system of a semantic domain in its classical, Saussurian, sense. Other reasons are that it is an inalienable part of some of the other approaches. Thus, the extensionist approach has first to perform traditional componential analysis of its core, or prototypical, vocabulary, while the methodologies seeking psychologically valid models, like that proposed by Romney and D'Andrade (1964), presuppose the availability of componential models to assess subsequently for cognitive credibility.

1.5 Summary

In this chapter, I have introduced componential analysis in a historical perspective. It was shown that the method is based on the Saussurean idea of 'system' in linguistics, in which the objects forming a system are described as a conjunction of smaller components that are necessary and sufficient to distinguish each object in the system from all others. Componential analysis originates in phonological distinctive feature analysis and is naturally extended to the other linguistic levels (morphology, semantics, etc). Kinship terminology studies in particular are initiated by the classical works of Goodenough, Lounsbury and some others and have gained wide popularity in both linguistics and anthropology, resulting in a significant number of componential models proposed in the literature for mostly 'exotic' languages. Some analysts believe that these models reveal 'psychological validity', or the world view of native speakers, while others assume that such models describe 'social-structural reality', or the rules of using kin terms in a society, and that the discovery of psychologically valid models requires subsequent psychological tests. Some scholars have proposed such tests, while others have introduced alternative ways to study kinship terminology (extensionist, algebraic, relational, grammatical approaches). Despite the existence of alternative approaches, classical componential analysis is indispensable to kinship studies. First, componential analysis is an inalienable part of some of the other approaches (for instance the extensionist method presupposes componential models of the 'core vocabulary' while the approaches looking for psychological validity presuppose the availability of componential models to be subsequently tested psychologically). Second, it is the only method that reveals the semantic system of kin terms and for this reason continues to be in the analytic repertoire of both current linguistics and current anthropology. And, third, componential models are essential not only for exposing semantic structure, but also for translation purposes and for historical semantic reconstruction.

2
Problems of componential analysis

A critical evaluation of the literature on componential analysis of kinship terminology reveals two common basic problems. Analysts have either failed to provide 'consistent' componential models (i.e. models defining kin terms by necessary and sufficient features) or have failed to list all componential models of specific data sets. The first problem has generally remained unnoticed, while the second was emphasized by Robbins Burling and attracted considerable attention in the literature, but without any feasible solutions proposed to solve it. This chapter discusses these two problems in detail and provides illustrations of the problems from the literature. Inconsistency, for example, is illustrated in several published models of English as well as in the analysis of Burmese. These proposals are shown either to fail to demarcate some kin terms or use redundant features or both. Redundancy is identified as a particularly acute problem and the logic and psychological reasons for its occurrence are briefly discussed. The problem of multiple solutions is illustrated with Bulgarian, showing that the alternative models, even when using a fixed number of dimensions, generate astronomical numbers. These numbers become even greater if redundant models are accepted. Both the problem of inconsistency and that of the failure to list all multiple solutions actually stem from the computational complexity of the task of componential analysis, forcing the conclusion that the task requires automation. Importantly, the needed computational tool should be able, in a principled manner, to reduce to manageable limits the formidable indeterminacy of completely unconstrained componential analysis.

2.1 Violation of consistency: examples from the literature

An adequate componential model, as discussed in Chapter 1, should be 'consistent' and provide conjunctive definitions of all kin terms in a kinship vocabulary such that each kin term is discriminated from the rest of the terms with components that are both necessary and sufficient. A violation of the sufficiency condition results in a failure to discriminate some term(s), whereas a violation of the necessity condition results in using components that are redundant and superfluous.

Below I give some illustrations of these shortcomings of solutions to kinship systems proposed in the literature. In the discussion, the formulations and notation of the original works is generally preserved.

2.1.1 Nogle on English

In his book *Method and Theory in the Semantics and Cognition of Kinship Terminology* (1974), Lawrence Nogle undertakes a componential analysis of American English kin terms. He notes the existence of three published componential models of English at the time, viz. Wallace and Atkins (1960), Romney and D'Andrade (1964) and Goodenough (1965), singling out the latter work for the rigour of the method and the completeness of the kinship terminology data used. Nogle writes: '[Goodenough] covered the complete set of kin terms, not a restricted set. Goodenough invited other analysts to construct their own systems [...] employing the rigorous analytic procedure he (Goodenough) set up. Below I have attempted just this' (1974: 62–4). Nogle thus claims to have based his analysis on Goodenough's extensive data (which I list in full in Chapter 4), so we should examine his proposal more closely.

Nogle proposes the following dimensions of contrast:

(1) Nuclear family, with values
    1.1 – nuclear (the nuclear family in Nogle's view includes Fa, Mo, Br, Si, So, Da, Hu, Wi, as well as all step-relatives)
    1.2 – nonnuclear
(2) Affinity, with values
    2.1 – affinal
    2.2 – consanguineal
(3) Generation, with values
    3.1 – ascending
    3.2 – contemporary
    3.3 – descending

(4) Affinity of 1st link, with values
    4.1 – consanguineal 1st link
    4.2 – affinal 1st link
(5) Lineality, with values
    5.1 – lineal
    5.2 – collateral
(6) Sex, with values
    6.1 – male
    6.2 – female.

Now, a closer inspection of how these dimensions fare in discriminating Goodenough's data set reveals that this set of six dimensions is *insufficient* to demarcate all kin terms. Thus, Nogle's features fail to set apart *great-grandfather* from *grandfather* since both lexemes are defined in terms of these dimensions as [nonnuclear & consanguineal & ascending generation & consanguineal 1st link & lineal & male]. A perfectly analogous situation obtains with the pair of respective female kin terms *great-grandmother* and *grandmother* which both share the components [nonnuclear & consanguineal & ascending generation & consanguineal 1st link & lineal & female]. Additionally, the pair *great-uncle* and *uncle* also fail discrimination, both having the same components, viz. [nonnuclear & consanguineal & ascending generation & consanguineal 1st link & collateral & male], and obviously the same would apply to their female counterpart pair *great-aunt* and *aunt*. In the kin terms of descending generation, the problem of demarcation persists and the pair *great-grandson* and *grandson* are both described – using Nogle's six dimensions – as having the components [nonnuclear & consanguineal & descending generation & consanguineal 1st link & lineal & male]; the same problem for analogous reasons faces the female counterpart kin terms *great-granddaughter* and *granddaughter*. In general, Nogle's features fail to distinguish between kin terms of the form *great-X* and *X*, where *X* stands for an appropriate form in this context. The reason is that he defines the dimension generation as only having three values, viz. ascending vs. contemporary vs. descending generation, while further values are apparently needed to accomplish the demarcations successfully (to be fair, Nogle does not explicitly list in his analysis (Table 2.1) the *great-X* terms although Goodenough does).

However, problems do not stop here. In terms of the features proposed by Nogle, the kin term *cousin* has the components [nonnuclear & consanguineal & consanguineal 1st link & collateral] – with no specified components for sex (as the term covers relatives of both sexes) and generation (as the term covers relatives of all generations). As a consequence of the failure to contrast on these latter dimensions, *cousin* cannot be set apart from any of the terms *great-uncle, great-aunt, uncle, aunt, niece* and *nephew*, all of which include the components that make up *cousin*. Finally, *nephew* cannot be discriminated from *son-in-law* since both have the components [nonnuclear & descending generation & collateral & male]; the terms do not contrast on the dimension of affinity of 1st link (as each has both consanguineal and affinal links) and on the dimension of affinity/consanguinity of relative (as each covers both consanguineal and affinal kin types). Analogous considerations hold for the pair *niece* and *daughter-in-law*.

In sum, if we take Nogle's claim to have used Goodenough's complete data set of American English, the six dimensions he proposes to handle the set violate the sufficiency condition of kin term definitions and fail to demarcate the following fourteen pairs of kin terms:

1. *great-grandfather vs. grandfather*
2. *great-grandmother vs. grandmother*
3. *great-uncle vs. uncle*
4. *great-aunt vs. aunt*
5. *great-grandson vs. grandson*
6. *great-granddaughter vs. granddaughter*
7. *great-uncle vs. cousin*
8. *great-aunt vs. cousin*
9. *uncle vs. cousin*
10. *aunt vs. cousin*
11. *cousin vs. niece*
12. *cousin vs. nephew*
13. *nephew vs. son-in-law*
14. *niece vs. daughter-in-law*

We may now look at the componential model proposed by Nogle (our Table 2.1 – his Table 1, p.64; for simplicity, the foster relatives are ignored here). The following remarks regarding the model are in order.

First, it can be observed that all kin terms of the form *great-X* are omitted from the analysis (as mentioned earlier). Second, Nogle apparently believes it is not possible to give a conjunctive definition of *uncle* and *aunt* and introduces somewhat artificially homonymity by listing them as separate entries, *uncle1* vs. *uncle2* and *aunt1* vs. *aunt2*, with affinal or consanguineal meaning, respectively. However in actual fact his features are perfectly sufficient to make the demarcation. Thus, *uncle*, in its usual meaning covering both affinal and consanguineal kin types, will have the components [nonnuclear & ascending generation & consanguineal 1st link & collateral & male], and *aunt* the components [nonnuclear & ascending generation & consanguineal 1st link & collateral & female].

Let us now show (Table 2.2) how, for example, *uncle* contrasts with the other terms from the domain (the situation with *aunt* will be analogous). It will be clear that *uncle* stays distinct from all female terms, and all terms that are not of ascending generation. So let us just focus on contrasts with the remaining terms, viz. *grandfather, father, father-in-law*, and *step-father*. Table 2.2 lists the actual contrasts that might be used to accomplish the demarcation.

Third, the kin term *cousin* is interpreted very narrowly, unlike Goodenough, as having the component of 'contemporary generation' (notated 3.2 in Table 2.1), while the term covers kin types of other generations as well (e.g. the contemporary generation PaSbCh, where Pa = parent, Sb = sibling, Ch = child, but also the ascending generation PaPaSbCh, etc.).

Fourthly, Nogle interprets the kin terms *nephew* and *niece* narrowly as possessing the component 'consanguineal' (notated 2.2 in Table 2.1), while the terms have some kin types which are consanguineal, and others which are affinal (e.g. *nephew* covers the consanguineal BrSo, etc., but also the affinal WiSiSo, etc.; *niece* covers the consanguineal BrDa, etc. but also the affinal WiSiDa, etc.).

The above considerations thus reveal some distortion of Goodenough's data and the usual conception of American English kinship terminology. Still, taking these dubious interpretations for granted, we may check the componential analysis presented in Table 2.1 with respect to its consistency in providing necessary and sufficient definitions of the kin terms. Again, the model presented violates the sufficiency condition and fails to discriminate the two pairs:

husband vs. step-brother
wife vs. step-sister

Thus, let us first look at the descriptions of *husband* and *step-brother* (rows 1 and 5 of Table 2.1). They differ only as regards the fourth dimension, in that the first kin term has the value 4.1 while the second has the value 0 (i.e. inapplicable). Since one cannot properly contrast an applicable feature with an inapplicable feature, the two terms fail discrimination. The situation is analogous with the pair *wife* and *step-sister*:

their only difference in Table 2.1 is in respect to the fourth dimension but they do not contrast along this dimension.

However, the problems do not stop here. The proposed componential model also violates in a number of cases the *necessity condition* and defines some kin terms with components that are redundant and must be omitted from the kin terms definitions (the zeroes in the table of course do not count anyway). Thus, consider again the kin term *husband*, having the definition [nuclear (1.1) & affinal (2.1) & contemporary generation (3.2) & consanguineal linking (4.1) & male (6.1)]. The first component 'nuclear' discriminates the term from all nonnuclear terms in the table, viz. *uncles, aunts, in-laws, grandparents, grandchildren, cousin, nephew* and *niece*. The second component 'affinal' demarcates the terms from all nuclear but non-affinal terms, viz. *father, mother, brother, sister, son* and *daughter*. The third component 'contemporary generation' distinguishes *husband* from all terms that are nuclear, affinal but not of contemporary generation, viz. *step-parents* and *step-children*. The only two kin terms that remain undiscriminated with *husband* so far are *step-sister* and *step-brother*, the sixth dimension, that of sex, doing the job in the former case. The sole undiscriminated pair then is *husband* vs. *step-brother*, which, as we have seen above, cannot be distinguished on the grounds of the fourth dimension. Therefore the listed value 4.1 for this dimension is redundant for *husband* and should be omitted.

An alternative way of arguing that a component is redundant in a definition of a kin term is to isolate the set of all kin terms distinguished from the original term by this component and then show that this set of terms is actually demarcated by other features (components), already used in the definition of the original term. Thus, looking at the definition of *husband* again, we see that the component denoted 4.1 discriminates the lexeme from the lexemes *step-father, step-mother, father-in-law* and *mother-in-law*, which have the component 4.2. However, it can be noted that the feature 'generation', already used in the definition of *husband*, successfully discriminates *husband*, which is of contemporary generation, from the very same set of terms, as all of them are of ascending generation. Therefore the component at issue is superfluous.

Below I give some further examples of violation of the necessity condition in Table 2.1.

Consider the definition of the kin term *father*: [nuclear (1.1) & consanguineal (2.2) & ascending generation (3.1) & lineal (5.1) & male (6.1)]. The component 'lineal' (5.1) however is redundant in this description.

Thus, the feature 'lineality' serves to discriminate *father* from the set of kin terms *brother, sister, uncle1, aunt1, uncle2, aunt2, cousin, nephew* and *niece*, all of which are collateral. At the same time, the term *father* is already assigned the component 'nuclear', which distinguishes it from *uncle1, aunt1, uncle2, aunt2, cousin, nephew* and *niece* (all of which are nonnuclear) and the component 'ascending generation' distinguishes *father* from *brother* and *sister* (which are of contemporary generation). Thus, the components 'nuclear' and 'contemporary generation', collectively, discriminate all the words the component 'lineal' demarcates, making the use of the latter superfluous. (The definition of the kin term *mother* also contains the component 'lineal', which is redundant for analogous reasons.)

By way of a final example, consider the definition of the kin term *uncle1*. The term is described in the table with six components, viz. [nonnuclear (1.2) & affinal (2.1) & ascending generation (3.1) & consanguineal linking relative (4.1) & collateral (5.2) & male (6.1)]. A closer look reveals that four components are sufficient to discriminate *uncle1* from the remaining lexemes, and the two components 'nonnuclear' and 'collateral' are redundant. Thus, the first component, 'nonnuclear', serves to distinguish *uncle1* from the set of kin terms *husband, wife, step-father, step-mother, step-brother, step-sister, step-son, step-daughter, father, mother, brother, sister, son* and *daughter*, which are all nuclear. However, the three components of *uncle1* 'affinal', 'ascending generation' and 'consanguineal linking relative', that must be used anyway in the definition of the term, do the same job, taken collectively: the feature 'affinal' discriminates *uncle1* from the consanguineals *father, mother, brother, sister, son* and *daughter*, the feature 'ascending generation' discriminates *uncle1* from the set of terms, which are not of ascending generation, viz. *husband, wife, step-brother, step-sister, step-son, step-daughter, brother, sister, son* and *daughter*, while the component 'consanguineal linking relative' distinguishes *uncle1* from the rest of the lexemes in the set of those discriminated by the redundant component 'nonnuclear', viz. the lexemes *step-father* and *step-mother*. In other words, the *uncle1*'s three components 'affinal', 'ascending generation' and 'consanguineal linking relative' are sufficient to successfully accomplish the differentiation, making Nogle's use of the component 'nonnuclear' superfluous.

We may now explain why the other component Nogle uses in the definition of *uncle1*, viz. 'collateral', is also redundant. This component may serve to discriminate *uncle1* from *father, mother, son, daughter, grandfather, grandmother, grandson, granddaughter*, all of which are lineal. However, another component, 'affinal' (2.1), that is already used in the definition of *uncle1*, discriminates this word from the very same set of words 'collateral' does, making the use of the latter component superfluous. (We may note that the definition of the kin term *aunt1* is redundant in the same way *uncle1* is and for analogous reasons.)

Our examples were only illustrative and do not exhaust all cases of violation of the necessity condition in Nogle's componential analysis. The full list of these is given in Table 2.3, in which the redundant components are enclosed in brackets. Summarizing, 17 kin term definitions are redundant out of 31 (ignoring zeroes). Of these, two lexemes, *uncle1* and *aunt2*, each have two redundant components.

2.1.2 Burling on Burmese

Robbins Burling, one of the leading theorists in componential analysis (to whose work we also turn later on in the chapter), proposes a componential model of the Burmese language in the famous collection *Formal Analysis* (1965). He employs the following six dimensions in his analysis:

(1) Affinity, with values
    C – consanguineal
    A – affinal
(2) Generation, with values
    the integers 1, 2, 3, etc.
(3) Lineality, with values
    L – lineal
    C – collateral
(4) Sex of kinsman, with values
    M – male
    F – female
(5) Relative age, with values
    E – elder
    Y – younger
(6) Speaker's sex, with values
    m – male
    f – female.

The componential model he presents of Burmese is given in Table 2.4 (ignore for the moment the brackets, so that all components, non-bracketed and bracketed, count).

It is immediately apparent from this analysis that Burling has a problem demarcating some of the Burmese words using this set of six dimensions and in order to do so he recourses to splitting each of them into homonymous lexemes. Thus, the word *qaphécî*, covering both grandfather and grandfather's elder brother (as seen from the full data set Burling lists and omitted here), is presented in the table as two separate lexemes, viz. *qaphécî1* (with meaning grandfather and hence marked as lineal in the table) and *qaphécî2* (with meaning grandfather's elder brother and hence marked as collateral). Similar considerations hold for the Burmese kin term *qaméicî*. The word *qaméicî* means either grandmother or grandmother's elder sister, but is presented in the table as two separate lexemes, viz. *qaméicî1* (with meaning grandmother and hence marked as lineal in the table) and *qaméicî2* (with meaning grandmother's elder sister and hence marked as collateral). The case with *yauʔkhamà1* and *yauʔkhamà2* is different from the above examples in that the kin term *yauʔkhamà* means either more generally both mother-in-law or father-in-law (*yauʔkhamà1*) or, more specifically, only mother-in-law (*yauʔkhamà2*), this inclusion of meaning making impossible in principle (i.e. regardless of chosen dimensions) the contrast between the two word meanings. The table also lists other pairs of kin terms which are not in principle distinguishable with the same meaning relation of inclusion between them, but I will ignore them here (in similar situations, other theorists than Burling would prefer to leave such kin terms out from a componential model, saying that they contrast at a different level).

Burling's proposed componential model of Burmese kinship vocabulary, besides the somewhat artificial splitting of kin terms in order not to violate the sufficiency condition, also has the shortcoming of providing redundant definitions of a number of kin terms. Below are some examples of kin terms defined with some superfluous components in Table 2.4.

The kin term *pín* meaning great-great-grandparent is described with two components: [consanguineal & fourth ascending generation]. However, apparently the generation feature is sufficient to single out this term from all the rest as there are no other terms of this generation in the data set; hence the component 'consanguineal' is redundant. Analogously, the kin term *pí* meaning great-grandparent is described with the components [consanguineal & third ascending generation], whereas the generation component alone puts apart the kin term, there being no other terms of this generation.

The kin term *báci* is assigned the definition [consanguineal & first ascending generation & collateral & male & elder relative age]. The component 'consanguineal' differentiates the term *báci* from the set of terms *yauʔkhamà1, yauʔkhamàqaphóu, yauʔkhamà2, yauʔcâ, mêimà, yauʔphà, khêqóu, yâumà, mayî, khémà, θameʔ* and *chwêimà*. The subset of this set comprising the terms *yauʔcâ, mêimà, yauʔphà, khêqóu, yâumà, mayî, khémà, θameʔ* and *chwêimà* is discriminated from the term *báci* by the dimension of generation, since neither of the former are of first ascending generation, which *báci* is. The rest of the kin terms from the original set, viz. *yauʔkhamà1, yauʔkhamàqaphóu* and *yauʔkhamà2*, are distinguished from *báci* by the feature 'lineal', as the latter is collateral. In effect, the components 'first ascending generation' and 'collateral' in the definition of *báci* suffice to define the kin term with no appeal to the component 'consanguineal', making it unnecessary.

The kin term *citó* is provided with the definition [consanguineal & first ascending generation & collateral & female & elder relative age]. The feature 'consanguineal', again, is redundant. Thus, it can serve to distinguish *citó* from the set of kin terms *yauʔkhamà1, yauʔkhamàqaphóu, yauʔkhamà2, yauʔcâ, mêimà, yauʔphà, khêqóu, yâumà, mayî, khémà, θameʔ* and *chwêimà*. However, the same set of terms is covered by using in the definition of *citó* the components 'first ascending generation' (distinguishing the term from the subset of terms *yauʔcâ, mêimà, yauʔphà, khêqóu, yâumà, mayî, khémà, θameʔ* and *chwêimà*) and 'collateral' (distinguishing the term from the subset of terms *yauʔkhamà1, yauʔkhamàqaphóu, yauʔkhamà2*).

Continuing with examples of redundant definitions of kin terms in Burling's componential model, consider the description of *yâumà*. The kin term *yâumà* is attributed the meaning [affinal & contemporary (zero) generation & collateral & female relative & female speaker's sex]. Here, the feature of zero generation is superfluous. Indeed, it discriminates a large set of kin terms, comprising *pín, pí, qaphôu, qaphécî1, qaphécî2, qaphôulêi, qaphwâ, qaméicî1, qaméicî2, qaphwâlêi, qaphéi, qaméi, báci, qûlêi, citó, dólêi, θâ, θamî, tú, túmà, myî, myiʔ, cuʔ, tî, yauʔkhamà1, yauʔkhamàqaphóu, yauʔkhamà2, θameʔ, chwêimà*. Despite its discriminative power, however, the same set of kin terms is differentiated collectively by the use of other features in the definition of *yâumà*. The component 'affinal' puts apart *yâumà* from the subset *pín, pí, qaphôu, qaphécî1, qaphécî2, qaphôulêi, qaphwâ, qaméicî1, qaméicî2, qaphwâlêi, qaphéi, qaméi, báci, qûlêi, citó, dólêi, θâ, θamî, tú, túmà, myî, myiʔ, cuʔ, tî* (none of which is affinal) and the component 'collateral' puts apart *yâumà* from the subset *yauʔkhamà1, yauʔkhamàqaphóu, yauʔkhamà2, θameʔ, chwêimà* (none of which is collateral). The feature 'zero generation' in the definition of *yâumà* therefore makes no contribution to the kin term's demarcation from the rest of the terms.

Another case in which the generally strongly discriminative (and therefore useful) feature of generation is superfluous is the definition of *mayî*. The kin term *mayî* is assigned the meaning [affinal & contemporary (zero) generation & collateral & female relative & elder relative age & female speaker's sex]. The set of kin terms discriminated from *mayî* by the component of zero generation includes the words *pín, pí, qaphôu, qaphécî1, qaphécî2, qaphôulêi, qaphwâ, qaméicî1, qaméicî2, qaphwâlêi, qaphéi, qaméi, báci, qûlêi, citó, dólêi, θâ, θamî, tú, túmà, myî, myi?, cu?, tî, yau?khamà1, yau?khamàqaphóu, yau?khamà2, θame?, chwêimà.* Of these, the subset comprising *pín, pí, qaphôu, qaphécî1, qaphécî2, qaphôulêi, qaphwâ, qaméicî1, qaméicî2, qaphwâlêi, qaphéi, qaméi, báci, qûlêi, citó, dólêi, θâ, θamî, tú, túmà, myî, myi?, cu?* and *tî* is differentiated from *mayî* by its component 'affinal', whereas the rest of the kin terms from the original set, viz. the lexemes *yau?khamà1, yau?khamàqaphóu, yau?khamà2, θame?, chwêimà*, are differentiated from *mayî* by its component 'collateral'.

We do not need to continue with further illustrations of redundant definitions in Burling's componential model of Burmese. The full set of these is given in Table 2.4, where the superfluous components are enclosed in brackets.

Summarizing: in Burling's componential model, with 41 terms in all, there are 37 which are redundant, i.e. only four are correct. Also, two kin terms, *qaphécî* and *qaméicî*, are split into homonymous pairs in order to allow conjunctive definitions.

2.1.3 Wallace and Atkins on English

In their classic paper, Wallace and Atkins (1960) suggest a componential analysis of English, which is briefly discussed in this section (a simplified version of this model, cleared from the problems below, was used as an illustration in Chapter 1). They assume the following data set of kin terms with their attendant kin types:

grandfather: FaFa ∨ MoFa
grandmother: FaMo ∨ MoMo
father: Fa
mother: Mo
brother: Br
sister: Si
son: So
daughter: Da

grandson: SoSo ∨ DaSo
granddaughter: SoDa ∨ DaDa
uncle: FaBr ∨ MoBr ∨ FaFaBr ∨ MoFaBr, etc.
aunt: FaSi ∨ MoSi ∨ FaFaSi ∨ MoFaSi, etc.
cousin: FaBrSo ∨ FaBrDa ∨ MoBrSo ∨ MoBrDa ∨ FaSiSo ∨ FaSiDa ∨
MoSiSo ∨ MoSiDa ∨ FaFaBrSo ∨ FaMoBrSo ∨ MoFaSiDa, etc.

The set of features (dimensions) they seem to find sufficient to
differentiate all kin terms is as follows:

(1) Sex of relative, with values
　　　a1 – male
　　　a2 – female
(2) Generation, with values
　　　b1 – two generations above ego
　　　b2 – one generation above ego
　　　b3 – ego's own generation
　　　b4 – one generation below ego
　　　b5 – two generations below ego
(3) Lineality, with values
　　　c1 – lineal
　　　c2 – co-lineal
　　　c3 – ablineal.

(Goodenough's definition of the values on this feature of lineality is
used: lineals are persons who are ancestors or descendants of ego;
co-lineals are non-lineals all of whose ancestors include, or are included
in, all the ancestors of ego; ablineals are consanguineal relatives who are
neither lineals nor co-lineal.)

Wallace and Atkins propose the following componential model of
English, stated in their notation (the convention is adopted that where a
term does not discriminate on a dimension, the letter for that dimension
is given without any numerical index):

grandfather:	a1b1c1
grandmother:	a2b1c1
father:	a1b2c1
mother:	a2b2c1
brother:	a1b3c2
sister:	a2b3c2

son:	a1b4c1
daughter:	a2b4c1
grandson:	a1b5c1
granddaughter:	a2b5c1
uncle:	a1b1c2 and a1b2c2
aunt:	a2b1c2 and a2b2c2
cousin:	abc3
nephew:	a1b4c2 and a1b5c2
niece:	a2b4c2 and a2b5c2

However, the definitions of kin terms involving two expressions connected by 'and', such as those for *uncle, aunt, nephew* and *niece*, are flawed. Taking for example *uncle* in the authors' conception of the term, it indeed denotes the kin types FaBr, MoBr, which are of one generation above ego (i.e. b1), and the kin types FaFaBr, MoFaBr, which are of two generations above ego (i.e. b2). Still, the definition of *uncle* as a1b1c2 *and* a1b2c2 (which, reshaped in more explicit form, is just [a1 & b1 & c2 & a1 & b2 & c2]) can only meaningfully designate that all kin types covered by the term are *both* of one generation above ego (i.e. b1) *and* of two generations above ego (i.e. b2), which is of course logically impossible, since all dimensions by definition have mutually exclusive values and hence no single word can be both of one generation above ego and of two generations above ego. The correct logical connective in the definition therefore should be the disjunction ∨ 'or', rather than the conjunction & 'and', but this in effect results in violation of the requirement that all kin term definitions must be conjunctive, not disjunctive. Similar considerations explain the infelicity of the componential definitions of the remaining kin terms with analogous definitions, viz. *aunt, nephew* and *niece*.

2.1.4 Wordick on English

In a paper appearing in *American Anthropologist*, Wordick (1973: 1249) makes the claim, though indeed in passing, that English can be handled by just three dimenisons, viz. (1) type, with values lineal vs. collateral vs. affinal, (2) generation removal, with values 1, 0, −1, and (3) sex of referent, with values male vs. female. This assertion, however, cannot be taken very seriously. Thus, from a first glance it is seen that we cannot distinguish between *father, grandfather, great-grandfather*, etc. insofar as they are all lineal males of ascending generation; the same applies to the female counterparts of these words, *mother, grandmother* and *great-grandmother*, which are all lineal females of ascending generation.

Things however cannot be remedied by simply letting the feature 'generation' take further numbers as values. There is a problem with the first feature, 'type', for its values lineal, collateral and affinal – under their usual interpretations – are not mutually exclusive, as feature values should be. Thus, relatives can be *both* collateral *and* affinal – for example, those designating *uncle, aunt*, etc. according to Wallace and Atkins (1960: 61), Goodenough (1965: 285), Nogle (1974: 64, and in other publications); under Goodenough's conception (1965: 285) relatives may be both lineal and affinal (e.g. *father-in-law*, etc.). A reinterpretation that does make these values mutually exclusive is also not a way out. For example, defining lineal and collateral to apply just to consanguineals, but not to affinals, we run into an impossibility to demarcate, say, *uncle* and *father*, for *uncle* would be neither lineal (obviously), nor collateral (having affinal kin types like FaSiHu), nor affinal (having consanguineal kin types like FaBr). So failing to achieve a contrast on the dimension of type, the terms will not contrast on the other two dimensions generation and sex either, for which they have the same values. Thus, Wordick's proposal turns out to be substantially flawed in failing to satisfy the sufficiency condition of componential definitions.

2.1.5 Two examples from phonology

So far we have seen a number of cases from kinship systems proposed in the literature that are unsound either with respect to the sufficiency condition, the necessity condition or both. From a linguistic methodological perspective, it is interesting to see whether published componential analyses at other levels of description may suffer from the same shortcomings. In this section, I briefly consider two examples from distinctive feature analysis in phonology, showing that published componential analyses in this branch are also not immune to the same weaknesses.

2.1.5.1 *Cherry, Halle and Jakobson*

In a classic paper in *Language*, Cherry, Halle and Jakobson (1953) propose a phonemic system for Russian. Their express goal is to provide definitions of Russian phonemes with necessary and sufficient conditions and therefore eliminate all redundancy in the system (one of the ideas – aside from the purely linguistic considerations – being to satisfy the requirements of information theory for performing the minimum number of steps for identification of each speech sound, an idea about language sounds incidentally abandoned later by Halle).

The authors describe the 42 Russian phonemes in terms of the following 11 binary (+/−) features:

(1) vocalic
(2) consonantal
(3) compact
(4) diffuse
(5) grave
(6) nasal
(7) continuant
(8) voiced
(9) sharp
(10) strident
(11) stressed.

Table 2.5 gives the resultant componential analysis in terms of the 11 binary (+/−) features used (ignore for the moment the brackets, so that all components, non-bracketed and bracketed, count). The notation in the table follows the IPA system of transcription, except in the following: a comma after a letter indicates palatalization; the accent mark is placed immediately before the vowel letter; and a strident stop is rendered by the same letter as the corresponding constrictive with the addition of a circumflex.

A closer look at the table reveals that all the eleven dimensions are indeed sufficient to differentiate each phoneme from all other phonemes in the system. However, a number of violations of the necessity condition can be observed.

Let us consider the definition of the phoneme /g,/, which comprises the features [−vocalic & +consonantal & +compact & +grave & −continuant & +voiced & +sharp]. The feature [−vocalic], however, is superfluous. It discriminates the set of phonemes /u 'u o e i 'i a 'a r r, l l,/. The subset /u 'u o e i 'i a 'a/ is differentiated by the component [+consonantal], /l l,/ is differentiated by [−continuant], /r/ by [+sharp] and /r,/ by [+voiced], that is, all phonemes discriminated by [−vocalic] are actually also discriminated by other features already used in the definition of /g,/.

The phoneme /z/ is defined in the table as the bundle of features [−vocalic & +consonantal & −compact & −grave & −nasal & +continuant & +voiced & −sharp]. The feature [−nasal] makes no contribution to the demarcation of /z/ from the other phonemes in the data set since the set it discriminates, viz. /n n, m m,/, is also discriminated by the feature [+voiced]. (The palatal counterpart phoneme /z,/ is redundant for the same reason.)

Finally, an example of a phoneme whose definition contains two redundant components. /b,/ is assigned the features [−vocalic & +consonantal & −compact & +grave & −nasal & −continuant & +voiced & +sharp]. The feature [+consonantal] discriminates the phonemes /u ′u o e i ′i a ′a/, the feature [−continuant] distinguishes /l l,/, the feature [+voiced] /r,/ and [+sharp] /r, l/, which comprises the set of all phonemes that [−vocalic] can discriminate. This circumstance makes the use of the latter in the definition of /b,/ redundant. Besides, [−nasal] is also unnecessary, as the set /n n, m m,/ it distinguishes is also distinguished by the feature [+voiced].

The full list of redundancies is exhibited in Table 2.5 (the superfluous features are enclosed in brackets). The observation one can make from the table is that there is a lot of redundancy in these authors' analysis: the 17 feature values enclosed in brackets are those components which are superfluous for the demarcation. 12 out of a total of 42 phonemes have an incorrect description. As a result of this, the average number of features in a definition of a phoneme turns out to comprise 6.14, rather than 6.5, components as suggested by Cherry, Halle and Jakobson (1953). Also, it is worth noting that some feature bundles are incorrect in more than one way; thus, the palatal phoneme /d,/ is assigned three superfluous feature values, and /d/, /ŝ/, and the palatal /b,/ two such values.

2.1.5.2 Spencer

It is interesting that not only large data sets, but also miniature ones can suffer from inconsistency. By way of a simple phonological illustration, consider the data set comprising only five elements, viz. the vowels /i e a o u/. In the introductory book on phonology *Phonology: Theory and Description*, Spencer (1996: 124) presents an 'underspecified matrix', i.e. 'a matrix with all redundancies extracted' of English vowels in terms of the features 'back', 'high' and 'low', see Table 2.6. (The place of redundant feature-values is left blank by Spencer.)

However, a closer look at Spencer's analysis shows that the feature bundle of the vowel /e/ is redundant, since the bundle [−back & −high & −low] contains the superfluous component [−low]. Thus, this definition of /e/ is intended to discriminate most economically this phoneme from the remaining phonemes /i a o u/. The feature [−back] in its definition distinguishes /e/ from /a o u/, all of which are [+back], and the feature [−high] distinguishes /e/ from /u/, the last sound to be distinguished (which is [+high]). The feature [−low] is obviously superfluous for the demarcation, contrary to what Spencer assumes, demonstrating that redundancy in discovering linguistic systems can creep in even in very simple systems of interrelations. This requires some explanation.

The first question relates to the logic of redundancy: Why is redundancy at all possible in ascribing a model to a data set (= language system)? The logical reason is the availability of more than one potential contrast between two system elements (i.e. when these elements are more 'dissimilar'), and instead of using just one, the model profiles an element using two or more contrasting features (= components). No such possibility exists for a pair of elements that differ in just one feature-value (i.e. when these elements are 'maximally similar'); this feature-value *must* be used anyway in the model to achieve contrast.

The second question relates to the psychology of redundancy, or to the question of why redundancy may creep into our analyses (as was the case in all our kinship and phonological illustrations). We believe that the emergence of such undesirable situations can be attributed to the computational complexity of the discrimination task, conforming to the redundancy-free requirement. The basic point is this. If we view human model-discovery as sequential acts of choosing a contrast between any two elements in the system, in order to avoid redundancy, at every point of this sequence at which alternatives exist, we must check all previous alternative decisions, such that are related to the current choice, and make the current choice in accordance with them, eventually *revising* our previous decisions.

By way of illustration, let us try to see how the redundant analysis in Table 2.6 might have crept in. Suppose we want to find the distinctive feature bundle of the phoneme /e/. Then its contrasts with the remaining elements in the system, viz. /i a o u/ are as follows (some elementary phonological knowledge is assumed):

The contrasts of /e/ with other vowels

(Step 1):	e ∼ i	[−high]				
(Step 2):	e ∼ a	[−back]	OR	[−low]		
(Step 3):	e ∼ o	[−back]	OR	[−round]		
(Step 4):	e ∼ u	[−back]	OR	[−high]	OR	[−round]

Let us view the discrimination process of /e/ from all other phonemes as a sequence of decisions that need to be made. At Step 1, we have no choice and must use the component [−high]. At Step 2, however, we do have a choice, between [−back] and [−low]. Suppose we choose

[−low]. Up to this moment, /e/ is profiled with two components [−high, −low]. At Step 3, we must add some of the features [−back] or [−round], since there is no other alternative for distinguishing /e/ from /o/, so, adding, say, [−back], we get the definition [−high & −low & −back]. At Step 4, we do not need to add a component, since /e/ discriminates from /u/ by components already in the definition of /e/. This results in a superfluous [−low]. Why? The reason is that at Step 2 we should have remembered that we had made a choice between [−low] and [−back], and at Step 3, we should have backtracked to this choice, and seen that we should have chosen not [−low], but [−back] instead, which is anyway needed for contrasting /e/ with the other vowels. This failure to revise our previous decision is thus the reason for the redundant component [−low] to creep in. We should note, however, that such a process, in which one needs to keep a record of all previous alternative decisions and be ready to revise them (called 'non-monotonic') may be difficult to perform even for computers, let alone human analysts. This computational complexity of the task is the basic reason for the inconsistencies we discussed of the componential models proposed by human agents.

2.2 Multiple solutions

2.2.1 Burling and the multiple solutions debate

In this section, I will be concerned with the problem of multiple componential models that can be arrived at, analysing the same data set. This problem was raised in a famous paper by Robbins Burling (1964), entitled 'Cognition and componential analysis: God's truth or hocus pocus?'.

Burling's basic point in this article is to show the large number of logically possible alternative componential models of any given set of kin terms. Thus, if there are three items in the kin term set (call the items a, b and c), one has three apparent choices: use a component which separates a from b and c; one which separates b from a and c; or one which separates c from a and b. The possibility of using components which are relevant for only a part of the set doubles the number of possibilities. Whereas for a three-term set the possibilities number 6, for any given four-kin term set they number 124. In general, the number of logically possible alternative componential models steeply increases with the increase of the number of kin terms that have to be discriminated. In Burling's opinion, there are no means to sensibly reduce this huge number of alternatives and the methods advocated are not equal to their goal – if this goal is to uncover 'psychological validity' – and the conduct of componential analysis is therefore 'hocus-pocus' rather than an enterprise that reveals 'God's truth'.

Burling's basic thrust was on the theoretical possibilities of choosing an indefinite number of ways to partition the space of relatives into kin terms and on the difficulty (or even, impossibility) of determining which features exactly are used in categorization by the native speakers of the language. In his response to Burling's challenge, Dell Hymes (1964) was less sceptical on the question, suggesting that further constraints from the culture, etc. will limit the possibilities. Hymes (1964: 118) writes that 'The analyst [...] is never in the situation of having to consider all logically possible sortings. His field procedure secures elimination of many of them by members of the culture, and he does all he can to devise questions, techniques, predictions which will discriminate among the alternatives that may remain.' Frake (1964), who also took part in the debate, seemed to share Dell Hymes's view, but his short comment was also largely theoretical, like those of the other commentators, and did not introduce any definiteness in the argument. Other theorists in the ethnosemantic field (e.g. Goodenough 1967) seemed to agree on the seriousness of the problem of multiple solutions, but not much was done to really try to resolve the difficulty. Thus, the practitioners of componential analysis continued to provide models with little or no concern for alternative analyses. Others attempted to further test a couple or so of alternative componential models with psychological methods (triad tests, etc.) in an attempt to choose 'psychologically valid' models, while still others substituted componential analysis with other methods (extensionists, etc.) in search of better methods for representing native speakers' categorization.

The review of the literature actually shows that the problem was never really understood in its depth, and the range of alternative solutions was not fully appreciated. One consensus point was however reached, and it was that it was not theoretical and programmatic studies, but analyses of concrete and exhaustive data sets that could resolve the multiple-solutions problem, and ultimately evaluate the utility of the componential analysis method. It became clear that whether one pursues the more ambitious goal of 'psychological validity' (as in ethnosemantics) or the more modest goal of revealing structural relationships (as in lexical semantics), the method should be empirically tested to see whether it can produce a manageable number of alternatives or not. What is needed then are not further programmatic statements and methodological arguments, but substantive descriptions of exhaustive language data sets. Burling, in his rejoinder, expressed this position as follows:

> I yield to no one in my admiration for Goodenough's analysis of Trukese kinship terminology, but Goodenough showed that his methods were possible by giving us an analysis of a whole system, and not by simply suggesting methods and illustrating them on scattered and artificially simple examples. In discussing my fear of the residue of indeterminacy, I said, 'I can be proved wrong by analyses which admit to no alternatives.' [...] I have the nagging fear that the reason full analyses have not been given is because the methods advocated are not equal to the goals. I would really like to be proved wrong, for I think componential analysis is lots of fun, but I will only be persuaded by substantive descriptions, not by methodological arguments. (Burling 1964: 121–2)

I turn in the next section to the discussion of whole and exhaustive data sets with the goal of assessing the problem of indeterminacy.

2.2.2 Explicating the problem: example from Bulgarian

Here, I provide componential analyses of two comprehensive data sets: the Bulgarian kin terms of reference and the kin terms of address. The models presented are consistent (i.e. with kin term definitions with necessary and sufficient conditions) and with all alternative solutions, guaranteed by the computer program KINSHIP (to be described in Chapter 3) with which they are produced. The models constructed employ a fixed set of standard features (dimensions), which are listed below, provided with some explanations and examples.

(1) Generation of relative, with feature values
  generation = 2
  generation = 1
  generation = 0
  generation = −1
  generation = −2, etc.

The value of the feature 'generation' can be any integer, including a range of integers (bounded by $\geq$ 'equal or greater than' or $\leq$ 'smaller or equal to'), as e.g. the cross-generational Bulgarian kin term *zet* with kin types SiHu and DaHu, meaning 'brother-in-law' or 'son-in-law', having the feature value generation $=\leq 0$.

(2) Sex of relative, with feature values
      sex = m – male
      sex = f – female

(3) Genealogical distance, with the integer feature values
      distance = 1
      distance = 2
      distance = 3, etc.

This feature, analogously to 'generation', can take as value any integer, including a range of integers (bounded by $\geq$ 'equal or greater than' or $\leq$ 'smaller or equal to'). The kin type Fa, for instance, has the value distance = 1, FaBr has the value distance = 2, and FaBrWi distance = 3.

(4) Affinity of relative, with three feature values
      affinity = cons – consanguineal, or absence of a marital tie
      affinity = aff-ego – affinal to ego, or marital tie directly to ego
      affinity = aff – affinal, marital tie, but not directly to ego

Examples: the kin type MoSi has the value affinity = cons, Wi has the value affinity = aff-ego, and SiHu has affinity = aff.

(5) Affinity of the 1st connecting relative (link), with feature values
      affinity 1st link = cons – consanguineal (first link is a blood relative)
      affinity 1st link = aff – affinal (first link is a relative by marriage)

Examples: the kin types F̱aSi, S̱iHu (where first link is underlined) both have the feature value affinity 1st link = cons, while W̱iMo, H̱uSi are both affinity 1st link = aff.

(6) Sex of the 1st connecting relative (link), with feature values
      sex 1st link = m – male
      sex 1st link = f – female

Examples: the kin types F̱a and F̱aSi (where first link is underlined) both have the feature value sex 1st link = m, while M̱o and W̱iSi are both sex 1st link = f.

(7) Generation of the last link, with the feature values
      generation last link = 1

generation last link = 0
generation last link = −1

The generations of the last links will be: Fa and Mo = 1; Si, Br, Hu and Wi = 0; So and Da = −1; hence, e.g., Fa<u>Mo</u> (where last link is underlined) will have the feature value generation last link = 1 for this feature, while <u>So</u> or So<u>So</u> will have the feature value generation last link = −1.

(8) Sex of the second connecting relative (link), with feature values
sex 2nd link = m – male
sex 2nd link = f – female

Examples: the kin types Fa<u>Fa</u>Si, Mo<u>Br</u> (where second link is underlined) both have the feature value sex 2nd link = m, while Fa<u>Mo</u>Si, Mo<u>Si</u> are both sex 2nd link = f.

(9) Affinity of the second connecting relative (link), with feature values
affinity 2nd link = cons – consanguineal
affinity 2nd link = aff – affinal

Examples: the kin types Fa<u>Fa</u>Si, Mo<u>Br</u> (where second link is underlined) both have the feature value affinity 2nd link = cons, while Br<u>Wi</u>Si, Si<u>Hu</u> are both affinity 2nd link = aff.

(10) Lineality, with the feature values:
lineality = lin – lineal
lineality = coll – collateral

(11) Seniority within one generation, with feature values
seniority = e – elder
seniority = y – younger.

2.2.2.1 *Bulgarian reference kin terms and their componential analyses*

Bulgarian kin terms have attracted some attention on the part of linguists who have looked at a number of problems related to this semantic domain, e.g. meaning shifts (Stoeva 1972), origin and dialectal distribution of some terms (Gălăbov 1986; Barbolova 2000), pragmatic viewpoint shift (Choi 1997). Data on Bulgarian reference kinship can be found in various places, e.g. in Mladenov (1979[1929]: 188–90) and Stojkov (1993[1962]: 323–4]; see also the references therein).

Consanguineals are listed in Comrie and Corbett (1993). Bulgarian has the following basic lexemes for designating relatives, which we give with glosses: *pradjado* 'great-grandfather', *prababa* 'great-grandmother', *djado* 'grandfather', *baba* 'grandmother', *bašta* 'father', *majka* 'mother', *vujčo* 'maternal uncle', *čičo* 'paternal uncle', *lelja* 'aunt', *brat* 'brother', *sestra* 'sister', *batko* 'elder brother', *kaka* 'elder sister', *bratovčedka* 'female cousin', *bratovčed* 'male cousin', *sin* 'son', *dăšterja* 'daughter', *plemennik* 'nephew', *plemennica* 'niece', *vnuk* 'grandson', *vnučka* 'granddaughter', *pravnuk* 'great-grandson', *pravnučka* 'great-granddaughter', *măž* 'husband', *žena* 'wife', *šurej* 'brother-in-law', *šurenajka* 'brother-in-law's wife', *dever* and *zet* and *badžanak* 'brother-in-law', *zălva* and *baldăza* and *snaha* and *etărva* 'sister-in-law', *svekăr* and *tăst* 'father-in-law', *svekărva* and *tăšta* 'mother-in-law', *vujna* and *strina* 'aunt', *lelin* and *tetin* 'uncle'.

These lexemes with their range of denotata are given below. This list is intended to be exhaustive and it covers practically all terms used in standard literary Bulgarian. However, some remarks are in order regarding the data. First, we omit numerous synonymous forms of the lexemes listed, which are basically dialectal variations (e.g. for *dăšterja* we have also *šterka*, *k'erka* (south-eastern dialects), *čerka* (north-west dialects)). Second, also omitted are certain definitely dialectal lexemes for designating relatives, such as *sestrinik* (SiSo) or *bratanec* (BrSo) or a group of words for designating husband's sisters according to their relative age: *kalina* (oldest HuSi), *malina* (HuSi younger than *kalina*), *hubavka* (HuSi younger than *malina*), *jabălka* (HuSi younger than *hubavka*), and *dunka* (youngest HuSi) (see Marinov (1892: 172–3), Gerov (1897: 159)). Third, insofar as the range of denotata of kin terms is concerned, we also follow literary, rather than dialectal, usages (thus, for example, for the lexeme *baba* 'grandmother' we list only the kin types FaMo and MoMo, given in standard Bulgarian dictionaries, but not also FaMoSi and MoMoSi, as the kin term is somewhere used). Finally, we note that for our purposes it is sufficient to limit the terminology to three generations above and below ego, though the Bulgarian prefix *pra-* just as the English word *great*, may be used any number of times to denote one-generation removal.

1. *pradjado*: FaFaFa ∨ FaMoFa ∨ MoFaFa ∨ MoMoFa
2. *prababa*: FaFaMo ∨ FaMoMo ∨ MoFaMo ∨ MoMoMo
3. *djado*: FaFa ∨ MoFa
4. *baba*: FaMo ∨ MoMo
5. *bašta*: Fa
6. *majka*: Mo
7. *vujčo*: MoBr

8. *čičo*: FaBr
9. *lelja*: FaSi
10. *tetka*: MoSi
11. *brat*: Br
12. *sestra*: Si
13. *batko*: elderBr
14. *kaka*: elderSi
15. *bratovčed*: MoSiSo ∨ MoBrSo ∨ FaSiSo ∨ FaBrSo ∨ MoMoSiDaSo ∨ MoMoSiSoSo ∨ MoMoBrDaSo ∨ MoMoBrSoSo ∨ MoFaSiDaSo ∨ MoFaSiSoSo ∨ MoFaBrDaSo ∨ MoFaBrSoSo ∨ FaMoSiDaSo ∨ FaMoSiSoSo ∨ FaMoBrDaSo ∨ FaMoBrSoSo ∨ FaFaSiDaSo ∨ FaFaSiSoSo ∨ FaFaBrDaSo ∨ FaFaBrSoSo
16. *bratovčedka*: MoSiDa ∨ MoBrDa ∨ FaSiDa ∨ FaBrDa ∨ MoMoSiDaDa ∨ MoMoSiSoDa ∨ MoMoBrDaDa ∨ MoMoBrSoDa ∨ MoFaSiDaDa ∨ MoFaSiSoDa ∨ MoFaBrDaDa ∨ MoFaBrSoDa ∨ FaMoSiDaDa ∨ FaMoSiSoDa ∨ FaMoBrDaDa ∨ FaMoBrSoDa ∨ FaFaSiDaDa ∨ FaFaSiSoDa ∨ FaFaBrDaDa ∨ FaFaBrSoDa
17. *sin*: So
18. *dăsterja*: Da
19. *plemennik*: BrSo ∨ SiSo
20. *plemennica*: BrDa ∨ SiDa
21. *vnuk*: SoSo ∨ DaSo
22. *vnučka*: DaDa ∨ SoDa
23. *pravnuk*: SoSoSo ∨ SoDaSo ∨ DaSoSo ∨ DaDaSo
24. *pravnučka*: DaDaDa ∨ SoSoDa ∨ SoDaDa ∨ DaSoDa
25. *măž*: Hu
26. *žena*: Wi
27. *šurej*: WiBr
28. *šurenajka*: WiBrWi
29. *dever*: HuBr
30. *zet*: SiHu ∨ DaHu
31. *badžanak*: WiSiHu
32. *zălva*: HuSi
33. *baldăza*: WiSi
34. *snaha*: BrWi ∨ SoWi
35. *etărva*: HuBrWi
36. *vujna*: MoBrWi
37. *strina*: FaBrWi
38. *lelin*: FaSiHu
39. *tetin*: MoSiHu
40. *svekăr*: HuFa

41. *svekǎrva*: HuMo
42. *tǎst*: WiFa
43. *tǎsta*: WiMo

This data set was explored with the set of 11 features described above (on pages 41–3), requiring that all alternative componential models be found. The analysis revealed that eight alternative overall feature (= dimension) sets are necessary and sufficient to discriminate all reference Bulgarian kin terms (two pairs of terms, viz. *batko-brat*, and *kaka-sestra* fail to discriminate from one another, since the meaning of the first part of the pair is included into the meaning of the second). These overall feature (dimension) sets are listed below:

All overall feature (dimension) sets

 I. {sex & sex 1st & affinity 1st & generation & distance & affinity}
 II. {sex & generation & sex 1st & affinity 1st & distance & affinity 2nd}
 III. {sex & sex 1st & generation & distance & affinity & affinity 2nd}
 IV. {sex & generation & sex 1st & affinity 1st & distance & generation last}
 V. {sex & lineality & affinity 2nd & sex 1st & affinity 1st & distance & generation last}
 VI. {sex & sex 1st & affinity 1st & distance & lineality & affinity & generation last}
 VII. {sex & sex 1st & affinity 1st & generation & sex 2nd & lineality & affinity & generation last}
 VIII. {sex & sex 1st & affinity 2nd & generation & sex 2nd & lineality & affinity & generation last}

To each overall feature set, there correspond an immense number of componential models, resulting from the different definitions that can be given to some kin terms, using only features from this overall feature set. We call such a concise representation of multiple componential models a *componential scheme*. For economy of space, in Table 2.7 we give just one componential scheme (produced by our KINSHIP program), viz. that corresponding to the dimension set I.

In a componential scheme, the different definitions of one kin term can freely combine with any other alternative definition of other terms to produce a componential model. Therefore, the total number of alternative componential models, Q, represented by a componential scheme, is equal to the product of the number of definitions, N, each individual term has obtained, expressed by the formula $Q = N1 \times N2 \times N3 \ldots \times Nm$. For example, assuming our data set to comprise only three terms, the first having two definitions, the second one, and the third four, we have $Q = 2 \times 1 \times 4 = 8$ componential analyses in all. In our particular case in Table 2.7, there are 21 terms having two definitions, three terms having three definitions, and eight terms having four definitions, i.e. we get $2^{21} \times 3^3 \times 4^8 = 3,710,851,743,744$. This is a very large number of componential models and so are the models corresponding to the other dimension sets, the total number of alternative componential analyses of the reference terms being the sum total of all these. In the following, we shall turn again to this question.

2.2.2.2 *Bulgarian vocative kin terms and their componential analyses*

The Bulgarian kin terms for address are given below. It may be mentioned that the vocatives vary dialectically. Also, some of the terms, although they definitely have vocative forms (e.g. *bratovčede, bratovčedke, bratko, sestro*), which are given in the list, are not very frequently used and the relatives designated by them are often called by their personal names instead.

1. *djado*: FaFa ∨ MoFa ∨ WiFa ∨ FaFaFa ∨ FaMoFa ∨ MoFaFa ∨ MoMoFa
2. *babo*: FaMo ∨ MoMo ∨ WiMo ∨ FaFaMo ∨ FaMoMo ∨ MoFaMo ∨ MoMoMo
3. *tatko*: Fa ∨ HuFa
4. *majko*: Mo ∨ HuMo
5. *vujčo*: MoBr
6. *čičo*: FaBr
7. *leljo*: FaSi
8. *tetko*: MoSi
9. *bratko*: Br
10. *sestro*: Si
11. *bate*: eBr
12. *kako*: eSi
13. *bratovčede*: MoSiSo ∨ MoBrSo ∨ FaSiSo ∨ FaBrSo ∨ MoMoSiDaSo ∨ MoMoSiSoSo ∨ MoMoBrDaSo ∨ MoMoBrSoSo ∨ MoFaSiDaSo ∨ MoFaSiSoSo ∨ MoFaBrDaSo ∨ MoFaBrSoSo ∨ FaMoSiDaSo ∨ FaMoSiSoSo ∨ FaMoBrDaSo ∨ FaMoBrSoSo ∨ FaFaSiDaSo ∨ FaFaSiSoSo ∨ FaFaBrDaSo ∨ FaFaBrSoSo

14. *bratovčedke*: MoSiDa ∨ MoBrDa ∨ FaSiDa ∨ FaBrDa ∨
    MoMoSiDaDa ∨ MoMoSiSoDa ∨ MoMoBrDaDa ∨
    MoMoBrSoDa ∨ MoFaSiDaDa ∨ MoFaSiSoDa ∨ MoFaBrDaDa
    ∨ MoFaBrSoDa ∨ FaMoSiDaDa ∨ FaMoSiSoDa ∨ FaMoBrDaDa
    ∨ FaMoBrSoDa ∨ FaFaSiDaDa ∨ FaFaSiSoDa ∨ FaFaBrDaDa ∨
    FaFaBrSoDa
15. *sine*: So
16. *dăste*: Da
17. *plemenniko*: BrSo ∨ SiSo
18. *plemennice*: BrDa ∨ SiDa
19. *măzo*: Hu
20. *ženo*: Wi
21. *zetko*: SiHu ∨ DaHu
22. *badžo*: WiSiHu
23. *snaho*: BrWi ∨ SoWi
24. *vujno*: MoBrWi
25. *strino*: FaBrWi
26. *lelinčo*: FaSiHu
27. *tetinčo*: MoSiHu

The KINSHIP system was run on this data set with the features described earlier, requiring that all alternative componential models be found. The system reported six alternative overall feature (= dimension) sets that are necessary and sufficient to discriminate the address forms data set. Again, two pairs of address terms, viz. *batko-brat*, and *kaka-sestra* fail to discriminate from one another, since the meaning of the first part of the pair is included into the meaning of the second.

All overall feature (dimension) sets

 I. {sex & generation last & generation & sex 1st & affinity 1st & distance}
 II. {sex & generation last & generation & sex 1st & distance & affinity}
 III. {sex & generation last & generation & sex 1st & affinity 1st & lineality & affinity}
 IV. {sex & generation last & generation & sex 1st & affinity 2nd & lineality & affinity}
 V. {sex & generation last & generation & sex 1st & affinity 1st & lineality & sex 2nd}
 VI. {sex & generation last & generation & sex 1st & affinity & lineality & sex 2nd}

The componential scheme given in Table 2.8 also represents a large number of componential models, as one term has two definitions, four terms have three definitions, four terms have four definitions, and one has five definitions, viz. we get $2^1 \times 3^4 \times 4^4 \times 5^1 = 207,360$ models. All componential analyses of the Bulgarian vocatives, corresponding to the six dimension sets, will be equal to the sum total of all these models.

2.2.2.3 The indeterminacy in Bulgarian

To give the complete picture of the indeterminacy resulting from processing our reference and address kin terms without imposing any constraints, below we summarize the results:

Reference kin terms

I. {sex & sex 1st & affinity 1st & generation & distance & affinity}, $2^{21} \times 3^3 \times 4^8 = 3,710,851,743,744$

II. {sex & generation & sex 1st & affinity 1st & distance & affinity 2nd}, $2^{17} \times 3^2 = 1,179,648$

III. {sex & sex 1st & generation & distance & affinity & affinity 2nd}, $2^{16} \times 3^2 \times 5^2 = 14,745,600$

IV. {sex & generation & sex 1st & affinity 1st & distance & generation last}, $2^{23} \times 3^8 \times 4^2 \times 5^4 \times 6^2 = 19,813,556,551,680,000$

V. {sex & lineality & affinity 2nd & sex 1st & affinity 1st & distance & generation last}, $2^{12} \times 3^2 \times 4^4 = 9,437,184$

VI. {sex & sex 1st & affinity 1st & distance & lineality & affinity & generation last}, $2^{13} \times 3^9 \times 4^3 \times 8^4 = 42,268,920,643,584$

VII. {sex & sex 1st & affinity 1st & generation & sex 2nd & lineality & affinity & generation last}, $2^9 \times 3^6 \times 4^4 \times 5^2 \times 6^8 \times 7^4 \times 9^2 \times 10^2 = 78,030,545,907,477,381,120,000$

VIII. {sex & sex 1st & affinity 2nd & generation & sex 2nd & lineality & affinity & generation last}, $2^{14} \times 3^3 \times 4^6 \times 5^9 \times 6^2 \times 8^2 = 2,717,908,992,000,000,000$

Address kin terms

I. {sex & generation last & generation & sex 1st & affinity 1st & distance}, $2^1 \times 3^4 \times 4^4 \times 5^1 = 207,360$

II. {sex & generation last & generation & sex 1st & distance & affinity}, $2^{10} \times 3^2 \times 4^4 \times 6^5 \times 7^1 = 128,421,199,872$

III. {sex & generation last & generation & sex 1st & affinity 1st & lineality & affinity}, $2^2 \times 3^6 \times 4^3 \times 6^2 = 6,718,464$

IV. {sex & generation last & generation & sex 1st & affinity 2nd & lineality & affinity}, $2^6 \times 3^2 \times 4^4 \times 6^1 \times 7^1 = 6{,}193{,}152$

V. {sex & generation last & generation & sex 1st & affinity 1st & lineality & sex 2nd}, $2^6 \times 3^1 \times 4^2 = 3{,}072$

VI. {sex & generation last & generation & sex 1st & affinity & lineality & sex 2nd}, $2^4 \times 3^{10} \times 4^7 = 15{,}479{,}341{,}056$

The total number of componential models of the reference terms then will equal the sum of all componential models corresponding to each of the eight reference componential schemes, and the total number of componential models of the address terms will equal the sum of all componential models corresponding to each of the six address componential schemes. These are astronomical numbers and the only conclusion we can draw is that the completely unconstrained componential analysis, in which the adequacy criterion is to provide all and only the 'correct' models corresponding to a kin term data set, leads to an intolerably large number of models. The indeterminacy in the componential analysis of Bulgarian kin terms is strongly reminiscent of the warning by Burling (1964), even though in his discussion he does not mention such huge numbers. Without some constraints which limit the indeterminacy in some principled manner the method itself seems in jeopardy.

2.2.3 Redundancy and multiple solutions

There are various factors introducing additional ambiguity in the analysis of kinship systems (like homonymity, the use of 'empty lexemes', redundancy and some others). Burling (1964) recognizes redundancy as a major factor in this respect. In this chapter, we also observed that redundancy quite commonly occurs in componential analysis practice, so it deserves our special attention.

Noricks (1987) undertakes, among other problems, the task of choosing a psychologically valid componential analysis of Niutao kinship terms (Niutao is a Polynesian language of Tuvalu). He tries to evaluate their cognitive validity, the measure of which is the ability to predict similarity judgments by Niutao native speakers in kin term triad tests. Noricks proposes four different overall features (= dimensions) that can partition the same data set, and within each of the four sets of alternative dimensions, comes up with two componential models: a nonredundant and a redundant one. Thus, he gets eight componential models in all, four nonredundant and four redundant. He then tests all eight models (using triad tests, estimating similarity judgments of subjects on kinship terms), reporting that one of the redundant models is significantly and consistently better supported by his experiments than the others.

We need not go into a detailed discussion of his results, but may focus on just one of his componential analyses. It employs the following semantic dimensions:

(1) Generation distance between ego and alter, with values
    1.1 – more than one generation distant
    1.2 – one generation distant
    1.3 – zero generation distant

(2) Affinity of alter, with values
    2.1 – consanguineal
    2.2 – affinal

(3) Presence of a coeval consanguineal pair of opposite sex in the genealogical chain between ego and alter, with values
    3.1 – present
    3.2 – absent

(4) Sex of the connecting relative between ego and alter, with values
    4.1 – female
    4.2 – male

(5) Generation seniority of alter, with values
    5.1 – senior
    5.2 – junior

(6) Sex of alter, with values
    6.1 – male
    6.2 – female.

Noricks then presents (Table 2.9) a componential scheme encompassing two componential analyses, one nonredundant, in which the only components that count are those given without brackets in the table, and one redundant, in which all the components, with and without parentheses, count. Note that e1, e2, ... etc. in angle brackets denote the empty cells in a row and are given for later reference.

We should now look at the number of potential redundant componential models corresponding to the componential scheme of Table 2.9. How many models are there? To find this, we should, first, find the number of all potential redundant definitions of each kin term and, second, compute their product (as we did above in the computation of all nonredundant models), since each redundant definition of a kin term can freely combine with all the redundant definitions of all other kin terms.

Let us turn to the first task, the computation of potentially redundant definitions of individual kin terms. Consider Noricks's redundant definition of the kin term *makupuna* (first row), presented with its numerical components: [1.1 & (2.1) & 5.2]. Here, Noricks marks one component, the one in brackets, viz. (2.1), as redundant. However, there are also three additional redundant components, viz. those employing dimensions Nos. 3, 4 or 6 (corresponding respectively to the empty cells <e1>, <e2> and <e3> in the table). (For the sake of simplicity, we assume here and in the following that all dimensions are applicable to all kin terms.) Thus, having four potential redundant components – one given in parenthesis and three in angle brackets in the table – we can use them individually or combine them in pairs, triples, etc. to obtain further redundant definitions of *makupuna*, containing respectively one, two, three, etc. redundant components.

Let us now consider the alternative redundant definitions of *makupuna* containing just one redundant component. In addition to Noricks's definition [1.1 & (2.1) & 5.2], we will get the alternatives [1.1 & <e1> & 5.2], [1.1 & <e2> & 5.2] and [1.1 & <e3> & 5.2], i.e. four alternatives in all.

We can proceed with definitions of the kin term *makupuna* with two redundant components. The possible two-way redundant combinations from four redundant components are six in number; hence the resultant definitions of the kin terms are [1.1 & (2.1) & <e1> & 5.2], [1.1 & (2.1) & <e2> & 5.2], [1.1 & (2.1) & 5.2 & <e3>], [1.1 & <e1> & <e2> & 5.2], [1.1 & <e1> & 5.2 & <e3>] and [1.1 & <e2> & 5.2 & <e3>].

We can also form triples from these four elements, in which case the resultant redundant definitions of *makupuna* become four in number: [1.1 & (2.1) & <e1> & <e2> & 5.2], [1.1 & (2.1) & <e1> & 5.2 & <e3>], [1.1 & (2.1) & <e2> & 5.2 & <e3>], [1.1 & <e1> & <e2> & 5.2 & <e3>].

Finally, we can form just one quadruple out of our four elements, yielding the kin term's definition with four redundant components: [1.1 & (2.1) & <e1> & <e2> & 5.2 & <e3>].

To rephrase the matter in more general and precise terms, the number of redundant definitions of a kin term depends on the number of potentially redundant components (= empty cells) that can be used in its definition (in the case under discussion, this number is four, corresponding to dimensions numbered 2, 3, 4 and 6). To obtain the number of redundant definitions with one, two, three, etc. redundant components, the following 'combinations formula', also referred to as 'r-combination' or 'n choose r', is used:

$$C(n, r) = n!/r!(n - r)!$$

where n is the number of all potentially redundant components and r is an n-way $(1, 2, \ldots n)$ combination of these components. Thus, for instance, in the case of definitions with two redundant components (i.e. $n = 4$, $r = 2$), we will get:

$$C(4, 2) = 4 \times 3 \times 2 \times 1 / 2 \times 1 \times (2 \times 1) = 6$$

All redundant definitions of *makupuna*, containing a different number of redundant components, should then be summed up to get the total number of such definitions for the kin term. This number is: $4 + 6 + 4 + 1 = 15$.

We need to find the number of redundant definitions of each kin term from Table 2.9. These are as follows (computed by the formula above):

	No. of redundant components	No. of redundant dfns
makupuna	4	15
tupuna	4	15
tamana	1	1
maatua	1	1
tama	2	3
tamatuangaane	1	1
maatuatuangaane	1	1
tuaatina	2	3
fungaono	4	15
maa	3	7
aavanga	3	7
taina	3	7
tuangaane	3	7

We can now proceed with the second step of our computation of all redundant componential models of Niutao kin terms in Table 2.9 by multiplying the numbers of redundant definitions of all kin terms: $15 \times 15 \times 1 \times 1 \times 3 \times 1 \times 1 \times 3 \times 15 \times 7 \times 7 \times 7 \times 7 = 72,930,375$. This turns out to be a huge number.

In his article, Noricks argues that the redundant model presented in Table 2.9 is 'a better performer' than the other seven models of the same data set he considers. We need not go into the details of his argumentation, but we cannot fail to ask why just this specific redundant model out of the 72,930,375 that we have calculated from his matrix? We could go further, and ask: What about the other redundant models, conforming to the other three dimension sets, which will have about as many alternatives?

In principle, all language systems (whether kinship or phonological) are potential candidates for assignment of a redundant model. As we have seen, this eventuality is commonly realized in actual componential analyses. Proposing a redundant model automatically legitimizes all other redundant models. This circumstance introduces the need to make a choice among a set of equally admissible redundant alternatives, a problem reminiscent of that of Buridan's ass, where an ass faced with two equidistant and equally desirable bales of hay starves to death because there are no grounds for preferring to go to one bale rather than the other. Our linguistic task of making a rational choice, unlike Buridan's ass's, would further be aggravated by the usually large number of alternatives. Once we accept redundancy as a correct practice in linguistic description, it automatically leads to multiple ambiguity of the models, over and above the formidable ambiguity already present in nonredundant analyses. In effect, allowing redundancy by proposing a redundant model opens the back door to a legion of additional, and equally legitimate, redundant models, a fact which renders making a rational choice difficult (Buridan's ass problem).

2.3 Summary

We have seen some examples of inconsistent componential analyses from the literature, which, even though not representative in a statistical sense of linguistic practice of the method, quite strongly suggest being more prototypical cases than mere exceptions. An obvious reason for this state of affairs is the enormous difficulty of distinguishing comparatively large sets of kin terms with only necessary and sufficient features, a circumstance which enforces the conclusion that the task of componential analysis must be automated. Analogously, exhibiting all alternative componential models also cannot be generated without such a means. Indeed, our analysis of Bulgarian kin terms results in an astronomical number of possible models, whose generation would have been impossible without machine computation, and constitutes an empirical test of the degree of indeterminacy that previous researchers were not in a position to perform. The difference between using and not using a computational tool, thus, is not a matter of economy of time and effort, but the difference between finding and not finding a correct solution at all.

The second important conclusion from this chapter is that a completely unconstrained componential analysis, looking only for necessary and sufficient definitions of kin terms, may be intolerably indeterminate; it therefore speaks strongly in favour of Burling's position downplaying the method. Indeed, empirical descriptions of particular languages may lead to a flood of alternatives. However, as will be seen in the next section, introducing some natural and intuitive constraints pertaining to simplicity tips the balance in the other direction. Simplicity is a basic meta-scientific requirement, strongly adopted in linguistics, and as the saying goes *simplex sigillum veri* ('simplicity is the seal of truth').

3
The KINSHIP system

The KINSHIP program is a general computational tool for componential analysis of kinship terminology, supporting approaches from different theoretical persuasions. It can adequately handle the problems outlined in Chapter 2. The program accepts as input the kin terms of a given language with their attendant kin types and produces a componential analysis of the kinship vocabulary. The produced analysis is 'consistent', in that all kin terms are assigned definitions with necessary (nonredundant) and sufficient conditions, but the system also allows of producing various degrees of redundancy ('partially' or 'fully' redundant models) in case the user is for some analytical reason interested in such models. In addition, the system can generate all alternative solutions to kinship systems. The problem of the multiplicity of alternative solutions to kinship systems is approached by introducing three simplicity criteria, two choosing a minimum number of overall features (dimensions) and minimum components in kin term definitions, and a third one minimizing the use of features in definitions and ensuring coherence among kin term definitions within the whole data set. In this chapter, I describe the basic functional capabilities of the program (or what the program does) and the essential algorithm of its operation (or how the program does it).

3.1 An overview of KINSHIP

A basic goal of KINSHIP is to support one standard approach to componential analysis, viz. that corresponding to what has usually been called '(social) structural reality' (Wallace and Atkins 1960; Wallace 1965). From the standpoint of this approach, the parsimony and the

56

logical consistency with which kin term usage is predicted are generally considered as the basic criteria by which the relative merit of (alternative) solutions are assessed. However, KINSHIP is designed as a general computational tool for performing componential analysis, and is hence not necessarily committed to this particular view. Thus, although we consider structural reality an essential aspect of kinship structure, and have implemented the system to be capable of quite faithful simulation of this approach, the user of the system is not forced to employ the system with the particular goal of parsimony in mind. If the analyst pursues the more ambitious goal of searching for cognitive validity (by psychological tests of cognitive validity of alternative models – see, for example, Romney and D'Andrade 1964, Wallace 1965, Rose and Romney 1979, Noricks 1987), this would presuppose the availability of all componential models, and not only the most concise, feature (dimension) sets, along with all, and not only the shortest, nonredundant kin term definitions. To support this need, KINSHIP can generate all alternative componential models. The system may also produce 'fully redundant' or 'partially redundant' componential models. In general, the kinship analyst may utilize the potential outputs of the system in ways that fit the particular goals pursued, if these outputs are in any sense relevant to those goals. It is worth noting that, inasmuch as the extensionist paradigm also presupposes performing componential analysis, our system can be used to this end as well, though indeed it would be practically more helpful in 'pure' componential analysis, which is as a rule much more difficult to conduct, owing to the need to find contrasting features covering all, not only the kernel, kin types of a kin term.

3.1.1 Input and outputs

The input of KINSHIP is a set of kin terms, the kinship vocabulary of a language, with their attendant kin types. By way of a simple illustration, in the following I shall use a small subset of the Bulgarian consanguineal kin terms: *čičo* 'uncle', *lelja* 'aunt', *bašta* 'father', *majka* 'mother', *brat* 'brother', *sestra* 'sister', *sin* 'son' and *dăšterja* 'daughter'. The Bulgarian data are presented on Table 3.1.

The system can produce, as already mentioned, the simplest componential analysis (conforming to criteria to be detailed in the chapter), as well as all alternative non-simplest componential structures (componential schemes, models with varying degree of redundancy, etc.), specified by the user of the system.

3.1.2 Further facilities

In addition to producing various componential structures, the KINSHIP system can be queried in a variety of ways to support componential investigations. Thus, for instance, some basic queries include:

i. what the attendant kin types of a given kin term are or what kin term corresponds to a given (set of) kin type(s)
ii. whether there exists cross-classification of kin types, i.e. one kin type is classed under two or more different kin terms (such kinds of data preclude complete discrimination of kin terms, so the system displays the faulty kin types)
iii. what the current features of the system are
iv. what kin type/kin term possesses what features
v. what semantic contrasts exist between a selected pair of kin terms
vi. what pairs of kin terms are indistinguishable in terms of the features used

Besides making these queries, the user is also free to specify a subset from the set of features already defined in the system and run the program using just these features. This option is useful when specific features are for some reason (structural, cultural or psychological) considered important by the analyst of a specific culture and we require an analysis in terms of these features alone.

I shall not elaborate here on the question of how these additional capabilities of the program might be used in investigating kinship structure (generally, the success of such an enterprise will depend on the analyst's skill and ingenuity), but will rather confine myself to giving just an example of how the system's report of its failure to discriminate between a pair of kin terms may hint the postulation of a novel feature to accomplish the discrimination.

The point at issue will be the componential analysis of English, and in particular, the definition of the kin term *cousin*, when conceived in its extended meaning (following Goodenough 1965) as covering not only relatives of zero generation, but also kin types of any generation. The lexeme *cousin* thus conceived is difficult to define conjunctively and is often somewhat artificially split into two homonymous words in order to conjunctively discriminate it from the rest of English kin terms. In an analysis of the comprehensive English data (Goodenough 1965) with the well-known set of features (dimensions) proposed by Kroeber (1909), the KINSHIP program reported that it cannot cleanly discriminate the pairs *cousin* and *grandson*; *cousin* and *granddaughter*; *cousin* and *nephew*;

cousin and *niece* (Pericliev and Valdés-Pérez 1998). This suggested that we look at the kin types of these pairs, given as Table 3.2.

Now, we can ask: what feature is possessed by all kin types of *cousin* that could serve as a potential contrast with the remaining kin terms? It is quite conspicuous in the data that all attendant kin types of *cousin* have as their first connecting link Pa, which is a relative of ascending generation, so a potential candidate is the feature 'generation of the first connecting link'. This feature indeed can discriminate *cousin* from *grandson/granddaughter* whose first connecting relative is Ch (i.e. generation $= -1$) and *nephew/niece* whose first connecting relatives are Sb and Sp (i.e. of generation $= 0$) (note Ch = child, Sb = sibling, Sp = spouse). In effect, the ability of the KINSHIP system to exhibit what pairs of kin terms are indistinguishable, in terms of the features used and what the attendant kin types of a given kin term are, readily suggests the new feature 'generation of the first connecting link' doing the job (and actually useful in the analysis of other languages as well).

3.2 The basic algorithm

The KINSHIP system algorithm comprises the following basic steps:

Step I. Extraction of feature values of kin types
Step II.1. Determining kin term components
Step II.2. Determining contrasting features between pairs of kin terms
Step III. Ensuring the simplicity of kinship models
Step III.1. Determining simplest overall feature (=dimension) sets
Step III.2. Determining simplest definitions of kin terms
Step III.3. Maximizing coherence of kin term definitions
Step IV. Inventing derived features
Step V. Producing different styles of kin term definitions

Each of these steps is described in more detail in the following paragraphs.

Step I. Extraction of feature values of kin types

The program is endowed with a set of features (or dimensions) and with subroutines that determine, for each kin type, the value the kin type has for the inspected feature. Over the years, various features have been defined in the system to suit the analysis of diverse languages. Currently, KINSHIP may use more than twenty features. It employs those of Kroeber (1909), viz. 'generation', 'lineal versus collateral', 'age difference in one generation', 'sex of the relative', 'sex of the first connecting relative', 'sex of the speaker', 'consanguineal versus affinal' and 'condition of the relative'. Greenberg writes about these features: 'Leaving aside some difficulties and complications, in principle any kin term in any language can be specified by means of them' (1980: 13). To alleviate some potential difficulties envisaged by Greenberg, we have also included the features 'genealogical distance', 'same vs. different sex of ego and alter', 'sex of the second connecting relative', 'Iroquois parallel' (see page 108 for a definition), 'matrilateral' and some others.

Below is a list of some of these features, accompanied where necessary by some explanatory examples (the definitions may differ in minor respects from those used for the analysis of Bulgarian in Chapter 2; further explanations may be given as necessary in Chapter 4). Then I will continue with the problem of how the values of features are extracted, using as illustration the small subset of the Bulgarian consanguineal kin terms in Table 3.1.

(1) Generation of relative, with feature values
$$\text{generation} = 2$$
$$\text{generation} = 1$$
$$\text{generation} = 0$$
$$\text{generation} = -1$$
$$\text{generation} = -2, \text{etc.}$$

The value of the feature 'generation' can be any integer, including a range of integers (bounded by $\geq$ 'equal or greater than' or $\leq$ 'smaller or equal to'), as e.g. the cross-generational Bulgarian kin term *zet* covering the kin types SiHu and DaHu, and meaning 'brother-in-law' or 'son-in-law', having the feature value generation $= \leq 0$.

(2) Sex of relative, with feature values
$$\text{sex} = \text{m} - \text{male}$$
$$\text{sex} = \text{f} - \text{female}$$

(3) Genealogical distance, with the integer feature values
$$\text{distance} = 1$$
$$\text{distance} = 2$$
$$\text{distance} = 3, \text{etc.}$$

This feature, analogously to 'generation', can take as value any integer, including a range of integers (bounded by $\geq$ 'equal or greater than' or $\leq$ 'smaller or equal to'). The kin type Fa has the value distance $= 1$, FaBr has the value distance $= 2$, and FaBrWi distance $= 3$.

(4) Affinity of relative, with two feature values
affinity = cons – consanguineal, or absence of a marital tie
affinity = aff – affinal, marital tie

Examples: the kin type MoSi has the value affinity = cons, while Wi and SiHu have the feature value affinity = aff.

(5) Affinity of the 1st connecting relative (link), with feature values
affinity 1st link = cons – consanguineal (first link is a blood relative)
affinity 1st link = aff – affinal (first link is a relative by marriage)

Examples: the kin types <u>Fa</u>Si, <u>Si</u>Hu (where first link is underlined) both have the feature value affinity 1st link = cons, while <u>Wi</u>Mo, <u>Hu</u>Si are both affinity 1st link = aff.

(6) Sex of the 1st connecting relative (link), with feature values
sex 1st link = m – male
sex 1st link = f – female

Examples: the kin types <u>Fa</u> and <u>Fa</u>Si (where first link is underlined) both have the feature value sex 1st link = m, while <u>Mo</u> and <u>Wi</u>Si are both sex 1st link = f.

(7) Generation of the last link, with the feature values
generation last link = 1
generation last link = 0
generation last link = – 1

The generations of the last links will be: Fa and Mo = 1; Si, Br, Hu and Wi = 0; So and Da = –1; hence, e.g., Fa<u>Mo</u> (where last link is underlined) will have the feature value generation last link = 1 for this feature, while <u>So</u> or So<u>So</u> will have the feature value generation last link = –1.

(8) Sex of the second connecting relative (link), with feature values
sex 2nd link = m – male
sex 2nd link = f – female

Examples: the kin types Fa<u>Fa</u>Si, Mo<u>Br</u> (where second link is underlined) both have the feature value sex 2nd link = m, while Fa<u>Mo</u>Si, Mo<u>Si</u> are both sex 2nd link = f.

(9) Affinity of the second connecting relative (link), with feature values
>   affinity 2nd link = cons – consanguineal
>   affinity 2nd link = aff – affinal

Examples: the kin types Fa<u>Fa</u>Si, Mo<u>Br</u> (where second link is underlined) both have the feature value affinity 2nd link = cons, while Br<u>Wi</u>Si, Si<u>Hu</u> are both affinity 2nd link = aff.

(10) Lineality, with the feature values:
>   lineality = lin – lineal
>   lineality = coll – collateral

(11) Seniority within one generation, with feature values
>   seniority = e – elder
>   seniority = y – younger

We may now turn to the question of how values of features are extracted from kin types. For the sake of simplicity, in the following discussion I assume just four features: 'generation', 'sex', 'distance' and 'lineality'. Given the input in Table 3.1, the program will determine the values for some of the above features in the following manner. For instance, the values of a kin type for the feature 'sex' can be established by the system by its last symbol (= link), knowing further the sex of all atomic relationships. Thus, the program can find that the kin type FaBr is sex = male, since its last link, viz. Br, is male, while FaSi is sex = female, since its last link, Si, is female. The feature 'generation' of a kin type can be found out as the sum of the generations of the links constituting this kin type, where the latter are +1 for the parental kin types Fa and Mo, −1 for the filial relationships So and Da, and 0 for all remaining relationships Br, Si, Hu and Wi. In this way, the program can compute that the kin type FaBr is generation = 1, since +1 +0 = 1. In a similar fashion, all feature values (components) are computed, and this is done for all kin types in the data set. The result of this computation for our illustrative kinship domain from Table 3.1, in which bundles of feature values are substituted for kin types, is given as Table 3.3.

Step II.1. Determining kin term components

At this step, the KINSHIP program transfers the components of the kin types into components of kin terms. This is accomplished by establishing those components that are possessed by *all* the kin types covered by a kin term. Thus, the kin term *čičo* covers the kin types FaBr and MoBr. Both these kin types have the components [generation = 1 & sex = m & distance = 2 & lineality=coll], as seen from Table 3.3, therefore the kin term *čičo* will have the same bundle of feature values. This transfer of the components of the kin types into components of kin terms is exhibited in Table 3.4.

A feature (dimension) is said to be 'applicable' to a kin term when all kin types covered by the term have a common value for that feature. Otherwise, the feature is 'inapplicable' or 'irrelevant' (as for instance, the feature 'sex' for the English word *cousin* or the feature 'matrilateral' for the English *son*). A pair of kin terms cannot contrast on an inapplicable feature (as we have seen in some examples from Chapter 2).

Step II.2. Determining contrasting features between pairs of kin terms

In order to find the dimensions of contrast, or contrasting features, that demarcate one kin term from another the program proceeds in the following way. It computes all unordered pairs of kin terms from the analysed vocabulary (i.e. combining the first kin term with the second, third, fourth, and so on, the second with the third, fourth, and so on until all possibilities are exhausted), and then computes all the possible contrasts for each pair.

The result from this computation of the contrasting features in our illustrative example from Table 3.1 is given in Table 3.5 (the slant line '/' in the table stands for a logical disjunction ∨ 'or').

Two kin terms contrast with respect to some feature (dimension) just in case the feature is applicable to both terms and besides they have *different values* for this feature. Thus, for instance, *brat* and *sestra* contrast along the dimension of sex since the former has feature value 'male' and the latter the feature value 'female'; *čičo* and *bašta* contrast along two dimensions, viz. distance and lineality, insofar as *čičo* is distance = 2 and lineality = collateral, whereas *bašta* is distance = 1 and lineality = lineal, and so on. The features sex and lineality have nominal values. In the case when the values of a feature are integers (as with distance and generation), where we have values such as 'greater or equal to', two kin terms contrast when their integer intervals do not intersect. Thus, for instance, the feature value generation => 3 will contrast with another that is generation = 2, but not with one that is generation = 3 or generation = 5. If no contrast is found between two kin terms, this fact is reported by the program and its operation proceeds with processing the remaining kin terms.

Table 3.5 shows the contrasting features for each pair of kin terms. Thus, for the pair *sin* vs. *čičo* the contrasting features are (generation ∨ distance ∨ lineality), those for the *majka* vs. *lelja* are (distance ∨ lineality), and so on. The task of kin term discrimination can be completed by randomly choosing for each term one contrasting feature from the alternatives given in Table 3.5, such that distinguishes this term from another term, then choosing another feature distinguishing the term from still another one, and so on, until the term is finally set apart from all other terms. Thus, for instance, to discriminate *čičo*, one needs to choose arbitrarily a feature (with its corresponding value) from each cell of the first row in Table 3.5. One such definition of *čičo* is [generation = 1 & sex = male & distance = 2 & lineality = collateral]. However, such a mode of constructing a definition may result in redundancy (as we have seen in Chapter 2) and in any case does not lead to producing simplest kinship models, therefore we proceed differently, as described below.

Step III. Ensuring the simplicity of kinship models

In order to achieve 'simple' componential models, the KINSHIP system employs three simplicity criteria involving the use of minimum overall features (dimensions), minimum components in kin term definitions and maximum 'coherence' in kin term definitions.

Step III.1. Determining simplest overall feature (=dimension) sets

In order to satisfy the first simplicity criterion, pertaining to choosing the minimum number of overall features, the KINSHIP system has to find out a minimum set of features that covers *all* pair-wise contrasts between the kin terms. (It is apparent that Table 3.5 is symmetrical with respect to the empty-cells diagonal, hence we may consider only half of it in order to find those contrasts.)

What does this task mean, and how shall we perform its computation? This task can actually be reduced to the familiar one from algorithmic theory of finding a *minimum set cover*. Given a set, whose members are other sets, a 'set cover' is defined as a set whose members include at least one member of each constituent set. A 'minimum set cover' then is defined as the set cover with the smallest cardinality (or the shortest set). Equivalently, we may rephrase the task as the conversion of a *conjunctive normal form* (CNF – i.e. a conjunction of disjunctions) into a *disjunctive normal form* (DNF – i.e. a disjunction of conjunctions). For these notions, see for example, Chang and Lee (1973).

In our illustrative case in Table 3.1, we obtain two alternative minimal set covers, each having three features (dimensions): {generation & sex & distance} or {generation & sex & lineality}. It will be easy to verify that either of these sets of features covers all cells of pair-wise contrasts. Thus, taking the feature set {generation & sex & distance}, it is seen from Table 3.5 that at least one of these features occurs in every cell of pair-wise contrasts.

Step III.2. Determining simplest definitions of kin terms

The program proceeds with the construction of a conjunctive definition (feature bundle) of each kin term, using one of the minimal sets of features (dimensions). Alternatively, both sets can be employed, in case we want to get alternatives with equally succinct feature sets.

The procedure uses as input information the simplest overall feature set(s), obtained at Step III.1, as well as the set of contrasting features, obtained at Step II.2, and given in Table 3.5. The simplest definition of a kin term, then, must use only features from the simplest feature set, and, additionally, must use the smallest number of features, such that are members of this simplest feature set. In order to achieve the second goal, the very same procedure of finding a minimal set cover, or conversion of CNF into DNF, is used as in Step II.1, the latter converting the conjunction of alternative pair-wise contrasting features of a kin term with all other kin terms from Table 3.5 into a DNF formula, in which every resultant disjunct represents a potential kin term definition.

By way of illustration, consider how the definition of the kin term *čičo* is constructed. Let us first assume that we are given the simplest overall feature set {generation & sex & distance} found above. Table 3.6, which is actually the first row of Table 3.5, gives the contrasts of *čičo* with all other kin terms in our illustrative kin domain. To construct a definition of *čičo*, we need to convert the above CNF into a DNF, which yields the two expressions: {sex & distance} ∨ {generation & sex & lineality}. Both these definitions of *čičo* are subsumed by the simplest feature set assumed, but the program will choose the first, as it is shorter.

Proceeding in an analogous manner with all kin terms from the examined kinship vocabulary, and again assuming the minimal feature set {generation & sex & distance}, gives the simplest componential analysis as shown in Table 3.7.

An alternative simplest model (see Table 3.8) is obtained using the minimal feature set {generation & sex & lineality}.

Step III.3. Maximize coherence of kin term definitions

This simplicity constraint is applied by KINSHIP only if alternative kin term definitions remain even after the application of the first two restrictions. This criterion minimizes the use of 'minor', i.e. infrequent, peripheral, features in kin term definitions. The basic idea is that in the alternative, equally short, definitions of one kin term, some features are *obligatory* and must be used, while others are *optional* and may or may not be used; from the optional features for one kin term, the criterion prefers the more frequent feature/s from a frequency hierarchy computed from the obligatory features used in the whole componential scheme. The basic effect from applying the criterion is to ensure that lexemes that *may* be defined with the same set of features, or dimensions (like, say, *father* and *mother*), but which differ only as regards values for these features, or dimensions (male vs. female), are *indeed* defined by the program in terms of identical dimensions. This move guarantees a maximal coherence, or coordination, of kin term definitions across the whole analysed data set and avoids 'cross-definitions', where semantically maximally close lexemes receive differing descriptions. This criterion is in accord with the results of Romney and D'Andrade (1964: 156), who found that such pairs as *father* vs. *mother*, etc., differing only as regards to 'sex', are placed by subjects adjacently 98 per cent of the time in a free recall experiment.

No kin terms from our miniature data set in Table 3.1 receive more than one definition with the illustrative dimensions of contrast, so for clarification of the method I will turn to the discussion of Bulgarian later in the chapter, as analysed with the three simplicity constraints described here. Another principled criterion trying to handle the coherence of kin term definitions across the whole kinship vocabulary is described in detail in Pericliev and Valdés-Pérez (1998: 302–4).

Step IV. Inventing derived features

The system disposes of a mechanism for *inventing derived features*, formed by combining old features by means of the logical operations conjunction, disjunction, implication and equivalence. This mechanism, reflecting interactions between features, can be used in the cases when the available features are insufficient to discriminate all kin terms.

The key idea of this mechanism is to express interactions between the given primitive features. Currently, we have implemented inventing novel derived features via combining two primitive features (combining three or more primitive features is also possible, but has not so far been done, owing to the likelihood of a combinatorial explosion):

i. Two binary (=Boolean) features P and Q are combined into a set of two-place functions, none of which is reducible to a one-place function or to the negation of another two-place function in the set. The resulting set consists of 'P-and-Q, P-or-Q, P-iff-Q, P-implies-Q, and Q-implies-P.
ii. Two nominal features M and N are combined into a single two-place nominal function M × N.
iii. Two numeric features X and Y are combined by forming their product and their quotient.

Both primitive and derived features are treated analogously in deciding whether two classes contrast by a feature, since derived features are legitimate Boolean, nominal or numeric features.

As an illustration, let us look at an indiscriminable pair of terms from the Australian aboriginal language Gooniyandi (McGregor 1996):

jaja: MoMo ∨ MoMoSi ∨ MoMoBr ∨ MoFaSiHu ∨ WiFaMo ∨ MoBrSoWi ∨ fDaSo ∨ fDaDa
ngoomara: WiMoFa

KINSHIP would form derived features, and would find that, for instance, the derived (binary) feature +/−[affinal 1st link-and-male-alter] discriminates the terms:

jaja	− <affinal 1st link-and-male alter>
ngoomara	+ <affinal 1st link-and-male alter>

Indeed, the sole kin type of *ngoomara*, viz. WiMoFa, is + affinal 1st link (Wi) *and* +male alter, whereas neither of the kin types of *jaja* have *both* these feature values at the same time. A further example of this mechanism will be given in Chapter 4 with Zapotec, an Oto-Manguean language.

Step V. Producing different styles of kin term definitions

Depending on the presence or absence of redundant values (components) in the definition of some kin term, three styles of kin term componential definitions are discernible. A 'redundant' component is one that is not necessary for accomplishing the demarcation of kin terms (and can therefore be deleted from the resultant description without destroying this demarcation). All three styles are actually observed in kinship practice, as we already noted in the previous chapters. The KINSHIP system is designed as a general tool for studying componential structure, so it supports some redundancy and can produce such structures. To describe these styles in what follows, we will assume that a minimum set S of features (dimensions) has already been identified.

Nonredundant kin term definition. The first style of kin term definitions, which we call 'nonredundant', is one in which each kin term is defined only with components which are both necessary and jointly sufficient to discriminate it from all other kin terms. This is the default operation of KINSHIP. The componential models, given in Tables 3.7 and 3.8, for instance are nonredundant. Thus, in Table 3.7, in the definition of *čičo*, the components sex = m and distance = 2, jointly, are sufficient to distinguish the kin term from all other terms: distance = 2 makes it distinct from *bašta, majka, brat, sestra, sin* and *dăšterja*, which all have distance = 1; sex = m distinguishes the kin term from *lelja*, which has sex = f. Any of these components is also necessary for the distinction: removing distance = 2 will lead to confusion of the term with all others possessing male sex (viz. *bašta, brat* and *sin*); removing sex = m will cause ambiguity with the other kin terms in the data set that have distance = 2, viz. *lelja*. The application of the computational mechanisms of set covers, or the conversion of a CNF into DNF, described above, guarantees the avoidance of redundancy.

It should be noted that a simplest componential model is necessarily nonredundant, but of course there are non-simplest models which are also nonredundant.

Fully redundant kin term definition. The second style, of kin term definitions, which we shall call 'fully redundant', simply lists, for every kin term, its component for every feature in S, without caring whether all these components are actually necessary for the demarcation. The resultant fully redundant componential analysis of our illustrative example from Table 3.1 – assuming the minimal feature set $S = \{$generation & sex & distance$\}$ – is given in Table 3.9.

In this analysis, the feature values will be sufficient to distinguish every kin term from all the rest. At the same time, it will also be apparent that some definitions will contain redundant components. Thus, as seen from Table 3.9, on the basis of the feature values for generation, the kin terms are apportioned into three subsets: *čičo, lelja, bašta, majka* (generation = 1), *brat* and *sestra* (generation = 0), and *sin* and *dăšterja* (generation = −1); within the first subset, the values of distance, further break it down into *čičo* and *lelja* on the one hand (having distance = 2), and *bašta* and *majka* on the other (having distance = 1), each individual kin term being distinguished from the rest by being either of male or female sex. The feature 'sex' suffices to completely demarcate each term within the remaining two subsets, those of generation = 0 and those of generation = − 1. It thus turns out that the values for distance of all the kin terms *sestra, brat, sin* and *dăšterja* are not, strictly speaking, necessary.

Partially redundant kin term definition. The third style of kin term definitions, which is called 'partially redundant', does not list indiscriminately for every kin term the values of all features in *S*. Rather, it embodies a procedure in which a consecutive partitioning of the space of kin terms along the given dimensions is executed, which is very much like that described in the previous paragraph (why this definition is redundant, we shall see shortly). In the procedure leading to this definition, a feature is selected and the values for this feature are listed in the definitions of all kin terms, unless a term is already completely discriminated from all remaining in the data set; if a term is already completely discriminated, the term's value for this feature is discarded, and does not enter as a component in its definition.

Two partially redundant componential analyses are shown in Table 3.10. In the first, only the bare values and the values in square brackets count (i.e. the components in angular brackets are ignored), whereas in the second only the bare values and those in angular brackets are valid components (i.e. the components in square brackets are ignored).

We will now look at how the first alternative partially redundant kin term definition is obtained. The procedure starts with the same feature set *S* = {generation & sex & distance} and selects the first feature, viz. generation. Since no kin term is yet completely discriminated, the values for generation are included in the definitions of all kin terms. (This gives column 1 of Table 3.10.) The kin terms are partitioned into three subsets, and no term is completely discriminated by the generation feature. Then we take the second feature (sex), and, as no term is decisively demarcated, we list its corresponding values in the definitions of all kin terms. (This gives column 2 of Table 3.10.) The terms *brat, sestra, sin* and *dăšterja* are now completely discriminated from the remaining terms because generation and sex cover all their cells of contrast, see Table 3.5. Finally, the last feature (distance) is chosen and its corresponding values are included in the definition of *čičo, lelja, bašta* and *majka*, but *not* in the definitions of *brat, sestra, sin* and *dăšterja*, which completes the analysis. It is now clear why the values for distance do not occur in the definitions of the latter terms.

The consecutive partitioning, described above, suggests that the *order* of applying the features may matter, and in fact it does. Thus, if we start the partitioning with distance, instead of with generation, we shall obtain the second alternative partially redundant definition (see Table 3.10, and note again that here only bare values, and those in square brackets, actually count). Starting with distance, the definitions of all kin terms will contain the corresponding values for this feature (column 3 of Table 3.10). No term is decisively demarcated, so we use the second feature, sex, and include its corresponding values in the definitions of all kin terms. Now, distance and sex jointly suffice to discriminate completely *čičo* and *lelja*, which may be verified from Table 3.10, so when, finally, the feature generation is used, its corresponding values will not be included in the definitions of these two kin terms, but only in those of the remaining ones. (The relative order of using sex is irrelevant as regards the introduction of a new alternative analysis.)

It will now be clear why these two analyses are redundant. The first contains the component generation $= 1$ in both the definition of *čičo* and in the definition of *lelja*, but in both cases this is not necessary, since the components distance $= 2$ and sex $= m$ suffice to completely distinguish *čičo* (FaBr $\vee$ MoBr), and the components distance $= 2$ and sex $= f$ do likewise for *lelja* (FaSi $\vee$ MoSi). Similar considerations hold for the second analysis where the occurrence of distance $= 1$ in the definitions of *brat*, *sestra*, *sin* and *dăšterja* are redundant. Thus, *brat* is distinguished by having generation $= 0$ and sex $= m$, *sestra* by having generation $= 0$ and sex $= f$, and so on. The analyses are only partially redundant since any one of them avoids some redundancy, unlike the fully redundant componential analysis.

3.3 Bulgarian re-analysed with KINSHIP's simplicity constraints

In Chapter 2, we looked at Bulgarian kin terms of reference and address and saw that each of these data sets allowed an immense number of alternative componential models. We may now examine how the three simplicity criteria of KINSHIP fare in an attempt to resolve the formidable indeterminacy.

Below I list the alternative feature (dimension) sets for the reference and the address kin terms from the previous analysis, along with the number of dimensions of each.

Reference kin terms

I. {sex & sex 1st & affinity 1st & generation & distance & affinity}   6
II. {sex & generation & sex 1st & affinity 1st & distance & affinity 2nd}   6
III. {sex & sex 1st & generation & distance & affinity & affinity 2nd}   6
IV. {sex & generation & sex 1st & affinity 1st & distance & generation last}   6
V. {sex & lineality & affinity 2nd & sex 1st & affinity 1st & distance & generation last}   7
VI. {sex & sex 1st & affinity 1st & distance & lineality & affinity & generation last}   7
VII. {sex & sex 1st & affinity 1st & generation & sex 2nd & lineality & affinity & generation last}   8
VIII. {sex & sex 1st & affinity 2nd & generation & sex 2nd & lineality & affinity & generation last}   8

Address kin terms

I. {sex & generation last & generation & sex 1st & affinity 1st & distance}   6
II. {sex & generation last & generation & sex 1st & distance & affinity}   6
III. {sex & generation last & generation & sex 1st & affinity 1st & lineality & affinity}   7
IV. {sex & generation last & generation & sex 1st & affinity 2nd & lineality & affinity}   7
V. {sex & generation last & generation & sex 1st & affinity 1st & lineality & sex 2nd}   7
VI. {sex & generation last & generation & sex 1st & affinity & lineality & sex 2nd}   7

These counts show that our first simplicity constraint, pertaining to selecting a minimum number of dimensions, will significantly reduce the indeterminacy in both data sets. Thus, choosing the simplest sets, which have six dimensions, will block four theoretically possible componential schemes (with their corresponding componential models) in both the reference and in the address vocabulary. However, several alternative simplest componential schemes still remain, so we additionally choose to combine the reference and the address vocabularies into a single unified data set, which, for completeness, is listed below. (An 'a-' prefix to a kin type designates an address form, while the absence of this prefix in a kin type designates a reference form.) The theoretical motivation behind this move is the call by componential analysts that comprehensive vocabularies are analysed, rather than only fragmentary data.

1. *pradjado*: FaFaFa ∨ FaMoFa ∨ MoFaFa ∨ MoMoFa
2. *prababa*: FaFaMo ∨ FaMoMo ∨ MoFaMo ∨ MoMoMo
3. *djado*: FaFa ∨ MoFa
4. *baba*: FaMo ∨ MoMo
5. *bašta*: Fa
6. *majka*: Mo
7. *vujčo*: MoBr
8. *čičo*: FaBr
9. *lelja*: FaSi
10. *tetka*: MoSi
11. *brat*: Br
12. *sestra*: Si
13. *batko*: eBr
14. *kaka*: eSi
15. *bratovčed*: MoSiSo ∨ MoBrSo ∨ FaSiSo ∨ FaBrSo ∨ MoMoSiDaSo ∨ MoMoSiSoSo ∨ MoMoBrDaSo ∨ MoMoBrSoSo ∨ MoFaSiDaSo ∨ MoFaSiSoSo ∨ MoFaBrDaSo ∨ MoFaBrSoSo ∨ FaMoSiDaSo ∨ FaMoSiSoSo ∨ FaMoBrDaSo ∨ FaMoBrSoSo ∨ FaFaSiDaSo ∨ FaFaSiSoSo ∨ FaFaBrDaSo ∨ FaFaBrSoSo
16. *bratovčedka*: MoSiDa ∨ MoBrDa ∨ FaSiDa ∨ FaBrDa ∨ MoMoSiDaDa ∨ MoMoSiSoDa ∨ MoMoBrDaDa ∨ MoMoBrSoDa ∨ MoFaSiDaDa ∨ MoFaSiSoDa ∨ MoFaBrDaDa ∨ MoFaBrSoDa ∨ FaMoSiDaDa ∨ FaMoSiSoDa ∨ FaMoBrDaDa ∨ FaMoBrSoDa ∨ FaFaSiDaDa ∨ FaFaSiSoDa ∨ FaFaBrDaDa ∨ FaFaBrSoDa
17. *sin*: So
18. *dăsterja*: Da
19. *plemennik*: BrSo ∨ SiSo
20. *plemennica*: BrDa ∨ SiDa
21. *vnuk*: SoSo ∨ DaSo
22. *vnučka*: DaDa ∨ SoDa
23. *pravnuk*: SoSoSo ∨ SoDaSo ∨ DaSoSo ∨ DaDaSo
24. *pravnučka*: DaDaDa ∨ SoSoDa ∨ SoDaDa ∨ DaSoDa
25. *măž*: Hu

26. *žena*: Wi
27. *šurej*: WiBr
28. *šurenajka*: WiBrWi
29. *dever*: HuBr
30. *zet*: SiHu ∨ DaHu
31. *badžanak*: WiSiHu
32. *zălva*: HuSi
33. *baldăza*: WiSi
34. *snaha*: BrWi ∨ SoWi
35. *etărva*: HuBrWi
36. *vujna*: MoBrWi
37. *strina*: FaBrWi
38. *lelin*: FaSiHu
39. *tetin*: MoSiHu
40. *svekăr*: HuFa
41. *svekărva*: HuMo
42. *tăst*: WiFa
43. *tăsta*: WiMo
44. *djado*: aFaFa ∨ aMoFa ∨ aWiFa ∨ aFaFaFa ∨ aFaMoFa ∨ aMoFaFa ∨ aMoMoFa
45. *babo*: aFaMo ∨ aMoMo ∨ aWiMo ∨ aFaFaMo ∨ aFaMoMo ∨ aMoFaMo ∨ aMoMoMo
46. *tatko*: aFa ∨ aHuFa
47. *majko*: aMo ∨ aHuMo
48. *vujčo*: aMoBr
49. *čičo*: aFaBr
50. *leljo*: aFaSi
51. *tetko*: aMoSi
52. *bratko*: aBr
53. *sestro*: aSi
54. *bate*: aelderBr
55. *kako*: aelderSi
56. *bratovčede*: aMoSiSo ∨ aMoBrSo ∨ aFaSiSo ∨ aFaBrSo ∨ aMoMoSiDaSo ∨ aMoMoSiSoSo ∨ aMoMoBrDaSo ∨ aMoMoBrSoSo ∨ aMoFaSiDaSo ∨ aMoFaSiSoSo ∨ aMoFaBrDaSo ∨ aMoFaBrSoSo ∨ aFaMoSiDaSo ∨ aFaMoSiSoSo ∨ aFaMoBrDaSo ∨ aFaMoBrSoSo ∨ aFaFaSiDaSo ∨ aFaFaSiSoSo ∨ aFaFaBrDaSo ∨ aFaFaBrSoSo
57. *bratovčedke*: aMoSiDa ∨ aMoBrDa ∨ aFaSiDa ∨ aFaBrDa ∨ aMoMoSiDaDa ∨ aMoMoSiSoDa ∨ aMoMoBrDaDa ∨ aMoMoBrSoDa ∨ aMoFaSiDaDa ∨ aMoFaSiSoDa ∨ aMoFaBrDaDa

∨ aMoFaBrSoDa ∨ aFaMoSiDaDa ∨ aFaMoSiSoDa ∨ aFaMoBrDaDa
∨ aFaMoBrSoDa ∨ aFaFaSiDaDa ∨ aFaFaSiSoDa ∨ aFaFaBrDaDa
∨ aFaFaBrSoDa

58. *sine*: aSo
59. *dăste*: aDa
60. *plemenniko*: aBrSo ∨ aSiSo
61. *plemennice*: aBrDa ∨ aSiDa
62. *măzo*: aHu
63. *ženo*: aWi
64. *zetko*: aSiHu ∨ aDaHu
65. *badžo*: aWiSiHu
66. *snaho*: aBrWi ∨ aSoWi
67. *vujno*: aMoBrWi
68. *strino*: aFaBrWi
69. *lelinčo*: aFaSiHu
70. *tetinčo*: aMoSiHu

Running KINSHIP on this new and larger corpus with the same set of features, adding only the binary feature 'reference' with the values ref(erence) and addr(ess), marking kin terms as reference vs. address, resulted in the following dimension sets, given with the number of their constituent members:

Overall feature sets of reference and address kin terms

I.   {sex & generation last & generation & sex 1st & affinity 1st & distance & reference}   7
II. {sex & generation last & generation & sex 1st & affinity 2nd & distance & affinity & reference}   8
III. {sex & generation last & generation & sex 1st & affinity 1st & sex 2nd & lineality & affinity & reference}   9
IV. {sex & generation last & generation & sex 1st & affinity 2nd & & sex 2nd & lineality & affinity & reference}   9

The program now outputs a single simplest overall feature set, comprising seven features, viz. Set I, which further reduces the ambiguity of Bulgarian kinship terminology. The componential scheme of the corpus is given as Table 3.11.

However, as seen from Table 3.11, there still remain a lot of alternative kin term definitions; practically, every Bulgarian kin term, analysed with the features at hand, allows more than one definition, and many terms admit of several descriptions. We do not need to compute their exact number (equal to the product of the number of definitions each individual term receives), since apparently the number of possible componential models is still immense.

The application of the second criterion further significantly reduces the models, since some kin terms have alternative definitions that are longer than the other, simpler, definitions for the same term. The longer definitions are blocked by the program. The terms that have descriptions thus discarded are: *pradjado* 'great-grandfather', *prababa* 'great-grandmother', *djado* 'grandfather', *baba* 'grandmother', *bašta* 'father', *majka* 'mother', *brat* 'brother', *sestra* 'sister', *batko* 'elder brother', *kaka* 'elder sister', *bratovčed* 'male cousin', *bratovčedka* 'female cousin', *badžanak* 'wife's sister's husband', *baldăza* 'wife's sister', *vujna* 'mother's brother's wife', *strina* 'father's brother's wife', *tetin* 'mother's sister's husband', *svekăr* 'husband's father', *tăsta* 'wife's mother' (all reference terms); and *bratko* 'brother', *sestro* 'sister', *bate* 'elder brother', *kako* 'elder sister', *bratovčede* 'male cousin', *măžo* 'husband', *ženo* 'wife', *zetko* 'sister's or daughter's husband', *badžo* 'wife's sister's husband' (all address terms). One example of such cases is the kin term *bašta* 'father', which has six definitions in all, the first four with four components, and the last two with five components and hence blocked:

bašta

[reference = ref & sex 1st link = m & generation = 1 & distance = 1]
[reference = ref & sex 1st link = m & distance = 1 & generation last link = 1]
[reference = ref & sex = m & generation = 1 & distance = 1]
[reference = ref & sex = m & distance = 1 & generation last link = 1]

[reference = ref & sex 1st link = m & affinity 1st link = cons & generation = 1 & generation last link = 1]
[reference = ref & affinity 1st link = cons & sex = m & generation = 1 & generation last link = 1]

Even after the application of the second criterion, there still remain many terms with multiple definitions and to these we apply the third simplicity criterion, which is computed as follows. From the set of remaining equally simple alternative definitions of each term, we find the 'obligatory features' that *must* be used, whatever alternative definition for that term is chosen. This is done by computing the intersection of these alternatives. For example, in the case of *bašta* above, the intersection, or obligatory features, are 'reference' and 'distance', as they recur in all four equally simple definitions, whereas the features 'sex', 'generation', 'sex 1st link', 'generation last link' and 'affinity 1st link' are optional, as they may or may not be used depending on what definition of the term we choose. We then compute the frequencies of obligatory uses of features for all terms comprising our data set. The frequency hierarchy thus obtained reflects the salience of features, the more frequent features being more salient than the less frequent ones. The frequency hierarchy in our case, computed from Table 3.11, is:

Frequency hierarchy (salience) of features

{reference = 60, sex = 47, distance = 45, generation = 29, sex 1st link = 27, generation last link = 23, affinity 1st link = 19}

Finally, the sum is computed from the frequencies of component features in each definition of a kin term and the definition with the highest score is selected. For example, for *bašta* we get the following scores:

bašta

1. [reference & sex 1st link & generation & distance]
   $60 + 27 + 29 + 45 = 161$
2. [reference & sex 1st link & distance & generation last link]
   $60 + 27 + 45 + 23 = 155$
3. [reference & sex & generation & distance]
   $60 + 47 + 29 + 45 = 181$
4. [reference & sex & distance & generation last link]
   $60 + 47 + 45 + 23 = 175$

and therefore the third definition with the highest score of 181 is chosen. We thus obtain a single definition of the term, viz. [reference = ref & sex = m & generation = 1 & distance = 1], out of four equally simple alternatives according to the previous criteria.

It should be emphasized that the third simplicity criterion is as intuitive and principled as the other two criteria, and in particular avoids undesired 'cross-definitions' in a componential model. Thus, as seen from Table 3.11, the term *majka* 'mother', the female counterpart of *bašta* 'father', is defined by KINSHIP with the same set of features and will differ only as regards the value (male vs. female) of one of these features, viz. 'sex'. The scores of the alternative definitions will be accordingly the same:

majka

1. [reference & sex 1st link & generation & distance]
   $60 + 27 + 29 + 45 = 161$
2. [reference & sex 1st link & distance & generation last link]
   $60 + 27 + 45 + 23 = 155$
3. [reference & sex & generation & distance]
   $60 + 47 + 29 + 45 = 181$
4. [reference & sex & distance & generation last link]
   $60 + 47 + 45 + 23 = 175$

and the chosen simplest definition will, again, be that with the highest score of 181, viz. [reference = ref & sex = f & generation = 1 & distance = 1]. Our criterion will force the choices 3 in both *bašta* and *majka*, but will avoid the 'cross-definitions' involving say choice 3 in *bašta*, but choice 2 in *majka*; choice 3 in *majka* but some other choice in *bašta*, etc. This ensures coordination, or cohesion, between the definitions of terms in the whole kinship domain and corresponds to the intuitions of native speakers.

Applying the third simplicity constraint on the alternatives stored in the componential scheme from Table 3.11, the KINSHIP program produces a unique simplest componential model of the Bulgarian kin terms listed in Table 3.12. It is not my goal here to make detailed commentaries of this unique model, but several remarks are in order.

First, a comment on the features used, viz. {sex & generation & distance & sex of 1st link & affinity of 1st link & generation of last link & reference}. The first four features Bulgarian uses are universally employed in the languages of the world, while Bulgarian prefers affinity of 1st link to another universal feature, affinity of relative, in order to be able to distinguish the cross-generational term *zet* 'S̲i̲Hu ∨ D̲a̲Hu' whose first linking relative (underlined) is consanguineal from *šurej* 'W̲i̲Br', whose first link is affinal, and the cross-generational *snaha* 'B̲r̲Wi ∨ S̲o̲Wi', whose first linking relative is consanguineal from *zălva* 'H̲u̲Si', where this link is affinal. Another uncommon feature Bulgarian uses (at least insofar as models proposed in the literature are concerned) is the generation of last link. This feature is indispensable for demarcating the Bulgarian vocative kin terms (note that it is an element of all overall feature sets for the address forms), and the failure to employ it results in a failure to discriminate the following vocative term pairs: *tatko-tetinčo, tatko-tetinčo, tatko-čičo, tatko-vujčo, majko-strino, majko-vujno, majko-tetko, majko-leljo.* The following illustrates how the vocative lexeme *tatko* 'father' is discriminated by this feature:

tatko Fa ∨ HuFa (generation last = 1) vs. *tetinčo* MoSiHu (generation last = 0)
tatko Fa ∨ HuFa (generation last = 1) vs. *lelinčo* FaSiHu (generation last = 0)
tatko Fa ∨ HuFa (generation last = 1) vs. *čičo* FaBr (generation last = 0)
tatko Fa ∨ HuFa (generation last = 1) vs. *vujčo* MoBr (generation last = 0)

Second, the definition of words for kinship in terms of semantic primitives may help dictionary definitions. The Bulgarian terminology is of a Sudanese type, characterized by descriptive kin terms, where most relatives are given separate names, rather than a classificatory one, in which sets of relatives are classified under a single label. As a consequence of this circumstance, Bulgarian dictionaries, rightly, predominantly define kinship words in terms of their attendant kin types, which generally yields concise and clear dictionary definitions. For example, *čičo* 'uncle' in the dictionary *Bălgarski tălkoven rečnik* (1973) is defined as '1. Father's brother relative to the children', and the extended non-kinship meaning as '2. An older man, relative or close to the family relative to the children'. How componential models can be used in lexicographic work is a complex problem, which we will not discuss here. Suffice it here to give just an example of how our model can serve this purpose. The extended non-kinship meaning 2, given by this dictionary, seems inaccurate in view of the fact that its componential definition, among others, includes the component generation = 1, or one generation above ego. This component should necessarily be present and therefore its omission may lead to a failure to distinguish this term from some other terms in the domain. Indeed, so defined, *čičo* 'uncle' may be confused with the older relatives *batko* 'older brother', which is of the same generation as ego, and *djado* 'grandfather', which is two generations away from ego. The same considerations for example hold for *lelja* 'aunt', and its extended non-kinship meaning should include reference to its being one generation above ego, if the term is to be distinguished from *kaka* 'elder sister' and *baba* 'grandmother'. Incidentally, the dictionary in question includes no definition of the extended meaning of *lelja*. Another remark in the same vein would be that in some cases the reference and vocative forms of one word may have slightly different meanings, which Bulgarian dictionaries as a rule fail to pinpoint, listing only the reference form. For instance, as seen from Table 3.12, in the componential definitions of *dajdo* (reference) [reference = ref & sex = m & generation = 2] and *djado* (vocative) [reference = addr & sex = m & generation = ≥ 2] the vocative designates relatives in the second and higher generations above ego, in contrast to the reference form, and therefore this fact should figure in its dictionary definition.

Concluding this section, we may say that the simplicity contstraints incorporated in KINSHIP perform very well for Bulgarian, totally eliminating the indeterminacy. The operation of the system in this regard, however, needs to be tested against further data sets, and to this problem I turn in Chapter 4.

4
Componential analyses of selected languages

In the previous chapter, I introduced the KINSHIP system and showed its successful operation on data from Bulgarian. In this chapter, I conduct componential analysis of a dozen other languages of Indo-European and non-Indo-European origin. The basic goals of these exercises in machine componential analysis are both to provide a further empirical test of the capacity of the program and to present 'adequate' models of the examined languages, many of which have not been analysed previously.

4.1 Introduction

As mentioned in Chapter 3, KINSHIP is endowed with about 20 overall features (dimensions). The following subset of 15 features was selected for the analysis of all languages below:

1. Sex of relative
2. Sex of speaker
3. Sex of 1st link
4. Sex of 2nd link
5. Generation of relative
6. Generation of 1st link
7. Generation of last link
8. Genealogical distance
9. Affinity of relative
10. Affinity of 1st link
11. Affinity of last link
12. Lineality
13. Seniority within one generation
14. Parallelity
15. Structural equivalence

Most of these features were explained in Chapter 3, but some further specifications may be added as required at appropriate places. Suffice it to say here that they include the standard features proposed by Kroeber (1909) ('generation', 'lineal versus collateral' 'age difference in one generation', 'sex of the relative', 'sex of the first connecting relative', 'sex of the speaker', 'consanguineal versus affinal'), but also some additional features pertaining to the first, second and last link of a kin type that turn out to be necessary in order to successfully demarcate the kin terms of specific languages.

The data subjected to study include the following languages: English (West Germanic), Swedish (East Germanic), Irish (Celtic), Spanish (Italic), Polish and Czech (West Slavic), Persian (Indo-Iranian), Albanian, Armenian (all belonging to the Indo-European), as well as Turkish (Altaic), Seneca (Iroquoian), Zapotec and Popoloca (Oto-Manguean), and Huave (language isolate). The set of examined languages includes predominantly Indo-European languages, covering to some extent most major branches of the family, and a couple of non-Indo-European languages. The choice of languages was partly determined by the fact that previous analysts have largely focussed on more 'exotic' languages, thus ignoring Indo-European ones, which, beyond doubt, also deserve attention, and partly because they cover the basic structural types (Eskimo, Sudanese, Iroquois, etc.). The particular data (kin terms and their attendant kin types) for the languages come from published accounts, dictionaries or other sources.

In the sequel, KINSHIP will start with the set of 15 features (dimensions) listed above and will output, for each language, the set of all alternative dimension sets that can serve for the discrimination of every kin term from its kinship vocabulary (thus highlighting its degree of ambiguity), as well as present its 'simplest' componential model(s), fulfilling our three simplicity criteria, pertaining to shortness of dimension set and kin term definitions and coherence of the latter. In case I am aware of previous componential analyses of the examined language, a concise comparison of the human and machine analyses will be made.

4.2 Exercises in machine componential analysis

4.2.1 English

English has been subjected to componential analyses in several works, notably by Wallace and Atkins (1960), Nogle (1974), Wordick (1973) and Goodenough (1965). The most comprehensive data set for American

(Yankee) kin terms is provided by Goodenough (1965) and we consider this set in our analysis below.

The kin terms with their attendant kin types are as follows:

1. *great-grandfather*: FaFaFa $\vee$ FaMoFa $\vee$ MoFaFa $\vee$ MoMoFa
2. *great-grandmother*: FaFaMo $\vee$ FaMoMo $\vee$ MoFaMo $\vee$ MoMoMo
3. *great-uncle*: MoMoBr $\vee$ MoFaBr $\vee$ FaMoBr $\vee$ FaFaBr
4. *great-aunt*: MoMoSi $\vee$ MoFaSi $\vee$ FaMoSi $\vee$ FaFaSi
5. *grandfather*: FaFa $\vee$ MoFa
6. *grandmother*: FaMo $\vee$ MoMo
7. *uncle*: MoBr $\vee$ FaBr $\vee$ FaFaSo $\vee$ FaMoSo $\vee$ MoFaSo $\vee$ MoMoSo $\vee$ FaSiHu $\vee$ FaSiHu $\vee$ MoSiHu $\vee$ MoSiHu $\vee$ FaFaDaHu $\vee$ FaMoDaHu $\vee$ MoMoDaHu $\vee$ MoFaDaHu
8. *aunt*: MoSi $\vee$ FaSi $\vee$ FaFaDa $\vee$ FaMoDa $\vee$ MoFaDa $\vee$ MoMoDa $\vee$ FaBrWi $\vee$ FaBrWi $\vee$ MoBrWi $\vee$ MoBrWi $\vee$ FaFaSoWi $\vee$ FaMoSoWi $\vee$ MoMoSoWi $\vee$ MoFaSoWi
9. *father*: Fa
10. *mother*: Mo
11. *son*: So
12. *daughter*: Da
13. *brother*: Br $\vee$ FaSo $\vee$ MoSo
14. *sister*: Si $\vee$ FaDa $\vee$ MoDa
15. *cousin*: MoSiDa $\vee$ MoBrDa $\vee$ FaSiDa $\vee$ FaBrDa $\vee$ MoSiSo $\vee$ MoBrSo $\vee$ FaSiSo $\vee$ FaBrSo $\vee$ MoMoSiDaDa $\vee$ MoMoSiSoDa $\vee$ MoMoBrDaDa $\vee$ MoMoBrSoDa $\vee$ MoFaSiSoDa $\vee$ MoFaBrDaDa $\vee$ MoFaBrSoDa $\vee$ FaMoSiDaDa $\vee$ FaMoSiSoDa $\vee$ FaMoBrSo $\vee$ FaFaSiDaDaDa $\vee$ FaFaSiDaDaDaDa
16. *nephew*: BrSo $\vee$ SiSo $\vee$ FaSoSo $\vee$ MoSoSo $\vee$ FaDaSo $\vee$ MoDaSo $\vee$ WiBrSo $\vee$ WiSiSo $\vee$ HuBrSo $\vee$ HuSiSo $\vee$ WiMoDaSo $\vee$ WiFaSoSo $\vee$ WiFaDaSo $\vee$ WiMoSoSo $\vee$ HuMoDaSo $\vee$ HuFaSoSo $\vee$ HuFaDaSo $\vee$ HuMoSoSo
17. *niece*: BrDa $\vee$ SiDa $\vee$ FaSoDa $\vee$ MoSoDa $\vee$ FaDaDa $\vee$ MoDaDa $\vee$ WiBrDa $\vee$ WiSiDa $\vee$ HuBrDa $\vee$ HuSiDa $\vee$ WiMoDaDa $\vee$ WiFaSoDa $\vee$ WiFaDaDa $\vee$ WiMoSoDa $\vee$ HuMoDaDa $\vee$ HuFaSoDa $\vee$ HuFaDaDa $\vee$ HuMoSoDa
18. *grandson*: SoSo $\vee$ DaSo
19. *granddaughter*: DaDa $\vee$ SoDa
20. *great-grandson*: SoSoSo $\vee$ SoDaSo $\vee$ DaSoSo $\vee$ DaDaSo
21. *great-granddaughter*: DaDaDa $\vee$ SoSoDa $\vee$ SoDaDa $\vee$ DaSoDa
22. *husband*: Hu
23. *wife*: Wi

24. *father-in-law*: WiFa ∨ HuFa ∨ WiMoHu ∨ HuMoHu
25. *mother-in-law*: WiMo ∨ HuMo ∨ WiFaWi ∨ HuFaWi
26. *son-in-law*: DaHu ∨ WiDaHu ∨ HuDaHu
27. *daughter-in-law*: SoWi ∨ WiSoWi ∨ HuSoWi
28. *brother-in-law*: HuBr ∨ WiBr ∨ WiMoSo ∨ WiFaSo ∨ HuMoSo ∨ HuFaSo ∨ WiMoHuSo ∨ WiFaWiSo ∨ HuMoHuSo ∨ HuFaWiSo ∨ SiHu ∨ FaDaHu ∨ MoDaHu ∨ MoHuDaHu ∨ FaWiDaHu
29. *sister-in-law*: HuSi ∨ WiSi ∨ WiFaDa ∨ WiMoDa ∨ HuFaDa ∨ HuMoDa ∨ WiMoHuDa ∨ WiFaWiDa ∨ HuMoHuDa ∨ HuFaWiDa ∨ BrWi ∨ FaSoWi ∨ MoSoWi ∨ MoHuSoWi ∨ FaWiSoWi
30. *step-father*: MoHu
31. *step-mother*: FaWi
32. *step-son*: HuSo ∨ WiSo
33. *step-daughter*: HuDa ∨ WiDa
34. *step-brother*: MoHuSo ∨ FaWiSo
35. *step-sister*: MoHuDa ∨ FaWiDa

Running KINSHIP with the selected 15 features on this data set yields a unique dimension (overall features) set comprising seven dimensions:

I. {sex & generation & distance & affinity & generation 1st link & generation last link & str equiv}

The feature 'structural equivalence' merits some explanation. Goodenough (1964: 231–2) and Goodenough (1965: 277) use the fact that certain affinal kin types, viz. the step-relatives, are structurally equivalent to primary consanguineal kin types; for example, under normal expectations, one's father's wife will be one's mother, etc. Thus, the following equivalences are valid:

(1) FaWi = Mo
(2) MoHu = Fa
(3) SpSo = So
(4) SpDa = Da
(5) PaSpSo = Br
(6) PaSpDa = Si (Sp=spouse, Pa=parent; below we shall also use the common abbreviations Ch=child and Sb=sibling)

Also, we observe that besides the structural equivalence between affinal and primary consanguineal kin types (i.e. rules (1)–(6)), there exists structural equivalence between some consanguineal and primary consanguineal kin types; for example, under normal expectations, one's father's (or mother's) son will be one's brother, etc. These equivalences are:

(7) PaSo=Br
(8) PaDa=Si

In our definition, the feature 'structural equivalence' is binary: kin types that match the left-hand part of one of the above eight rules get the value 'eq(univalent)' while those that do not match any left-hand part of a rule get the value 'non-eq(univalent)'. For instance, *step-father* (MoHu) will be described as 'str equiv = eq' (as it matches equivalence rule (2)), whereas *father* (Fa) will be described as 'str equiv = non-eq' (as it does not match any equivalence rule).

We note that the idea of structural equivalence is also incorporated in the definition of the feature 'generation of last link' (which should more properly be called 'generation of last link or its structural equivalent'). We first observe that an equivalence relation may apply not only to whole kin types, but also between parts, or sequences of links within a kin type. For example, under normal expectations, my mother's husband's daughter's husband is actually my sister's husband, i.e. *MoHuDa*Hu should be considered as SiHu, since the initial, italicized, sequence of the former kin type is of course equivalent to Si (see rule (6)) and can be substituted for it. Analogously, Wi*MoHuSo* can naturally be considered as WiBr since the italicized last sequence of the kin type is structurally equivalent to Br (by rule (5)) and hence can be substituted for it. We use the foregoing natural transformations in the definition of our feature generation of the last link, and determine the generation of the last link *only after* the equivalence substitution has been made (if possible); thus, the generation of the last link of the above kin type WiMoHuSo will be 0 since it is equivalent to WiBr, and the generation of Br is 0.

It is worthwhile to illustrate how one can verify whether the kin types of a kin term possess the feature 'generation of last link (or its structural equivalent)'. The procedure is as follows. If the last two or three symbols of a kin type are structural equivalents to some primary consanguine – according to the above list of eight equivalences – the generation of this consanguine is taken as the feature value. If not, then the generation of the last symbol (= link) is the feature value. The following is an illustration of how one determines that *brother-in-law* is generation last link (or structural equivalent) = 0 (the last link/structural equivalent is underlined):

brother-in-law	*Ultimate value*	*Reasoning*
HuB<u>r</u>	= 0	since Br=0
WiB<u>r</u>	= 0	since Br=0
Wi<u>MoSo</u>	= 0	since PaSo=Br=0 (by (7))
Wi<u>FaSo</u>	= 0	since PaSo=Br=0 (by (7))
Hu<u>MoSo</u>	= 0	since PaSo=Br=0 (by (7))
Hu<u>FaSo</u>	= 0	since PaSo=Br=0 (by (7))
Wi<u>MoHuSo</u>	= 0	since PaSpSo=Br=0 (by (5))
Wi<u>FaWiSo</u>	= 0	since PaSpSo=Br=0 (by (5))
Hu<u>MoHuSo</u>	= 0	since PaSpSo=Br=0 (by (5))
Hu<u>FaWiSo</u>	= 0	since PaSpSo=Br=0 (by (5))
Si<u>Hu</u>	= 0	since Hu=0
FaDa<u>Hu</u>	= 0	since Hu=0
MoDa<u>Hu</u>	= 0	since Hu=0
MoHuDa<u>Hu</u>	= 0	since Hu=0
FaWiDa<u>Hu</u>	= 0	since Hu=0

The second column shows the ultimate value and the third column the reason for assigning this value (the relevant substitutions made). In the first two, and in the last five, rows there are no valid structural equivalents, and hence the last links Br and Hu are considered, which are both of generation last link = 0, while in the remaining cases there is a valid structural equivalence whose primary consanguineal counterpart is in all cases Br = 0.

With theses specifications made, we note that many of the kin terms in the data set obtain several definitions in terms of the seven overall features, sufficient for demarcation of all kin terms. Some examples are:

great-grandfather

[generation 1st link = 1 & sex = m & generation last link = 1 & distance = 3]
[sex = m & generation last link = 1 & distance = 3 & affinity = cons]
[sex = m & generation = 3]

great-grandmother

[generation 1st link = 1 & sex = f & generation last link = 1 & distance = 3]

[sex = f & generation last link = 1 & distance = 3 & affinity = cons]
[sex = f & generation = 3]

son

[generation 1st link = −1 & sex = m & generation last link = −1 &
   generation = −1]
[generation 1st link = −1 & sex = m & generation = −1 & affinity =
   cons]
[generation 1st link = −1 & sex = m & distance = 1]
[sex = m & generation last link = −1 & distance = 1]
[sex = m & generation = −1 & distance = 1]

daughter

[generation 1st link = −1 & sex = f & generation last link = −1 &
   generation = −1]
[generation 1st link = −1 & sex = f & generation = −1 & affinity =
   cons]
[generation 1st link = −1 & sex = f & distance = 1]
[sex = f & generation last link = −1 & distance = 1]
[sex = f & generation = −1 & distance = 1]

Thus, there is potentially a huge number of componential models corresponding to the seven dimensions, since each definition of a kin term can freely combine with all definitions of the other terms. More specifically, in the whole English vocabulary, there are eight kin terms with two definitions, six terms with three, and six with four definitions, and finally, four terms with five definitions, resulting in $2^8 \times 3^6 \times 4^6 \times 5^4 = 477,757,440,000$ models in all. However, the application of our simplicity criteria, selecting the shortest and coherent definitions of terms, successfully blocks all alternatives (choosing in each of the above illustrative cases the last definition, employing the features 'sex', 'generation' and eventually 'distance'). This unique simplest model is given in Table 4.1.

It is worthwhile to briefly compare our analysis with componential analyses known in the literature, specifically with regards to the consistency (conjunctiveness) of definitions and parsimony. I begin with the proposals critically reviewed in Chapter 2.

The model of Wallace and Atkins (1960) is more economical, using only the three dimensions 'sex', 'generation' and 'lineality' (the latter absent altogether from our analysis). However their data is much less exhaustive and is limited to consanguineals only. Besides, even in their smaller set, some kin terms (*uncle, aunt, nephew* and *niece*), as already mentioned, are not correctly described with conjunctive definitions, but are rather split into homonymous lexemes to camouflage the failure of the dimensions employed to cover the full range of reference of the terms.

Nogle (1974) examines a larger data set, comprising both consanguineal and affinal relatives, and his model is more parsimonious than ours, using six dimensions (nuclear family, sex, generation, affinity of relative, affinity of 1st link, lineality), some of which are absent from our analysis. However, Nogle's treatment faces a number of serious problems, as we saw earlier. First, although his data set is indeed larger than Wallace and Atkins (1960), it is not as exhaustive as that of Goodenough (1965), whose data, he claims, he undertakes to inspect; thus, for instance, some kin terms like *great-grandfather, great-grandmother, great-uncle, great-uncle* are absent altogether, while others like *cousin* are interpreted very narrowly, unlike Goodenough, as having only kin types of contemporary generation, while the term covers kin types of other generations as well (note the contemporary generation PaSbCh, but also the ascending generation PaPaSbCh, etc.). Secondly, Nogle's features are insufficient to discriminate a whole set of 14 pairs of kin terms (see Chapter 2, Section 2.1.1). Thirdly, Nogle wrongly believes that it is not possible to give a conjunctive definition of *uncle* and *aunt* (as we saw, a common problem in the analysis of English) and without any need introduces homonymity by listing them as separate entries, with affinal or consanguineal meaning respectively (in actual fact, his features are perfectly sufficient to make the demarcation). And, finally, Nogle's analysis is inconsistent in that it uses many redundant kin term definitions, 17 definitions being redundant out of 31 analysed terms.

Wordick (1973) suggests that English can be analysed in terms of only three dimenisons, viz. 'type' (with values lineal vs. collateral vs. affinal), 'generation' (with values 1, 0, −1) and 'sex of relative' (male vs. female). Apparently, however, with this set alone, we cannot distinguish, as mentioned earlier, between *father, grandfather, great-grandfather,* etc., insofar as they are all lineal males of ascending generation; the same applies to the female counterparts of these words, *mother, grandmother* and *great-grandmother*, which are all lineal females of ascending generation.

We may now look at the most ambitious treatment of American English by Ward Goodenough. Goodenough (1965) uses nine features, so the model discovered by KINSHIP is more economical with its seven features of contrast. This is basically due to our use of multi-valued features whereas Goodenough shows a preference for binary, or sometimes ternary, features. Also, Goodenough seems unable to give a *conjunctive* definition of a number of kin terms, and lists as separate lexemes e.g. *uncle* (consanguineal meaning) and *uncle* (affinal meaning) and some others, like *nephew, niece*, etc. (see Table VI on p. 279, and Table X on p. 285 of Goodenough 1965, where this is less evident, but is nevertheless seen in the use of features, and the 'same-as-above' entry in the table). Put differently, for these kin terms Goodenough has not found components shared by all their attendant kin types such that they also serve to contrast these from other kin terms. Our analysis does not encounter this problem, say with a kin term like *uncle*, owing to the introduction of the new feature 'generation of last link' (or its structural equivalent). Referring to our Table 4.1, *uncle* is described with three features, 'generation of relative', 'sex of alter' (both used by Goodenough), but also with 'generation of last link' or its structural equivalent, the latter feature possessed by all its attendant kin types, both consanguineal and affinal, and hence eliminating the need to artificially introduce homonymity in the term. As a final contrast, Goodenough's analysis has three 'no lexeme' entries, whereas ours has none – thus showing a somewhat better regularity in the kinship paradigm. Schneider (1965: 295) also notes an excessive use of empty lexemes in Goodenough's treatment. Thus, our model seems preferable to that proposed by Goodenough in terms both of consistency of definitions and parsimony.

Finally, the model in Table 4.1 seems more credible than the closely related analysis discovered by KINSHIP earlier and described in Pericliev and Valdés-Pérez (1998). The earlier model is indeed more parsimonious, using six features on the full data set (in contrast to the present, which uses seven), but this effect of economy, as one looks in retrospect, has perhaps been partly achieved at the expense of some resultant infelicity in the definition of some features. Thus, in the earlier treatment, the feature 'affinity of relative' has the three values, 'consanguineal' (= absence of marital tie, e.g. Mo), 'affinal-ego' (= marital tie directly to ego, e.g. Wi) and 'affinal' (= marital tie, but not directly to ego, e.g. BrWi), which allows the earlier model to dispense with the feature 'distance' we need for the present model. This looks a somewhat artificial move and I now prefer to define the feature 'affinity of relative' with the 'standard' two values 'affinal' (both Wi and BrWi) and 'consanguineal' (Mo) and reconcile myself to the addition of a further dimension in the analysis.

4.2.2 Swedish

The other Germanic language I will deal with is Swedish. The consanguineal kin terms with their ranges of reference are given below:

1. *fader*: Fa
2. *moder*: Mo
3. *farfar*: FaFa
4. *morfar*: MoFa
5. *farmor*: FaMo
6. *mormor*: MoMo
7. *son*: So
8. *dotter*: Da
9. *broder*: Br
10. *syster*: Si
11. *farbror*: FaBr
12. *morbror*: MoBr
13. *faster*: FaSi
14. *moster*: MoSi
15. *sonson*: SoSo
16. *dotterson*: DaSo
17. *sondotter*: SoDa
18. *dotterdotter*: DaDa
19. *brorson*: BrSo
20. *systerson*: SiSo
21. *brordotter*: BrDa
22. *systerdotter*: SiDa
23. *kusin*: FaBrSo ∨MoBrSo ∨ FaSiSo ∨ MoSiSo ∨ FaBrDa ∨ MoBrDa ∨ FaSiDa ∨ MoSiDa

Running KINSHIP with the selected 15 features on this data set shows a significant indeterminacy: there exist 14 different dimension sets that suffice to demarcate the kin terms. These dimension sets are as follows:

   I. {sex 2nd link & sex 1st link & generation & distance}
  II. {sex & sex 1st link & generation & distance}
 III. {sex 2nd link & generation last link & generation & sex 1st link & generation 1st link}
 IV. {sex & generation last link & generation & sex 1st link & generation 1st link}
  V. {sex 2nd link & generation last link & sex 1st link & generation 1st link & distance}

VI. {sex & generation last link & sex 1st link & generation 1st link & distance}
VII. {sex 2nd link & generation & sex 1st link & generation 1st link & lineality}
VIII. {sex & generation & sex 1st link & generation 1st link & lineality}
IX. {sex 2nd link & generation & sex 1st link & generation last link & lineality}
X. {sex & generation & sex 1st link & generation last link & lineality}
XI. {sex 2nd link & sex 1st link & generation 1st link & distance & lineality}
XII. {sex & sex 1st link & generation 1st link & distance & lineality}
XIII. {sex 2nd link & sex 1st link & generation last link & distance & lineality}
XIV. {sex & sex 1st link & generation last link & distance & lineality}

There are two shortest dimension sets (Set I and Set II), which comprise four dimensions each. The other sets have five dimensions. Choosing Set I, yields the unique componential model presented in Table 4.2, in which each kin term obtains a unique definition with no recourse to our simplicity constraints related to kin term definitions. In contrast, choosing Set II, some terms are assigned more than one description, as for instance:

fader
[sex 1st link = m & generation = 1 & distance = 1]
[sex = m & generation = 1 & distance = 1]

moder
[sex 1st link = f & generation = 1 & distance = 1]
[sex = f & generation = 1 & distance = 1]

In actual fact, there are six kin terms, each with two definitions, resulting in $2^6 = 64$ models. This ambiguity is resolved using our criterion for coherence, yielding the unique simplest model given in Table 4.3.

4.2.3 Irish

The kinship terminology of Irish comprises the following set:

1. *mathair*: Mo
2. *athair*: Fa
3. *mac*: So
4. *inion*: Da

5. *deanthair*: Br
6. *deirfiur*: Si
7. *aintin*: MoSi $\vee$ FaSi $\vee$ MoFaBrDa $\vee$ MoMoBrDa $\vee$ MoFaSiDa $\vee$ MoMoSiDa $\vee$ FaFaBrDa $\vee$ FaMoBrDa $\vee$ FaFaSiDa $\vee$ FaMoSiDa
8. *uncail*: MoBr $\vee$ FaBr $\vee$ MoFaBrSo $\vee$ MoMoBrSo $\vee$ MoFaSiSo $\vee$ MoMoSiSo $\vee$ FaFaBrSo $\vee$ FaMoBrSo $\vee$ FaFaSiSo $\vee$ FaMoSiSo
9. *nia*: BrSo $\vee$ SiSo
10. *neacht*: BrDa $\vee$ SiDa
11. *seanmhathair*: FaMo $\vee$ MoMo
12. *seanathair*: FaFa $\vee$ MoFa
13. *garmhac*: SoSo $\vee$ DaSo
14. *garinion*: DaDa $\vee$ SoDa
15. *col gaolta*: MoSiDa $\vee$ MoBrDa $\vee$ FaSiDa $\vee$ FaBrDa $\vee$ MoSiSo $\vee$ MoBrSo $\vee$ FaSiSo $\vee$ FaBrSo

KINSHIP discovers that four different dimension sets may be employed to handle the Irish data, viz.:

I. {sex & distance & generation}
II. {sex & generation last link & generation 1st link & generation}
III. {sex & generation 1st link & lineality & generation}
IV. {sex & generation last link & lineality & generation}

There is a unique simplest set, Set I, which comprises three dimensions, the remaining ones having four members. Using Set I, no ambiguous kin term definitions are obtained, hence this results in a unique componential model given in Table 4.4.

4.2.4 Spanish

The Spanish data subjected to componential analysis are given below:

1. *bizabuelo*: FaFaFa $\vee$ FaMoFa $\vee$ MoFaFa $\vee$ MoMoFa
2. *bizabuela*: FaFaMo $\vee$ FaMoMo $\vee$ MoFaMo $\vee$ MoMoMo
3. *abuelo*: FaFa $\vee$ MoFa
4. *abuela*: FaMo $\vee$ MoMo
5. *tio-abuelo*: MoMoBr $\vee$ MoFaBr $\vee$ FaMoBr $\vee$ FaFaBr
6. *tia-abuela*: MoMoSi $\vee$ MoFaSi $\vee$ FaMoSi $\vee$ FaFaSi
7. *tio*: MoBr $\vee$ FaBr
8. *tia*: MoSi $\vee$ FaSi
9. *madre*: Mo
10. *padre*: Fa

11. *hermana*: Si
12. *hermano*: Br
13. *prima*: MoSiDa ∨ MoBrDa ∨ FaSiDa ∨ FaBrDa ∨ MoMoSiDaDa ∨ MoMoSiSoDa ∨ MoMoBrDaDa ∨ MoMoBrSoDa ∨ MoFaSiDaDa ∨ MoFaSiSoDa ∨ MoFaBrDaDa ∨ MoFaBrSoDa ∨ FaMoSiDaDa ∨ FaMoSiSoDa ∨ FaMoBrDaDa ∨ FaMoBrSoDa ∨ FaFaSiDaDa ∨ FaFaSiSoDa ∨ FaFaBrDaDa ∨ FaFaBrSoDa
14. *primo*: MoSiSo ∨ MoBrSo ∨ FaSiSo ∨ FaBrSo ∨ MoMoSiDaSo ∨ MoMoSiSoSo ∨ MoMoBrDaSo ∨ MoMoBrSoSo ∨ MoFaSiDaSo ∨ MoFaSiSoSo ∨ MoFaBrDaSo ∨ MoFaBrSoSo ∨ FaMoSiDaSo ∨ FaMoSiSoSo ∨ FaMoBrDaSo ∨ FaMoBrSoSo ∨ FaFaSiDaSo ∨ FaFaSiSoSo ∨ FaFaBrDaSo ∨ FaFaBrSoSo
15. *hijo*: So
16. *hija*: Da
17. *sobrino*: BrSo ∨ SiSo
18. *sobrina*: BrDa ∨ SiDa
19. *nieto*: SoSo ∨ DaSo
20. *nieta*: SoDa ∨ DaDa
21. *biznieto*: SoSoSo ∨ SoDaSo ∨ DaSoSo ∨ DaDaSo
22. *biznieta*: SoSoDa ∨ SoDaDa ∨ DaSoDa ∨ DaDaDa
23. *marido*: Hu
24. *esposa*: Wi
25. *suegra*: WiMo ∨ HuMo
26. *suegro*: WiFa ∨ HuFa
27. *yerno*: DaHu
28. *nuera*: SoWi
29. *cuñado*: HuBr ∨ WiBr
30. *cuñada*: HuSi ∨ WiSi

Running the KINSHIP system, with its 15 features, on this data set reveals a massive indeterminacy insofar as dimension sets are concerned. Thus, there are 18 such sets, which I list below:

  I. {sex & distance & generation & affinity}
 II. {sex & generation last link & generation 1st link & distance & affinity 1st link}
III. {sex & generation 1st link & generation & distance & affinity 1st link}
 IV. {sex & generation last link & generation & distance & affinity 1st link}
  V. {sex & generation last link & generation 1st link & distance & affinity last link}

VI. {sex & affinity 1st link & generation & distance & affinity last link}

VII. {sex & generation 1st link & generation & distance & affinity last link}

VIII. {sex & generation last link & generation & distance & affinity last link}

IX. {sex & generation last link & distance & generation 1st link & affinity}

X. {sex & generation last link & generation 1st link & generation & affinity 1st link & affinity last link}

XI. {sex & generation 1st link & lineality & generation & affinity 1st link & affinity last link}

XII. {sex & generation last link & lineality & generation & affinity 1st link & affinity last link}

XIII. {sex & generation last link & lineality & affinity 1st link & distance & affinity last link}

XIV. {sex & generation last link & lineality & distance & affinity 1st link & affinity}

XV. {sex & generation last link & lineality & distance & affinity last link & affinity}

XVI. {sex & generation last link & generation 1st link & affinity last link & generation & affinity}

XVII. {sex & generation 1st link & lineality & affinity last link & generation & affinity}

XVIII. {sex & generation last link & lineality & affinity last link & generation & affinity}

Our simplicity criterion pertaining to overall feature sets chooses the shortest set, in the case of Spanish, Set I, comprising four features (the others having five component members). Using this four-member set, all kin term definitions are unique, with no need to apply a further simplicity criterion. This unique simplest componential analysis is stated in Table 4.5.

4.2.5 Polish

The West Slavic language Polish uses the following kinship terminological set:

1. *pradziad*: FaFaFa ∨ FaMoFa ∨ MoFaFa ∨ MoMoFa
2. *prababka*: FaFaMo ∨ FaMoMo ∨ MoFaMo ∨ MoMoMo
3. *dziad*: FaFa ∨ MoFa
4. *babka*: FaMo ∨ MoMo

5. *ojciec*: Fa
6. *matka*: Mo
7. *wuj*: MoBr
8. *stryj*: FaBr
9. *ciotka*: MoSi ∨ FaSi
10. *syn*: So
11. *córka*: Da
12. *siostra*: Si
13. *brat*: Br
14. *siostra-stryjeczna*: FaBrDa
15. *siostra-cioteczna*: FaSiDa ∨ MoSiDa
16. *siostra-wujeczna*: MoBrDa
17. *brat-stryjeczna*: FaBrSo
18. *brat-cioteczna*: FaSiSo ∨ MoSiSo
19. *brat-wujeczna*: MoBrSo
20. *bratanek*: BrSo
21. *siostrzeniec*: SiSo
22. *bratanica*: BrDa
23. *siostzenica*: SiDa
24. *wnuk*: SoSo ∨ DaSo
25. *wnuczka*: DaDa ∨ SoDa
26. *prawnuk*: SoSoSo ∨ SoDaSo ∨ DaSoSo ∨ DaDaSo
27. *prawnuczka*: DaDaDa ∨ SoSoDa ∨ SoDaDa ∨ DaSoDa
28. *maż*: Hu
29. *żona*: Wi
30. *swiekr*: HuFa
31. *teść*: WiFa
32. *swiekra*: HuMo
33. *teściowa*: WiMo
34. *szwagier*: HuBr ∨ WiBr
35. *szwagrowa*: HuSi

KINSHIP discovers great indeterminacy as regards possible dimension sets: there are 15 such sets, ranging from six to eight features. Our simplicity constraint on dimensions selects Set I and Set II as the simplest ones, thus significantly diminishing the indeterminacy.

I. {sex 2nd link & sex & sex 1st link & generation & affinity 1st link & distance}

II. {sex 2nd link & sex & sex 1st link & generation & affinity & distance}

III. {sex 2nd link & sex & generation last link & sex 1st link & generation 1st link & affinity 1st link & distance}
IV. {sex 2nd link & sex & generation last link & sex 1st link & lineality & affinity 1st link & distance}
V. {sex 2nd link & sex & generation last link & sex 1st link & generation 1st link & affinity last link & distance}
VI. {sex 2nd link & sex & sex 1st link & generation 1st link & generation & affinity last link & distance}
VII. {sex 2nd link & sex & sex 1st link & generation last link & generation & affinity last link & distance}
VIII. {sex 2nd link & sex & generation last link & sex 1st link & generation 1st link & affinity & distance}
IX. {sex 2nd link & sex & generation last link & sex 1st link & lineality & affinity & distance}
X. {sex 2nd link & sex & generation last link & generation & sex 1st link & generation 1st link & affinity 1st link & affinity last link}
XI. {sex 2nd link & sex & generation & sex 1st link & generation 1st link & lineality & affinity 1st link & affinity last link}
XII. {sex 2nd link & sex & generation & sex 1st link & generation last link & lineality & affinity 1st link & affinity last link}
XIII. {sex 2nd link & sex & generation last link & generation & sex 1st link & generation 1st link & affinity & affinity last link}
XIV. {sex 2nd link & sex & generation & sex 1st link & generation 1st link & lineality & affinity & affinity last link}
XV. {sex 2nd link & sex & generation & sex 1st link & generation last link & lineality & affinity & affinity last link}

Using Set I to accomplish the analysis, some kin terms obtain ambiguous definitions, as for instance:

dziad

[sex 2nd link = m & generation = 2]
[sex = y & generation = 2]

babka

[sex 2nd link = n & generation = 2]
[sex = n & generation = 2]

There are actually 19 kin terms with two definitions, one with three and one with four, giving $2^{19} \times 3^1 \times 4^1 = 6,291,456$ models in all. These are reduced to a unique model, applying the coherence simplicity constraint, the paradigm given as Table 4.6. The situation is similar when KINSHIP accomplishes componential analysis with Set II, so we need not enter into further details; see Table 4.7.

It is interesting to note that Polish must use the uncommon feature 'sex of 2nd link', witnessed by the inclusion of the feature in all 15 alternative dimension sets. This dimension of contrast (along with the feature 'sex of 1st link') is necessary in Polish to distinguish the lexemes designating male cousin, viz. *brat stryjeczny* 'FaBrSo', *brat cioteczny* 'FaSiSo $\vee$ MoSiSo' and *brat wujeczny* 'MoBrSo', as well as those for female cousin, *sestra stryjeczna* 'FaBrDa', *sestra cioteczna* 'FaSiDa $\vee$ MoSiDa' and *sestra wujeczna* 'MoBrDa'. KINSHIP has also discovered that this somewhat infrequent feature might potentially be employed by languages such as Turkish and Hindi as well.

4.2.6 Czech

The West Slavic language Czech uses the following kinship terminology:

1. *děd*: FaFa $\vee$ MoFa
2. *babička*: FaMo $\vee$ MoMo
3. *strýc*: MoBr $\vee$ FaBr
4. *teta*: MoSi $\vee$ FaSi
5. *matka*: Mo
6. *otec*: Fa
7. *sestra*: Si
8. *bratr*: Br
9. *syn*: So
10. *dcera*: Da
11. *bratanec*: MoSiDa $\vee$ MoBrDa $\vee$ FaSiDa $\vee$ FaBrDa
12. *synovec*: BrSo $\vee$ SiSo
13. *neteř*: BrDa $\vee$ SiDa
14. *vnuk*: SoSo $\vee$ DaSo
15. *vnučka*: DaDa $\vee$ SoDa
16. *muž*: Hu
17. *žena*: Wi
18. *tchán*: WiFa $\vee$ HuFa
19. *tchyně*: WiMo $\vee$ HuMo
20. *zeť*: DaHu
21. *snacha*: SoWi
22. *švagr*: HuBr $\vee$ WiBr $\vee$ SiHu
23. *švagrová*: HuSi $\vee$ WiSi $\vee$ BrWi

KINSHIP finds 18 sets of overall features which suffice to distinguish all kin terms in the Czech vocabulary:

I. {sex & generation & distance & affinity}

II. {sex & generation last link & generation 1st link & distance & affinity 1st link}

III. {sex & generation 1st link & generation & distance & affinity 1st link}

IV. {sex & generation last link & generation & distance & affinity 1st link}

V. {sex & generation & distance & affinity 1st link & affinity last link}

VI. {sex & generation & distance & generation 1st link & affinity last link}

VII. {sex & generation 1st link & distance & generation last link & affinity last link}

VIII. {sex & generation & distance & generation last link & affinity last link}

IX. {sex & generation last link & generation 1st link & distance & affinity}

X. {sex 2nd link & sex 1st link & generation & distance & affinity}

XI. {sex 2nd link & sex 1st link & generation last link & generation 1st link & distance & affinity 1st link}

XII. {sex 2nd link & sex 1st link & generation 1st link & generation & distance & affinity 1st link}

XIII. {sex 2nd link & sex 1st link & generation last link & generation & distance & affinity 1st link}

XIV. {sex 2nd link & sex 1st link & generation & distance & affinity 1st link & affinity last link}

XV. {sex 2nd link & sex 1st link & generation & distance & generation 1st link & affinity last link}

XVI. {sex 2nd link & sex 1st link & generation 1st link & distance & generation last link & affinity last link}

XVII. {sex 2nd link & sex 1st link & generation & distance & generation last link & affinity last link}

XVIII. {sex 2nd link & sex 1st link & generation last link & generation 1st link & distance & affinity}

Our simplicity criteria, again, prove effective in reducing these alternatives, selecting just one dimension set, Set I, as the simplest, having four features (sets range from four to six features each). Using Set I, results in the unique simplest model on Table 4.8, obtained without recourse to any further simplicity constraints.

4.2.7 Persian

The Indo-Iranian language Persian has the following kinship vocabulary (synonymous kin terms are separated by a slash '/'):

1. *mādar*: Mo
2. *pedar*: Fa
3. *pesar*: So
4. *doxtar*: Da
5. *amu*: FaBr
6. *dāi*: MoBr
7. *amme*: FaSi
8. *xāle*: MoSi
9. *barādar*: Br
10. *xāhar*: Si
11. *mādar-bozorg*: FaMo ∨ MoMo
12. *pedar-bozorg*: FaFa ∨ MoFa
13. *nave/nabire*: SoSo ∨ DaSo ∨ DaDa ∨ SoDa
14. *pedar-jad*: FaFaFa ∨ FaMoFa ∨ MoFaFa ∨ MoMoFa
15. *mādar -jad*: FaFaMo ∨ FaMoMo ∨ MoFaMo ∨ MoMoMo
16. *bājenāq*: HuBr ∨ WiBr ∨ SiHu
17. *xāhar -zan*: WiSi
18. *xāhar -šowhar*: HuSi

KINSHIP discovers six different sets of contrasting dimensions, from four and five constituent members:

I. {sex & sex 1st link & generation & distance}
II. {sex & generation last link & sex 1st link & generation 1st link & distance}
III. {sex & lineality & sex 1st link & generation 1st link & distance}
IV. {sex & distance & sex 1st link & generation last link & affinity}
V. {sex & generation last link & sex 1st link & generation & affinity}
VI. {sex & lineality & sex 1st link & generation & affinity}

The simplest four-member set, Set I, is unique. Analysing Persian with this set, results in some kin terms having more than one definition, as for example:

mādar

[sex 1st link = f & generation = 1 & distance = 1]
[sex = f & generation = 1 & distance = 1]

pedar

[sex 1st link = m & generation = 1 & distance = 1]
[sex = m & generation = 1 & distance = 1]

Eight kin terms obtain two definitions, hence there are $2^8 = 256$ alternative componential models. Of these, the program selects a unique simplest model, after the application of the coherence simplicity constraint; see Table 4.9.

4.2.8 Albanian

The Albanian language has the following kinship vocabulary (synonymous kin terms are separated by a slash '/'):

1. *nene/mami*: Mo
2. *ate*: Fa
3. *bir/djale*: So
4. *vajze/bije*: Da
5. *vellai*: Br
6. *vellackoja*: Bry
7. *moter*: Si
8. *moterz*: Siy
9. *nip*: SoSoSo ∨ SoDaSo ∨ DaSoSo ∨ DaDaSo
10. *mbese*: DaDaDa ∨ SoSoDa ∨ SoDaDa ∨ DaSoDa ∨BrDa ∨ SiDa
11. *gjyshe*: FaMo ∨ MoMo
12. *gjysh*: FaFa ∨ MoFa
13. *daje*: MoBr ∨ FaBr
14. *teze*: MoSi ∨ FaSi
15. *kusherire*: MoSiDa ∨ MoBrDa ∨ FaSiDa ∨ FaBrDa ∨ MoMoSiDaDa ∨ MoMoSiSoDa ∨ MoMoBrDaDa ∨ MoMoBrSoDa ∨ MoFaSiDaDa ∨ MoFaSiSoDa ∨ MoFaBrDaDa ∨ MoFaBrSoDa ∨ FaMoSiDaDa ∨ FaMoSiSoDa ∨ FaMoBrDaDa ∨ FaMoBrSoDa ∨ FaFaSiDaDa ∨ FaFaSiSoDa ∨ FaFaBrDaDa ∨ FaFaBrSoDa
16. *kusheri*: MoSiSo ∨ MoBrSo ∨ FaSiSo ∨ FaBrSo ∨ MoMoSiDaSo ∨ MoMoSiSoSo ∨ MoMoBrDaSo ∨ MoMoBrSoSo ∨ MoFaSiDaSo ∨ MoFaSiSoSo ∨ MoFaBrDaSo ∨ MoFaBrSoSo ∨ FaMoSiDaSo ∨ FaMoSiSoSo ∨ FaMoBrDaSo ∨ FaMoBrSoSo ∨ FaFaSiDaSo ∨ FaFaSiSoSo ∨ FaFaBrDaSo ∨ FaFaBrSoSo

17. *nipi*: BrSo ∨ SiSo
18. *vjeherra*: HuMo
19. *vjeherr*: HuFa
20. *dhender*: DaHu
21. *nuse*: SoWi

Running KINSHIP on this data set, the program fails to discriminate two pairs of kin terms, viz. *vellai*: 'Br' vs. *vellackoja* 'Bry' and *moter* 'Si' vs. *moterz* 'Siy'. These pairs are indistinguishable in principle, however, since the meaning of one of the words in the pairs includes the meaning of the other (e.g. *brother* includes *younger brother*). The program isolates seven dimension sets, comprising from four to six dimensions. Three of these, Sets I–III, are simplest, having four component members:

I.   {sex & generation 1st link & distance & generation last link}
II. {sex & generation & distance & generation last link}
III. {sex & generation & distance & affinity}
IV. {sex & affinity last link & generation & distance & affinity 1st link}
V.   {sex & affinity last link & distance & generation & generation 1st link}
VI. {sex & lineality & generation 1st link & distance & affinity}
VII. {sex & lineality & affinity last link & distance & affinity 1st link & generation 1st link}

Accomplishing the analysis with Set I, 11 out of the 21 kin terms of Albanian obtain more than one definition, for example:

bir/djale

[generation 1st link = −1 & sex = m & distance = 1]
[sex = m & generation last link = −1 & distance = 1]

vajze/bije

[generation 1st link = −1 & sex = f & distance = 1]
[sex = f & generation last link = −1 & distance = 1]

vellai

[generation 1st link = 0 & sex = m & generation last link = 0]
[generation 1st link = 0 & sex = m & distance = 1]
[sex = m & generation last link = 0 & distance = 1]

The resultant alternative componential models employing Set I are $2^8 \times 3^3 = 6,912$. An analogous situation obtains using Set II for the analysis: we get $2^6 \times 3^4 = 5,184$ alternative models. In each of the two cases, the application of the coherence constraint reduces these alternative models to a unique one; see Table 4.10 and Table 4.11. Accomplishing the analysis with Set III, in contrast, does not generate any ambiguity in kin term definitions, and hence the program does not need additionally to apply any further simplicity restrictions to achieve a unique paradigm; see Table 4.12.

4.2.9 Armenian

The kinship vocabulary of Modern Eastern Armenian, according to Dum-Tragut (2009), is as follows (synonymous kin terms are separated by a slash '/' and morphological alternatives are given in brackets):

1. *hayr*: Fa
2. *mayr*: Mo
3. *pap*: FaFa ∨ MoFa
4. *tat*: FaFaMo ∨ FaMoMo ∨ MoFaMo ∨ MoMoMo
5. *ordi*: So
6. *ełbayr*: Br
7. *k'uyr*: Si
8. *t'oř(nik)*: SoSo ∨ DaSo ∨ DaDa ∨ SoDa
9. *horełbayr*: FaBr
10. *k'eři*: MoBr
11. *horak'uyr*: FaSi
12. *morak'uyr*: MoSi
13. *ełborordi*: BrSo
14. *k'eřordi*: SiSo
15. *ełbor ałjik*: BrDa
16. *k'roj ałjik*: SiDa
17. *morak'roj tła/ałjik*: MoSiSo ∨ MoSiDa
18. *horak'roj tła/ałjik*: FaSiSo ∨ FaSiDa
19. *k'eřu tła/ałjik*: MoBrSo ∨ MoBrDa
20. *horełbor tła/ałjik*: FaBrSo ∨ FaBrDa
21. *hars*: SoWi
22. *p'esa*: DaHu
23. *amusin*: Hu
24. *kin*: Wi
25. *skesrayr*: HuFa
26. *skesur*: HuMo
27. *tagr/tegr*: HuBr
28. *tagerakin*: HuBrWi

29. *tal*: HuSi
30. *aner*: WiFa
31. *zok'anč'*: WiMo
32. *anerjag*: WiBr
33. *k'eni*: WiSi
34. bajanał: WiSiHu
35. *k'e?rakin/k'e?rekin*: MoBrWi

KINSHIP discovers a flood of alternative dimension sets, combining in different ways the 15 features it uses at the start:

I. {sex 1st link & sex 2nd link & distance & generation & affinity}
II. {sex 1st link & sex 2nd link & generation last link & generation 1st link & distance & affinity 1st link}
III. {sex 1st link & sex 2nd link & generation 1st link & generation & distance & affinity 1st link}
IV. {sex 1st link & sex 2nd link & generation last link & generation & distance & affinity 1st link}
V. {sex 1st link & sex 2nd link & generation last link & generation 1st link & distance & affinity last link}
VI. {sex 1st link & sex 2nd link & affinity 1st link & generation & distance & affinity last link}
VII. {sex 1st link & sex 2nd link & generation 1st link & generation & distance & affinity last link}
VIII. {sex 1st link & sex 2nd link & generation last link & generation & distance & affinity last link}
IX. {sex 1st link & sex 2nd link & generation last link & distance & generation 1st link & affinity}
X. {sex & sex 1st link & parallelity & distance & generation & affinity}
XI. {sex & sex 1st link & parallelity & generation last link & generation 1st link & distance & affinity 1st link}
XII. {sex & sex 1st link & parallelity & generation 1st link & generation & distance & affinity 1st link}
XIII. {sex & sex 1st link & parallelity & generation last link & generation & distance & affinity 1st link}
XIV. {sex 1st link & sex 2nd link & generation last link & lineality & affinity 1st link & distance & affinity last link}
XV. {sex & sex 1st link & parallelity & generation last link & generation 1st link & distance & affinity last link}
XVI. {sex & sex 1st link & parallelity & affinity 1st link & generation & distance & affinity last link}

XVII. {sex & sex 1st link & parallelity & generation 1st link & generation & distance & affinity last link}

XVIII. {sex & sex 1st link & parallelity & generation last link & generation & distance & affinity last link}

XIX. {sex 1st link & sex 2nd link & generation last link & lineality & distance & affinity 1st link & affinity}

XX. {sex & sex 1st link & parallelity & generation last link & distance & generation 1st link & affinity}

XXI. {sex 1st link & sex 2nd link & generation last link & lineality & distance & affinity last link & affinity}

XXII. {sex 1st link & sex & parallelity & generation last link & generation 1st link & generation & affinity 1st link & affinity last link}

XXIII. {sex 1st link & sex & sex 2nd link & generation last link & generation 1st link & generation & affinity 1st link & affinity last link}

XXIV. {sex 1st link & sex & parallelity & generation 1st link & lineality & generation & affinity 1st link & affinity last link}

XXV. {sex 1st link & sex & sex 2nd link & generation 1st link & lineality & generation & affinity 1st link & affinity last link}

XXVI. {sex 1st link & sex & parallelity & generation last link & lineality & generation & affinity 1st link & affinity last link}

XXVII. {sex 1st link & sex & sex 2nd link & generation last link & lineality & generation & affinity 1st link & affinity last link}

XXVIII. {sex & sex 1st link & parallelity & generation last link & lineality & affinity 1st link & distance & affinity last link}

XXIX. {sex & sex 1st link & parallelity & generation last link & lineality & distance & affinity 1st link & affinity}

XXX. {sex & sex 1st link & parallelity & generation last link & lineality & distance & affinity last link & affinity}

XXXI. {sex 1st link & sex & parallelity & generation last link & generation 1st link & affinity last link & generation & affinity}

XXXII. {sex 1st link & sex & sex 2nd link & generation last link & generation 1st link & affinity last link & generation & affinity}

XXXIII. {sex 1st link & sex & parallelity & generation 1st link & lineality & affinity last link & generation & affinity}

XXXIV. {sex 1st link & sex & sex 2nd link & generation 1st link & lineality & affinity last link & generation & affinity}

XXXV. {sex 1st link & sex & parallelity & generation last link & lineality & affinity last link & generation & affinity}

XXXVI. {sex 1st link & sex & sex 2nd link & generation last link & lineality & affinity last link & generation & affinity}

Of these 36 alternatives, ranging from five to eight constituent members, the program selects a unique set, Set I, as the simplest alternative. Some ambiguous kin term definitions using this dimension set are:

hars

[sex 1st link = m & generation = −1 & affinity = aff]
[sex 2nd link = f & generation = −1 & affinity = aff]

p'esa

[sex 1st link = f & generation = −1 & affinity = aff]
[sex 2nd link = m & generation= −1 & affinity = aff]

There are in total five kin terms, each having two significata, i.e. we get $2^5 = 32$ componential models before the application of further simplicity restrictions. The unique simplest model after their application is listed as Table 4.13.

4.2.10 Turkish

The kinship vocabulary of Turkish, a language belonging to the Altaic family, comprises 39 kin terms, viz.:

1. *büyük baba*: FaFa ∨ MoFa
2. *babaanne*: FaMo
3. *anneanne*: MoMo
4. *baba*: Fa
5. *ana*: Mo
6. *oğul*: So
7. *kız*: Da
8. *teyze kızı*: MoSiDa
9. *dayı kızı*: MoBrDa
10. *hala kızı*: FaSiDa
11. *amca kızı*: FaBrDa
12. *teyze oğlu*: MoSiSo
13. *dayı oğlu*: MoBrSo
14. *hala oğlu*: FaSiSo
15. *amca oğlu*: FaBrSo
16. *dayı*: MoBr
17. *amca*: FaBr
18. *teyze*: MoSi
19. *hala*: FaSi
20. *yeğen*: BrSo ∨ SiSo
21. *kız yeğen*: BrDa ∨ SiDa

22. *büyük dede*: FaFaFa ∨ FaMoFa ∨ MoFaFa ∨ MoMoFa
23. *torun*: SoSo ∨ DaSo
24. *kız torun*: DaDa ∨ SoDa
25. *kardes*: Br
26. *kız dardes*: Si
27. *koca*: Hu
28. *karı*: Wi
29. *kayınpeder*: WiFa ∨ HuFa
30. *kaynana*: WiMo ∨ HuMo
31. *kayın*: WiBr ∨ HuBr
32. *baldız*: WiSi
33. *görümce*: HuSi
34. *bacanak*: WiSiHu
35. *elti*: HuBrWi
36. *yenge*: BrWi ∨ FaBrWi ∨ MoBrWi
37. *enişte*: SiHu ∨ FaSiHu ∨ MoSiHu
38. *damat*: DaHu
39. *gelin*: SoWi

KINSHIP finds that more than a dozen dimension sets, from seven to eight members, suffice for the analysis of Turkish:

   I. {sex 1st link & sex & parallelity & generation & distance & affinity last link & affinity 1st link}

  II. {sex 1st link & sex & sex 2nd link & generation & distance & affinity last link & affinity 1st link}

 III. {sex 1st link & sex & parallelity & generation & distance & affinity & affinity 1st link}

 IV. {sex 1st link & sex & sex 2nd link & generation & distance & affinity & affinity 1st link}

  V. {sex 1st link & sex & parallelity & generation last link & generation 1st link & generation & affinity last link & affinity 1st link}

 VI. {sex 1st link & sex & sex 2nd link & generation last link & generation 1st link & generation & affinity last link & affinity 1st link}

 VII. {sex 1st link & sex & parallelity & generation 1st link & lineality & generation & affinity last link & affinity 1st link}

VIII. {sex 1st link & sex & sex 2nd link & generation 1st link & lineality & generation & affinity last link & affinity 1st link}

 IX. {sex 1st link & sex & parallelity & generation last link & lineality & generation & affinity last link & affinity 1st link}

X. {sex 1st link & sex & sex 2nd link & generation last link & lineality & generation & affinity last link & affinity 1st link}

XI. {sex 1st link & sex & parallelity & generation last link & generation 1st link & distance & affinity last link & affinity 1st link}

XII. {sex 1st link & sex & sex 2nd link & generation last link & generation 1st link & distance & affinity last link & affinity 1st link}

XIII. {sex 1st link & sex & parallelity & generation last link & generation 1st link & distance & affinity & affinity 1st link}

XIV. {sex 1st link & sex & sex 2nd link & generation last link & generation 1st link & distance & affinity & affinity 1st link}

The first four of these are simplest. Applying Set I, some kin terms obtain more than one definition, as for instance:

kayın

[affinity 1st link = aff & sex = m & generation = 0 & distance = 2]

[affinity 1st link = aff & sex = m & affinity last link = cons & generation = 0]

[sex = m & affinity last link = cons & generation = 0 & distance = 2]

baldız

[sex 1st link = f & affinity 1st link = aff & sex = f & generation = 0 & distance = 2]

[sex 1st link = f & affinity 1st link = aff & sex = f & affinity last link = cons & generation = 0]

[sex 1st link = f & sex = f & affinity last link = cons & generation = 0 & distance = 2]

The theoretically possible componential models, conforming to Set I, owing to the different definitions of kin terms, are $2^{15} \times 3^7 \times 4^2 \times 5^2 = 28,665,446,400$. The application of our constraints pertaining to kin term definitions, however, successfully reduces this huge number to a single simplest paradigm, given as Table 4.14. The situation with indeterminacy is analogous, when we analyse Turkish using the other three dimension sets, so we need not give further numbers.

4.2.11 Seneca

In this section, KINSHIP rediscovers the classical analysis of Lounsbury (1965) of the kinship system of the Amerindian language Seneca belonging to the Iroquoian family (Pericliev 2010: 80–2).

The data on consanguineal relations, as presented in Leech (1974), are given below. In a kin type formula, the prefixes m and f denote the sex of the speaker (respectively 'male' or 'female'), whereas the suffixes e and y denote seniority within one generation (respectively 'elder' or 'younger'):

1. $ha^{?}nih$: Fa $\lor$ FaBr $\lor$ FaMoSiSo $\lor$ FaFaBrSo $\lor$ FaMoBrSo $\lor$ FaFaSiSo $\lor$ FaFaFaBrSoSo
2. $no^{?}y\bar{e}h$: Mo $\lor$ MoSi $\lor$ MoMoSiDa $\lor$ MoFaBrDa $\lor$ MoMoBrDa $\lor$ MoFaSiDa $\lor$ MoMoMoSiDaDa
3. $hakhno^{?}s\bar{e}h$: MoBr $\lor$ MoMoSiSo $\lor$ MoFaBrSo $\lor$ MoMoBrSo $\lor$ MoFaSiSo $\lor$ MoMoMoSiDaSo
4. $ake{:}hak$: FaSi $\lor$ FaMoSiDa $\lor$ FaFaBrDa $\lor$ FaMoBrDa $\lor$ FaFaSiDa $\lor$ FaFaFaBrSoDa
5. $hahtsi^{?}$: Bre $\lor$ MoSiSoe $\lor$ FaBrSoe $\lor$ MoMoSiDaSoe $\lor$ FaFaBrSoSoe $\lor$ MoFaBrDaSoe $\lor$ FaMoSiSoSoe $\lor$ MoMoBrDaSoe
6. $he^{?}k\bar{e}{:}^{?}$: Bry $\lor$ MoSiSoy $\lor$ FaBrSoy $\lor$ MoMoSiDaSoy $\lor$ FaFaBrSoSoy $\lor$ MoFaBrDaSoy $\lor$ FaMoSiSoSoy $\lor$ MoMoBrDaSoy
7. $ahtsi^{?}$: Sie $\lor$ MoSiDae $\lor$ FaBrDae $\lor$ MoMoSiDaDae $\lor$ FaFaBrSoDae $\lor$ MoFaBrDaDae $\lor$ FaMoSiSoDae $\lor$ MoMoBrDaDae
8. $khe^{?}k\bar{e}{:}^{?}$: Siy $\lor$ MoSiDay $\lor$ FaBrDay $\lor$ MoMoSiDaDay $\lor$ FaFaBrSoDay $\lor$ MoFaBrDaDay $\lor$ FaMoSiSoDay $\lor$ MoMoBrDaDay
9. $aky\bar{a}{:}^{?}se{:}^{?}$: MoBrSo $\lor$ FaSiSo $\lor$ MoMoSiSoSo $\lor$ FaFaBrDaSo $\lor$ MoFaBrSoSo $\lor$ FaMoSiDaSo $\lor$ MoMoBrSoSo $\lor$ MoBrDa $\lor$ FaSiDa
10. $he{:}awak$: (for male Speaker) mSo $\lor$ mBrSo $\lor$ mMoSiSoSo $\lor$ mFaBrSoSo $\lor$ mMoBrSoSo $\lor$ mFaSiSoSo $\lor$ mMoMoSiDaSoSo
11. $he{:}awak$: (for female Speaker) fSo $\lor$ fSiSo $\lor$ fMoSiDaSo $\lor$ fFaBrDaSo $\lor$ fMoBrDaSo $\lor$ fFaSiDaSo $\lor$ fMoMoSiDaDaSo
12. $khe{:}awak$: (for male Speaker) mDa $\lor$ mBrDa $\lor$ mMoSiSoDa $\lor$ mFaBrSoDa $\lor$ mMoBrSoDa $\lor$ mFaSiSoDa $\lor$ mMoMoSiDaSoDa
13. $khe{:}awak$: (for female Speaker) $\lor$ fDa $\lor$ fSiDa $\lor$ fMoSiDaDa $\lor$ fFaBrDaDa $\lor$ fMoBrDaDa $\lor$ fFaSiDaDa $\lor$ fMoMoSiDaDaDa
14. $hey\bar{e}{:}w\bar{o}{:}t\bar{e}^{?}$: mSiSo $\lor$ mMoSiDaSo $\lor$ mFaBrDaSo $\lor$ mMoBrDaSo $\lor$ mFaSiDaSo $\lor$ mMoMoSiDaDaSo
15. $hehs\bar{o}^{?}neh$: fBrSo $\lor$ fMoSiSoSo $\lor$ fFaBrSoSo $\lor$ fMoBrSoSo $\lor$ fFaSiSoSo $\lor$ fMoMoSiDaSoSo
16. $khey\bar{e}{:}w\bar{o}{:}t{\sim}e^{?}$: mSiDa $\lor$ mMoSiDaDa $\lor$ mFaBrDaDa $\lor$ mMoBrDaDa $\lor$ mFaSiDaDa $\lor$ mMoMoSiDaDaDa
17. $khehs\bar{o}^{?}neh$: fBrDa $\lor$ fMoSiSoDa $\lor$ fFaBrSoDa $\lor$ fMoBrSoDa $\lor$ fFaSiSoDa $\lor$ fMoMoSiDaSoDa

(Our kin formula MoMoMoSiDaDa is incorrectly given as MoMoSiDaDa by Leech, which was signalled by KINSHIP.)

Running KINSHIP on the above data, we obtained a simplest dimension set, comprising the following five features:

I. {sex & sex speaker & seniority & parallelity & generation}

The feature (Iroquoian) 'parallelity' merits an explanation. This feature reflects the anthropological distinction between parallel and cross cousins, and for a kin type to have the value 'parallel' there should be an equivalence of sex between the two kin of the generation above ego (whichever of those is junior); otherwise, the kin type is 'non-parallel' (or cross). This means that, for senior generation kin, a kin type is parallel only if there is a sex equivalence between ego's linking parent (= first link in kin type) and alter (= last link in kin type); for junior generation, sex equivalence between ego and alter's linking parent (penultimate link in kin type); and for kin of the same generation as ego, sex equivalence between ego's linking parent and alter's linking parent.

With these dimensions, no kin term in the vocabulary receives more than one definition and the program generates the unique componential model listed as Table 4.18, without using further constraints. The model is identical to the one proposed by Lounsbury (1965), and thus KINSHIP replicates Lounsbury's discovery. Both discoveries are performed under the same initial conditions, or have started with the same data, so KINSHIP may be said to replicate an outstanding linguistic achievement. At the same time, we note that one of the contributions of Lounsbury was the invention of a new feature 'parallelity', which KINSHIP only used as previously defined by us, so its discovery does not fully measure up to Lounsbury's achievement (but see the derived feature invented by the program in the next section).

4.2.12   Zapotec

The kinship vocabulary of Zapotec, an Oto-Manguean language, subjected to componential analysis below, is based on the collection of unpublished data on Middle American kinship vocabularies by A. Kimball Romney (1967):

1. *šoza$^{\textit{?}}$gul*: FaFa ∨ MoFa
2. *šna$^{\textit{?}}$agul*: FaMo ∨ MoMo
3. *šoza$^{\textit{?}}$*: Fa
4. *šna$^{\textit{?}}$*: Mo

5. *bulča$^?$*: mBr
6. *rjila$^?$*: fSi
7. *zana$^?$*: mSi ∨ fBr
8. *rji$^?$na$^?$*: So ∨ Da
9. *rsna$^?$*: SoSo ∨ DaDa ∨ SoDa ∨ DaSo
10. *tio*: FaBr ∨ MoBr
11. *tia*: FaSi ∨ MoSi
12. *primo kiu$^?$*: MoSiDa ∨ MoBrDa ∨ FaSiDa ∨ FaBrDa ∨ MoMoSiDaDa ∨ MoMoSiSiDa ∨ MoMoBrDaDa ∨ MoMoBrSiDa ∨ MoFaSiSiDa ∨ MoFaBrDaDa ∨ MoFaBrSiDa ∨ FaMoSiDaDa ∨ FaMoSiSiDa ∨ FaMoBr ∨ FaFaSiSiDa ∨ FaFaBrDaDa ∨ FaFaBrSiDa ∨ MoSiSiMoBrSi ∨ FaSiSiFaBrSi ∨ MoMoBrDaSi ∨ MoMoBrSiSi ∨ MoFaSiDaSi ∨ MoFaSiSiSi ∨ MoFaBrDaSi ∨ MoFaBrSiSi ∨ FaMoSiSiSi ∨ FaMoBrDaSi ∨ FaMoBrSiSi ∨ FaFaSiDaSi ∨ FaFaSiSiSi ∨ FaFaBrDa
13. *sobrinukin$^?$*: BrSo ∨ SiSo ∨ BrDa ∨ SiDa

Running KINSHIP with the available 15 features on this data set, the program reports that it cannot cleanly distinguish the kin term *zana$^?$* 'mSi ∨ fBr', which a male speaker uses for sister and a female speaker uses for brother, from either of the terms *bulča$^?$* 'mBr', which a male speaker uses for brother, and *rjila$^?$* 'fSi', which a female speaker applies to sister. Being incapable of demarcating terms by simple features alone, the system has recourse to its mechanisms for inventing derived features (see Chapter 3, Section 3.2). KINSHIP combines two of the relevant primitive features from its current inventory into a derived feature, which is a logical formula for conjunction, disjunction, implication or equivalence, as required. In this particular case, the relevant primitive features needed to distinguish the terms are the binary features 'sex of speaker' and 'sex of relative (alter)' and the required formula is an equivalence relation (iff), holding between these binary features. The new complex feature, which I will denote by <sex sp – iff – sex rel>, is also binary and will be possessed by any kin type which either designates a male speaker and a male relative or designates a female speaker and a female relative (or, in other terms, may be said to have the value 'parallel'); otherwise, or in the case when a kin type designates different sexes of speaker and relative, the feature will take the value 'cross'. (This new derived feature is in some respects reminiscent of, but is not identical to, the Senecan feature 'parallelity', which is hard-wired in the program and used in the componential models of other languages.) With the derived feature at our disposal, the demarcation of the problematic kin terms is cleanly done: *zana*$^?$ 'mSi $\vee$ fBr' is <sex sp – iff – sex rel> = cross (as the sister of a male and the brother of a female are both cross), whereas both *bulča*$^?$ 'mBr' and *rjila*$^?$ 'fSi' are <sex sp – iff – sex rel> = par (as a brother of a male speaker and a sister of a female speaker are both parallel). Hence *zana*$^?$ is now distinguishable from both *bulča*$^?$ and *rjila*$^?$.

The KINSHIP system discovers that eight dimension sets, ranging from four to five dimensions, suffice to discriminate the lexemes in the vocabulary. These dimensions are:

   I. {sex & generation & distance & <sex sp – iff – sex rel>}

  II. {sex & generation last link & generation 1st link & distance & <sex sp – iff – sex rel>}

 III. {sex 2nd link & sex 1st link & generation & distance & <sex sp – iff – sex rel>}

 IV. {sex & generation 1st link & lineality & distance & <sex sp - iff – sex rel>}

  V. {sex & generation last link & lineality & distance & <sex sp – iff – sex rel>}

 VI. {sex 2nd link & sex 1st link & generation last link & generation 1st link & distance & <sex sp – iff – sex rel>}

VII. {sex 2nd link & sex 1st link & generation 1st link & lineality & distance & <sex sp – iff – sex rel>}

VIII. {sex 2nd link & sex 1st link & generation last link & lineality & distance & <sex sp – iff – sex rel>}

Set I, comprising four features, three primitive and one derived, is simplest, and the analysis with this set leads to the unique simplest model given in Table 4.19, with no need to apply further simplicity criteria.

4.2.13 Popoloca

Popoloca is another Oto-Manguean language. The data set below comes from Romney (1967):

1. *tači*$^?$*na*: FaFa $\vee$ MoFa
2. *nači*$^?$*na*: FaMo $\vee$ MoMo
3. $^?$*apanaa*: Fa
4. $^?$*amanaa*: Mo
5. *s*$^?$*onaa*: Br
6. *thakhoonaa*: Si
7. *ča*$^?$*na*: So $\vee$ Da
8. *čand*$^?$*inaa*: SoSo $\vee$ DaDa $\vee$ SoDa $\vee$ DaSo

9. $či^{\textit{?}}ninaa$: FaBr $\vee$ MoBr
10. $khva^{\textit{?}}naa$: FaSi $\vee$ MoSi
11. $čauv^{\textit{?}}e$: MoSiDa $\vee$ MoBrDa $\vee$ FaSiDa $\vee$ FaBrDa $\vee$ MoSiSo $\vee$ MoBrSo $\vee$ FaSiSo $\vee$ FaBrSo $\vee$ BrSo $\vee$ SiSo $\vee$ BrDa $\vee$ SiDa

There are 12 dimension sets, sufficing to handle the data:

   I. {sex & generation last link & generation 1st link & generation}
  II. {sex & generation last link & lineality & generation}
 III. {sex & generation last link & generation 1st link & distance}
 IV. {sex & generation & generation 1st link & distance}
  V. {sex & generation last link & lineality & distance}
 VI. {sex & generation & lineality & distance}
VII. {sex 2nd link & sex 1st link & generation last link & generation 1st link & generation}
VIII. {sex 2nd link & sex 1st link & generation last link & lineality & generation}
 IX. {sex 2nd link & sex 1st link & generation last link & generation 1st link & distance}
  X. {sex 2nd link & sex 1st link & generation & generation 1st link & distance}
 XI. {sex 2nd link & sex 1st link & generation last link & lineality & distance}
XII. {sex 2nd link & sex 1st link & generation & lineality & distance}

Of these, six are simplest and comprise four features. None of the six sets generates only unambiguous kin term definitions. The number of theoretically possible componential models using each of these dimension sets is respectively: $2^4 = 16$ (Set I), $2^4 = 16$ (Set II), $2^5 \times 3^2 = 288$ (Set III), $2^5 \times 3^1 = 96$ (Set IV), $2^2 = 4$ (Set V), and $2^7 = 128$ (Set VI). Applying the coherence constraint results in unique models in each case; see Tables 4.20–4.25.

4.2.14 Huave

Huave is a language isolate spoken by the indigenous Huave people on the Pacific coast of the Mexican state of Oaxaca. The data set we consider again comes from the collection of Middle America kinship systems in Romney (1967):

1. $šèèč$: FaFa $\vee$ MoFa
2. $nčéy$: FaMo $\vee$ MoMo

3. *téàt*: Fa
4. *mí m*: Mo
5. *kóh*: Bre ∨ Sie
6. *číìg*: Bry ∨ Siy
7. *kwál*: So ∨ Da
8. *ntáh*: Wi
9. *òkwáàc*: WiFa ∨ WiMo
10. *nòh*: Hu
11. *píw*: HuFa ∨ HuMo
12. *kùnyádà*: mWiSi ∨ mWiBr ∨ mHuSi ∨ mHuBr ∨ mSiWi ∨ mBrWi ∨ mSiHu ∨ mBrHu
13. *híy*: SoWiFa ∨ SoWiMo ∨ DaWiFa ∨ DaWiMo ∨ SoHuFa ∨ SoHuMo ∨ DaHuFa ∨ DaHuMo

KINSHIP finds 14 alternative dimension sets for the relatively small kinship vocabulary of Huave. The size of these sets ranges from six to seven features. It is interesting to note that quite a number of the overall feature sets, viz.10, are simplest (comprising six features), which creates a significant indeterminacy in the potential componential models at the level of dimensions, in contrast to the usual indeterminacy *within* one dimension set we witnessed earlier.

I. {sex 2nd link & sex 1st link & seniority & generation last link & distance & affinity 1st link}
II. {sex & sex 1st link & seniority & generation last link & distance & affinity 1st link}
III. {sex 2nd link & sex 1st link & seniority & generation & distance & affinity 1st link}
IV. {sex & sex 1st link & seniority & generation & distance & affinity 1st link}
V. {sex 2nd link & sex 1st link & seniority & distance & generation & affinity last link}
VI. {sex & sex 1st link & seniority & distance & generation & affinity last link}
VII. {sex 2nd link & sex 1st link & seniority & generation last link & distance & affinity}
VIII. {sex & sex 1st link & seniority & generation last link & distance & affinity}
IX. {sex 2nd link & sex 1st link & seniority & generation & distance & affinity}
X. {sex & sex 1st link & seniority & generation & distance & affinity}

XI. {sex 2nd link & sex 1st link & seniority & generation last link & distance & generation 1st link & affinity last link}

XII. {sex & sex 1st link & seniority & generation last link & distance & generation 1st link & affinity last link}

XIII. {sex 2nd link & sex 1st link & seniority & generation last link & distance & lineality & affinity last link}

XIV. {sex & sex 1st link & seniority & generation last link & distance & lineality & affinity last link}

Using some of the simplest dimension sets, some kin terms are defined with more than one feature bundle. For instance, consider the following terms when applying the features in Set II:

téàt

[sex 1st link = m & generation last link = 1 & distance = 1]
[sex = m & generation last link = 1 & distance = 1]

mí m

[sex 1st link = f & generation last link = 1 & distance = 1]
[sex = f & generation last link = 1 & distance = 1]

ntáh

[sex 1st link = f & affinity 1st link = aff & distance = 1]
[affinity 1st link = aff & sex = f & distance = 1]

Other sets (Set I, Set V and Set VII) do not lead to ambiguous definitions of kin terms. In general, the indeterminacy in componential models within these dimension sets is of medium degree and varies from 1 to 1024 models. After the application of the further simplicity constraints within each componential scheme, in all cases KINSHIP produces unique models, listed as Tables 4.26–4.35.

4.3 Summary of results

In the previous section, 14 languages were subjected to componential analysis with the KINSHIP program. The program used 15 features (dimensions), listed in Section 4.1, and it was required to produce all alternative dimension sets for these languages. Additionally, the program generated the simplest componential models for the languages, fulfilling our simplicity criteria, pertaining to choosing the shortest dimension set and shortest definition of each kin term, as well as the condition on the coherence of definitions of kin terms within the kinship vocabulary.

We should now evaluate the operation of the program from two perspectives. First, we need to assess how KINSHIP manages to discriminate the kin terms of the analysed languages, and, second, how successfully it handles the multiple solutions problem, which is believed by some to be a threat to the method of componential analysis.

Regarding the first problem, we may say that KINSHIP fares quite well in showing the contrasts between the lexemes of the studied languages using the selected set of 15 primitive features. These have proved sufficient to demarcate all kin terms of the analysed 15 languages (14 languages in this chapter, plus Bulgarian from Chapter 3); in one case (Zapotec), the program having to invent a new, derived, feature, combining two primitive features from its current inventory. The examined languages are structurally diverse, some of them to a certain extent being prototypes of the basic structural types, viz. Eskimo (e.g. English), Sudanese (e.g. Turkish) or Iroquois (Seneca), a circumstance which attests to the generality of KINSHIP and the selected features. At the same time, in view of the enormous diversity of kinship systems worldwide, it goes without saying that not all languages could be successfully analysed with the current set of primitive features (or derived features therefrom). To handle all structural variety, it would be necessary to define new features, add further rules for structural equivalence (as we did for English, following Goodenough), and the KINSHIP system, as it stands, is implemented generally enough to allow such expansions. Making the program applicable to any random instance from the thousands of world languages is an ambitious task (if at all possible, in the literal sense) which requires enormous data-intensive research, which is beyond the scope of the present book.

Regarding the second problem, that of multiple solutions, we may say that generally our simplicity constraints perform quite well. As seen from Table 4.36, from 15 analysed languages in all, nine have unique componential models, and most of the others have just several simplest models, the exceptions being Popoloca and Huave with six and ten models respectively, which seems acceptable from an analytical point of view. We observe that the reason for the indeterminacy, in all cases, is the presence of multiple dimension sets; our simplicity constraints on kin term definitions eliminate all ambiguity within one dimension set (and the number of simplest componential models equals the number of simplest dimension sets).

A closer look at the simplest alternative dimension sets reveals that a further intuitive and natural choice can be made regarding their constituent members. Thus, let us consider the equally simple dimension sets for Swedish, comprising four features:

I. {*sex 2nd link* & sex 1st link & generation & distance}
II. {*sex* & sex 1st link & generation & distance}

The difference between these two sets amounts to the alternative use of the (italicized) feature 'sex 2nd link' (in the first set) as against the use of the feature 'sex' (in the second set). However, it would be natural to prefer the feature 'sex' to the feature 'sex 2nd link' in the description of Swedish, and of any language for that matter, for the following two reasons. First, from a methodological perspective, it would be preferable to use features that are universally present in languages rather than features that are more language-specific, so 'sex' becomes the natural choice over 'sex 2nd link', as the former is universal and the latter is much less common in the world languages (and for that reason the former, but not the latter, is included in the standard feature set proposed by Kroeber 1909). Secondly, from a cognitive perspective, the feature 'sex', marking the sex of the referenced relative is more salient than the feature 'sex 2nd link', marking the sex of just one linking relative in the chain of potentially many relatives forming a kin type. Owing to these considerations, Set II, employing the feature 'sex', looks a considerably better choice to make than Set I, using the feature 'sex 2nd link'.

An examination of the remaining cases in our analyses where there exist equally simple dimension sets shows that we are on the right track and thus can further reduce the indeterminacy of componential analysis by choosing the more universal features that refer to the description of the referenced relative rather than to some linking relative. The features we used for the analyses in the book naturally fall into these two groups:

More universal features	*Less universal features*
Sex of relative	Sex of 1st link
Sex of speaker	Sex of 2nd link
Generation of relative	Generation of 1st link
Genealogical distance	Generation of last link
Affinity of relative	Affinity of 1st link
Lineality	Affinity of last link
Seniority within one generation	Parallelity
	Structural equivalence

With this categorization at hand, we may look at the remaining languages with alternative dimension sets. For Polish, we have the following two simplest dimension sets, comprising six features:

I. {sex 2nd link & sex & sex 1st link & generation & *affinity 1st link* & distance}
II. {sex 2nd link & sex & sex 1st link & generation & *affinity* & distance}

A choice needs to be made between the (italicized) features 'affinity 1st link' (first set) and 'affinity' (second set). Here, the feature 'affinity' should be preferred over 'affinity 1st link' as the more universal one, and hence, ultimately, Set II.

For Albanian, we have the following three simplest dimension sets, comprising five features:

I. {sex & *generation 1st link* & distance & *generation last link*}
II. {sex & generation & distance & *generation last link*}
III. {sex & generation & distance & *affinity*}

The first two dimension sets employ the less salient and universal features ('generation 1st link' and 'generation last link') in comparison to the more universal feature 'affinity' used in Set III, hence the latter set should be selected.

For Turkish, we have the following four simplest dimension sets, comprising seven features:

I. {sex 1st link & sex & *parallelity* & generation & distance & affinity last link & affinity 1st link}
II. {sex 1st link & sex & sex 2nd link & generation & distance & *affinity last link* & affinity 1st link}
III. {sex 1st link & sex & *parallelity* & generation & distance & affinity & affinity 1st link}
IV. {sex 1st link & sex & sex 2nd link & generation & distance & *affinity* & affinity 1st link}

Set I and Set III employ the less common feature (Senecan) 'parallelity', besides other less universal features, so can be ignored as good choices. In the remaining dimension sets that do not employ this feature, Set II uses 'affinity last link' as contrasted to Set IV using 'affinity' instead. 'Affinity' is more universal than 'affinity last' link', hence Set IV, using the former, should be selected.

Popoloca's kin terms may be distinguished from one another using the following six four-member feature sets:

I. {sex & generation last link & generation 1st link & generation}
II. {sex & generation last link & lineality & generation}
III. {sex & generation last link & generation 1st link & distance}
IV. {sex & generation & generation 1st link & distance}
V. {sex & generation last link & lineality & distance}
VI. {sex & generation & lineality & distance}

Of these six dimensions sets, only Set VI contains exclusively universal features from our list, so this set should ultimately be selected in the componential analysis of the language.

Finally, Huave has ten simplest feature sets, each having six features, as follows:

I. {sex 2nd link & sex 1st link & seniority & generation last link & distance & affinity 1st link}
II. {sex & sex 1st link & seniority & generation last link & distance & affinity 1st link}
III. {sex 2nd link & sex 1st link & seniority & generation & distance & affinity 1st link}
IV. {sex & sex 1st link & seniority & generation & distance & affinity 1st link}
V. {sex 2nd link & sex 1st link & seniority & distance & generation & affinity last link}
VI. {sex & sex 1st link & seniority & distance & generation & affinity last link}
VII. {sex 2nd link & sex 1st link & seniority & generation last link & distance & affinity}
VIII. {sex & sex 1st link & seniority & generation last link & distance & affinity}
IX. {sex 2nd link & sex 1st link & seniority & generation & distance & affinity}
X. {sex & sex 1st link & seniority & generation & distance & affinity}

Of these ten dimension sets, Set X contains only one less universal feature from our list (viz. 'sex 1st link') in contrast to all other sets containing more than one such feature. Therefore, this dimension set should be selected.

In sum, the informally sketched procedure of selection of dimension sets that preferably employ more universal features results, in our illustrative cases, in unique dimension sets and hence in unique componential models. Similar results could be expected examining further languages. Therefore, a componential analysis incorporating this new criterion, in addition to our three previous simplicity criteria, convincingly resolves the indeterminacy problem altogether and in a principled way, thus revitalizing the role of componential analysis as an analytical tool in kinship terminology studies whose predominant goal is uniqueness of models.

5
Conclusion

The linguistic method of componential analysis was transferred to kinship terminological studies by Ward Goodenough and Floyd Lounsbury in the 1960s and this led to the wide popularity of the method for several decades. A large number of componential models were proposed in both the linguistic and anthropological literature for mostly 'exotic' languages. Some analysts believed that these models revealed 'psychological validity', or the world view of native speakers, while others assumed that such models describe 'social-structural reality', or the rules of using kin terms in a society, and the discovery of psychologically valid models required subsequent psychological tests. Some scholars proposed such tests, while others introduced alternative ways to study kinship terminology (extensionist, algebraic or relational). Despite the existence of alternative approaches, however, classical componential analysis continues to be an indispensable tool in kinship studies. First, componential analysis is an inalienable part of some of the other approaches (e.g. the extensionist method presupposes componential models of the 'core vocabulary', while the approaches looking for psychological validity often presuppose the availability of componential models to be subsequently tested psychologically). Second, it is the only method that reveals the semantic system of kin terms and for this reason continues to be in the analytic repertoire of both current linguistics and current anthropology. And, third, componential models are essential not only for exposing semantic structure, but also for constructing dictionary definitions, for translation purposes and for historical reconstruction.

A critical evaluation of the literature on componential analysis of kinship terms reveals two common basic problems. Analysts have either failed to provide 'consistent' componential models (i.e. models defining kin terms by necessary and sufficient features) or have failed to list all componential models of a specific data set. The first problem has generally remained unnoticed, while the second was emphasized by Robbins Burling and attracted considerable attention in the literature, but without any feasible solutions proposed to solve it. In this book, I discuss these two problems in detail and provide ample illustrations of the problems from the literature. Inconsistency, for instance, is illustrated in published models of English, which fail to demarcate some kin terms or use redundant features, or both. Redundancy is identified as a particularly acute problem and the logic and psychological reasons for its occurrence are discussed. The problem of multiple solutions is illustrated with Bulgarian, showing that the alternative models, even when using a fixed number of dimensions, amount to astronomical numbers. These numbers become even greater if redundant models are accepted. It is shown that both problems actually stem from the computational complexity of the task of componential analysis, leading to the conclusion that the task requires automation. The difference between using and not using a computational tool is not a matter of economy of time and effort, but the difference between finding and not finding a correct solution at all.

The KINSHIP program is designed to handle these two problems, and more generally, to serve as a computational aid in the study of kinship terminology by analysts of different theoretical persuasions. The program accepts as input the standard information used by linguists (kin terms with their attendant kin types, or relatives) and produces componential analyses in terms of the usual features (sex, generation, etc.). A detailed description of the algorithm was given by working out a simple example. The features (= dimensions) used by the program (which are about 20) were explained, as well as how they are computed for kin types and how the kin terms' conjunctive definitions are produced containing just the necessary and sufficient components for demarcation of any term from all others in the kinship vocabulary. The simplicity constraints introduced in the system in order to limit the indeterminacy of componential models were described. They pertain to dimensions and components in kin term definitions and prescribe using the least number of dimensions and components in a componential model. Whenever alternative definitions of a kin term still remain – and this is usually the case and the most common source of multiplicity of solutions – a third constraint chooses only those components in the definition of a kin term that are 'coherent' across the definitions of other 'semantically similar' kin terms in the analysed vocabulary (to the effect that, for instance, terms like *father* and *mother* will be defined analogously and with the same features, with the exception that the first will get the component sex = male, whereas the latter will get sex = female). The Bulgarian language was used as an illustration of the huge number of models arrived at with totally unconstrained analysis, targeting only the use of necessary and sufficient components. The illustrative example shows in detail how this huge number of alternatives is reduced to a unique model after the application of our simplicity criteria.

KINSHIP is a sophisticated computational tool and has mechanisms for the invention of new features (dimensions) in cases when those present in the system are insufficient to successfully analyse a specific kinship terminological system. These mechanisms are based on combining the elementary features by the logical operations of conjunction, disjunction, implication, etc. The KINSHIP system also possesses some additional facilities, designed to make it more user-friendly. These include checking the 'correctness' of input (for example, that no cross-classification of kin types occurs), querying the system in various ways (e.g. about kin terms and attendant kin types, about the features currently used by the system, semantic contrasts between a selected pair of kin terms), etc.

The KINSHIP system was applied in the book on 15 comprehensive data sets in order to test how it handles the problems of consistency and indeterminacy of models. Computer-generated componential models were presented of languages from Indo-European and from other language families. Previous literature on componential analysis focussed predominantly on 'exotic' languages, so Indo-European languages were largely ignored. We have filled this gap by analysing languages from most major branches of Indo-European. The addition of languages from some non-Indo-European families is intended, first, to extend the empirical basis for testing our program by covering most structural types (Eskimo, Sudanese, Iroquois, etc.), and second, to illustrate the system's power, by sketching the use of new, invented features by the program, in the case of languages failing to succumb to modelling with the classical Kroeber's features (sex, generation, etc.). The test is performed, employing an inventory of 15 feature, requiring that all generated models by the KINSHIP program are the simplest (using our inventory of features) and, besides, include all alternative feature sets. The selected features prove sufficient to demarcate all kin terms in the studied vocabularies, and the incorporated simplicity criteria prove effective in reducing a potentially unlimited to unique or a manageable number of models.

Some interesting aspects of the generated models of specific languages are also worth mentioning. Thus, for example, some analyses of American English, which have received much attention in the literature, are shown to be deficient in a number of ways, amended by our model. The model we propose for English is not only the simplest (with a previous one, also generated by KINSHIP), but the only one managing to describe all kin terms from Goodenough's exhaustive data set with conjunctive definitions. Our model for Bulgarian makes conspicuous some inaccuracies in the definitions of some kin terms in the standard Bulgarian dictionaries, thus providing ways to correct them. Remarkably, KINSHIP has re-discovered Lounsbury's classic analysis of the Seneca language from the Iroquois family.

The overall results from the operation of KINSHIP should be evaluated quite positively. First, the program was an indispensable computational aid in the critical evaluation of previous practices of the method and in making conspicuous the common problems of inconsistency and huge unnoticed ambiguity in manually performed componential analyses. This, in effect, led to better understanding of these problems and to proposals for their solution. Second, the program was successfully used to generate a sizable number of consistent and definite componential models of Indo-European and non-Indo-European languages; some of these models are the first componential analyses of the languages, while others – re-analyses – improve on previous ones. And last but not least, our study of the componential method has important implications for the application of the approach to tasks other than kinship semantics (e.g. phonological distinctive feature analysis), where the notion of linguistic system is essential, and hence similar problems are bound to be encountered. The computational machinery described in the book is general enough to be also applicable to these tasks and thus to make them practicable.

Appendix: Tables

Table 1.1 Componential analysis of English consanguineals

grandfather	[sex = m & generation = 2 & lineality = lin]
grandmother	[sex = f & generation = 2 & lineality = lin]
father	[sex = m & generation = 1 & lineality = lin]
mother	[sex = f & generation = 1 & lineality = lin]
brother	[sex = m & generation = 0 & lineality = lin]
sister	[sex = f & generation = 0 & lineality = lin]
son	[sex = m & generation = − 1 & lineality = lin]
daughter	[sex = f & generation = − 1 & lineality = lin]
grandson	[sex = m & generation = − 2 & lineality = lin]
granddaughter	[sex = f & generation = − 2 & lineality = lin]
uncle	[sex = m & generation = 1 & lineality = colin]
aunt	[sex = f & generation = 1 & lineality = colin]
cousin	[lineality = ablin]
nephew	[sex = m & generation = − 1 & lineality = colin]
niece	[sex = f & generation = − 1 & lineality = colin]

Table 1.2 Relational analysis of English (after Wallace 1970)

cousin		child of	sibling of	parent of	
uncle/aunt			sibling of	parent of	
nephew/niece		child of	sibling of		
brother/sister			sibling of		
father/mother				parent of	
son/daughter		child of			
son/daughter-in-law	spouse of	child of			
brother/sister-in-law	spouse of		sibling of		spouse of

Table 2.1 Nogle's componential model of English

	Nuclear (1)	Affinity (2)	Generation (3)	Affinity 1st (4)	Lineality (5)	Sex (6)
husband	1.1	2.1	3.2	4.1	0	6.1
wife	1.1	2.1	3.2	4.1	0	6.2
step-father	1.1	2.1	3.1	4.2	0	6.1
step-mother	1.1	2.1	3.1	4.2	0	6.2
step-brother	1.1	2.1	3.2	0	0	6.1
step-sister	1.1	2.1	3.2	0	0	6.2
step-son	1.1	2.1	3.3	0	0	6.1
step-daughter	1.1	2.1	3.3	0	0	6.2
father	1.1	2.2	3.1	0	5.1	6.1
mother	1.1	2.2	3.1	0	5.1	6.2
brother	1.1	2.2	3.2	0	5.2	6.1
sister	1.1	2.2	3.2	0	5.2	6.2
son	1.1	2.2	3.3	0	5.1	6.1
daughter	1.1	2.2	3.3	0	5.1	6.2
uncle1	1.2	2.1	3.1	4.1	5.2	6.1
aunt1	1.2	2.1	3.1	4.1	5.2	6.2
father-in-law	1.2	2.1	3.1	4.2	0	6.1
mother-in-law	1.2	2.1	3.1	4.2	0	6.2
brother-in-law	1.2	2.1	3.2	0	0	6.1
sister-in-law	1.2	2.1	3.2	0	0	6.2
son-in-law	1.2	2.1	3.3	0	0	6.1
daughter-in-law	1.2	2.1	3.3	0	0	6.2
grandfather	1.2	2.2	3.1	0	5.1	6.1
grandmother	1.2	2.2	3.1	0	5.1	6.2
grandson	1.2	2.2	3.3	0	5.1	6.1
granddaughter	1.2	2.2	3.3	0	5.1	6.2
uncle2	1.2	2.2	3.1	0	5.2	6.1
aunt2	1.2	2.2	3.1	0	5.2	6.2
cousin	1.2	2.2	3.2	0	5.2	0
nephew	1.2	2.2	3.3	0	5.2	6.1

Source: Nogle (1974: 64).

Table 2.2 Contrasts demarcating *uncle*

uncle (collateral)	vs.	*grandfather* (lineal)
uncle (collateral *or* nonnuclear)	vs.	*father* (lineal *or* nuclear)
uncle (consanguineal 1st link)	vs.	*father-in-law* (affinal 1st link)
uncle (nonnuclear)	vs.	*step-father* (nuclear)

Table 2.3 Redundancy in Nogle's componential model of English (redundant components enclosed in brackets)

	Nuclear (1)	Affinity (2)	Generation (3)	Affinity 1st (4)	Lineality (5)	Sex (6)
husband	1.1	2.1	3.2	(4.1)	(0)	6.1
wife	1.1	2.1	3.2	(4.1)	(0)	6.2
step-father	1.1	2.1	3.1	(4.2)	(0)	6.1
step-mother	1.1	2.1	3.1	(4.2)	(0)	6.2
step-brother	1.1	2.1	3.2	(0)	(0)	6.1
step-sister	1.1	2.1	3.2	(0)	(0)	6.2
step-son	1.1	2.1	3.3	(0)	(0)	6.1
step-daughter	1.1	2.1	3.3	(0)	(0)	6.2
father	1.1	2.2	3.1	(0)	(5.1)	6.1
mother	1.1	2.2	3.1	(0)	(5.1)	6.2
brother	1.1	2.2	3.2	(0)	(5.2)	6.1
sister	1.1	2.2	3.2	(0)	(5.2)	6.2
son	1.1	2.2	3.3	(0)	(5.1)	6.1
daughter	1.1	2.2	3.3	(0)	(5.1)	6.2
uncle1	(1.2)	2.1	3.1	4.1	(5.2)	6.1
aunt1	(1.2)	2.1	3.1	4.1	(5.2)	6.2
father-in-law	1.2	2.1	3.1	4.2	(0)	6.1
mother-in-law	1.2	2.1	3.1	4.2	(0)	6.2
brother-in-law	1.2	2.1	3.2	(0)	(0)	6.1
sister-in-law	1.2	2.1	3.2	(0)	(0)	6.2
son-in-law	1.2	2.1	3.3	(0)	(0)	6.1
daughter-in-law	1.2	2.1	3.3	(0)	(0)	6.2
grandfather	1.2	2.2	3.1	(0)	5.1	6.1
grandmother	1.2	2.2	3.1	(0)	5.1	6.2
grandson	1.2	2.2	3.3	(0)	5.1	6.1
granddaughter	1.2	2.2	3.3	(0)	5.1	6.2
uncle2	(1.2)	2.2	3.1	(0)	5.2	6.1
aunt2	(1.2)	2.2	3.1	(0)	5.2	6.2
cousin	1.2	2.2	3.2	(0)	(5.2)	(0)
nephew	(1.2)	2.2	3.3	(0)	5.2	6.1
niece	(1.2)	2.2	3.3	(0)	5.2	6.2

Table 2.4 Burling's componential model of Burmese and its redundancy (redundant components enclosed in brackets)

	Affinity (1)	Generation (2)	Lineality (3)	Alter Sex (4)	Age (5)	Ego's Sex (6)
pín	(C)	4				
pí	(C)	3				
qaphôu	(C)	2		M		
qaphécî1	(C)	2	L	M		
qaphécî2	(C)	2	C	M	E	
qaphôulêi	(C)	2	C	M	Y	
qaphwâ	(C)	2		F		
qaméicî1	(C)	2	L	F		
qaméicî2	(C)	2	C	F	E	
qaphwâlêi	(C)	2	C	F	Y	
qaphéi	C	1	L	M		
qaméi	C	1	L	F		
báci	(C)	1	C	M	E	
qûlêi	(C)	1	C	M	Y	
citó	(C)	1	C	F	E	
dólêi	(C)	1	C	F	Y	
qakóu	(C)	0	C	M	E	
nyi	C	0	(C)	M	Y	m
máun	C	0	(C)	M	Y	f
qamà	C	0	(C)	F	E	
nyímà	C	0	(C)	F	Y	
θâ	C	−1	L	M		
θamî	C	−1	L	F		
tú	(C)	−1	C	M		
túmà	(C)	−1	C	F		
myî	(C)	−2				
myiʔ	(C)	−3				
cuʔ	(C)	−4				
tî	(C)	−5				
yauʔkhamà1	A	1	(L)			
yauʔkhamàqaphóu	A	1	(L)	M		
yauʔkhamà2	A	1	(L)	F		
yauʔcâ	(A)	0	L	M		
mêimà	(A)	0	L	F		
yauʔphà	A	(0)	C	M		m
khêqóu	A	(0)	C	M		f
yâumà	A	(0)	C	F		f
mayî	A	(0)	C	F	E	m
khémà	A	(0)	C	F	Y	m
θameʔ	A	(−1)	L	M		
chwêimà	A	(−1)	L	F		

Table 2.5 Cherry *et al.*'s componential model of Russian phonemes and its redundancy (redundant components enclosed in brackets)

	(1)	(2)	(3)	(4)	(5)	(6)	(7)	(8)	(9)	(10)	(11)
k	−	+	+		+		−	−	−		
$k,$	−	+	+		+		−	−	+		
g	−	+	+		+		−	+	−		
$g,$	(−)	+	+		+		−	+	+		
x	−	+	+		+		+				
c	−	+	+		−		−				
$\int$	−	+	+		−		+	−			
3	−	+	+		−		+	+			
t	−	+	−		−	−	−	−	−	−	
$t,$	−	+	−		−	−	−	−	+		
d	−	+	−		−	(−)	−	+	−	(−)	
$d,$	(−)	+	−		−	(−)	−	+	+	(−)	
s	−	+	−		−	−	+	−	−		
$s,$	−	+	−		−	−	+	−	+		
z	−	+	−		−	(−)	+	+	−		
$z,$	−	+	−		−	(−)	+	+	+		
s	−	+	−		−	−	−	(−)	(−)	+	
n	−	+	−		−	+			−		
$n,$	−	+	−		−	+			+		
p	−	+	−		+	−	−	−	−		
$p,$	−	+	−		+	−	−	−	+		
b	−	+	−		+	(−)	−	+	−		
$b,$	(−)	+	−		+	(−)	−	+	+		
f	−	+	−		+	(−)	+	−	−		
$f,$	−	+	−		+	(−)	+	−	+		
v	−	+	−		+	(−)	+	+	−		
$v,$	−	+	−		+	(−)	+	+	+		
m	−	+	−		+	+			−		
$m,$	−	+	−		+	+			+		
$'u$	+	−	−	+	+						+
u	+	−	−	+	+						−
$'o$	+	−	−	−	+						
$'e$	+	−	−	−	−						
$'i$	+	−	−	+	−						+
i	+	−	−	+	−						−
$'a$	+	−	+								+
a	+	−	+								−
r	+	+					−		−		
$r,$	+	+					−		+		
l	+	+					+		−		
$l,$	+	+					+		+		
j	−	−									

Table 2.6 Spencer's redundant model of the system of five vowels /i, e, a, o, u/ (redundant components enclosed in brackets)

Vowels	back	high	low
i	−	+	
e	−	−	(−)
a			+
o	+	−	−
u	+	+	

Table 2.7 Componential scheme of Bulgarian reference terms with dimension set {sex, sex 1st link, affinity 1st link, generation, distance, affinity}

pradjado
[sex = m & generation = 3]

prababa
[sex = f & generation = 3]

djado
[sex = m & generation = 2]

baba
[sex = f & generation = 2]

bašta
[sex last link = m & generation = 1 & distance = 1]
[sex = m & generation = 1 & distance = 1]

majka
[sex last link = f & generation = 1 & distance = 1]
[sex = f & generation = 1 & distance = 1]

vujčo
[sex last link = f & affinity 1st link = cons & sex = m & generation = 1 &
   distance = 2]
[sex last link = f & sex = m & generation = 1 & affinity = cons]

čičo
[sex last link = m & affinity 1st link = cons & sex = m & generation = 1 &
   distance = 2]
[sex last link = m & sex = m & generation = 1 & distance = 2 & affinity = cons]

lelja
[sex last link = m & sex = f & generation = 1 & affinity = cons]
[sex last link = m & affinity 1st link = cons & sex = f & generation = 1 &
   distance = 2]

tetka
[sex last link = f & affinity 1st link = cons & sex = f & generation = 1 &
   distance = 2]
[sex last link = f & sex = f & generation = 1 & distance = 2 & affinity = cons]

brat
[sex last link = m & affinity 1st link = cons & generation = 0 & distance = 1]
[sex last link = m & generation = 0 & distance = 1 & affinity = cons]
[affinity 1st link = cons & sex = m & generation = 0 & distance = 1]
[sex = m & generation = 0 & distance = 1 & affinity = cons]

sestra
[sex last link = f & affinity 1st link = cons & generation = 0 & distance = 1]
[sex last link = f & generation = 0 & distance = 1 & affinity = cons]
[affinity 1st link = cons & sex = f & generation = 0 & distance = 1]
[sex = f & generation = 0 & distance = 1 & affinity = cons]

batko
[sex last link = m & affinity 1st link = cons & generation = 0 & distance = 1]
[sex last link = m & generation = 0 & distance = 1 & affinity = cons]
[affinity 1st link = cons & sex = m & generation = 0 & distance = 1]
[sex = m & generation = 0 & distance = 1 & affinity = cons]

kaka
[sex last link = f & affinity 1st link = cons & generation = 0 & distance = 1]
[affinity 1st link = cons & sex = f & generation = 0 & distance = 1]
[sex last link = f & generation = 0 & distance = 1 & affinity = cons]
[sex = f & generation = 0 & distance = 1 & affinity = cons]

bratovčed
[affinity 1st link = cons & sex = m & generation = 0 & $D \geq 3$]
[sex = m & generation = 0 & $D \geq 3$ & affinity = cons]

bratovčedka
[affinity 1st link = cons & sex = f & generation = 0 & $D \geq 3$]
[sex = f & generation = 0 & $D \geq 3$ & affinity = cons]

sin
[sex last link = m & generation = -1 & distance = 1]
[sex = m & generation = -1 & distance = 1]

dǎšterja
[sex last link = f & generation = -1 & distance = 1]
[sex = f & generation = -1 & distance = 1]

plemennik
[sex = m & generation = -1 & distance = 2 & affinity = cons]

plemennica
[sex = f & generation = -1 & distance = 2 & affinity = cons]

vnuk
[sex = m & generation = -2 & affinity = cons]

vnučka
[sex = f & generation = -2 & affinity = cons]

pravnuk
[sex = m & generation = -3 & distance = 3]
[sex = m & generation = -3 & affinity = cons]

Table 2.7 (Continued)

pravnučka
[sex = f & generation = − 3 & distance = 3]
[sex = f & generation = − 3 & affinity = cons]

mǎž
[sex last link = m & affinity 1st link = aff & distance = 1]
[sex last link = m & affinity = aff-ego]
[affinity 1st link = aff & sex = m & distance = 1]
[sex = m & affinity = aff-ego]

žena
[sex last link = f & affinity 1st link = aff & distance = 1]
[affinity 1st link = aff & sex = f & distance = 1]
[sex last link = f & affinity = aff-ego]
[sex = f & affinity = aff-ego]

šurej
[sex last link = f & affinity 1st link = aff & sex = m & generation = 0 &
  distance = 2]

šurenajka
[sex last link = f & affinity 1st link = aff & sex = f & distance = 3]
[sex last link = f & sex = f & generation = 0 & distance = 3 & affinity = aff]

dever
[sex last link = m & sex = m & generation = 0 & affinity = aff]
[sex last link = m & sex = m & generation = 0 & distance = 2]

zet
[sex last link = f & affinity 1st link = cons & generation = ≤0 & affinity = aff]
[sex last link = f & affinity 1st link = cons & distance = 2 & affinity = aff]
[affinity 1st link = cons & sex = m & generation = ≤0 & affinity = aff]
[affinity 1st link = cons & sex = m & distance = 2 & affinity = aff]

badžanak
[affinity 1st link = aff & sex = m & distance = 3]
[sex = m & generation = 0 & distance = 3 & affinity = aff]

zǎlva
[sex last link = m & affinity 1st link = aff & sex = f & generation = 0 &
  distance = 2]

baldǎza
[sex last link = f & sex = f & generation = 0 & distance = 2]

snaha
[sex last link = m & affinity 1st link = cons & generation = ≤0 & affinity = aff]
[affinity 1st link = cons & sex = f & generation = ≤0 & affinity = aff]
[sex last link = m & affinity 1st link = cons & distance = 2 & affinity = aff]
[affinity 1st link = cons & sex = f & distance = 2 & affinity = aff]

etǎrva
[sex last link = m & affinity 1st link = aff & distance = 3]
[sex last link = m & generation = 0 & distance = 3 & affinity = aff]

vujna
[sex last link = f & affinity 1st link = cons & sex = f & affinity = aff]
[sex last link = f & sex = f & generation = 1 & distance = 3]

strina
[sex last link = m & affinity 1st link = cons & sex = f & generation = 1 &
 affinity = aff]
[sex last link = m & sex = f & generation = 1 & distance = 3]
[sex last link = m & affinity 1st link = cons & sex = f & distance = 3 &
 affinity = aff]

lelin
[sex last link = m & affinity 1st link = cons & sex = m & affinity = aff]
[sex last link = m & sex = m & generation = 1 & distance = 3]
[sex last link = m & sex = m & distance = 3 & affinity = aff]

tetin
[sex last link = f & affinity 1st link = cons & sex = m & generation = 1 &
 affinity = aff]
[sex last link = f & sex = m & generation = 1 & distance = 3]
[sex last link = f & affinity 1st link = cons & sex = m & distance = 3 &
 affinity = aff]

svekăr
[sex last link = m & affinity 1st link = aff & sex = m & generation = 1]
[sex last link = m & sex = m & generation = 1 & distance = 2 & affinity = aff]

svekărva
[sex last link = m & affinity 1st link = aff & sex = f & generation = 1]
[sex last link = m & sex = f & generation = 1 & distance = 2 & affinity = aff]

tăst
[sex last link = f & affinity 1st link = aff & sex = m & generation = 1]
[sex last link = f & sex = m & generation = 1 & distance = 2 & affinity = aff]

tăsta
[sex last link = f & affinity 1st link = aff & sex = f & generation = 1]
[sex last link = f & sex = f & generation = 1 & distance = 2 & affinity = aff]

132

Table 2.8 Componential scheme of Bulgarian address terms with dimension set {sex, generation, generation last link, sex 1st link, affinity 1st link, distance}

djado
[sex = m & generation = ≥2]

babo
[sex = f & generation = ≥2]

tatko
[sex = m & generation = 1 & generation last link = 1]

majko
[sex = f & generation = 1 & generation last link = 1]

vujčo
[sex last link = f & sex = m & generation = 1 & distance = 2 & generation last link = 0]

čičo
[sex last link = m & sex = m & distance = 2 & generation last link = 0]

leljo
[sex last link = m & sex = f & generation = 1 & distance = 2 & generation last link = 0]

tetko
[sex last link = f & sex = f & distance = 2 & generation last link = 0]

bratko
[sex last link = m & affinity 1st link = cons & generation = 0 & distance = 1]
[sex last link = m & affinity 1st link = cons & distance = 1 & generation last link = 0]
[affinity 1st link = cons & sex = m & generation = 0 & distance = 1]
[sex last link = m & affinity 1st link = cons & sex = m & generation = 0 & generation last link = 0]
[affinity 1st link = cons & sex = m & distance = 1 & generation last link = 0]

sestro
[sex last link = f & affinity 1st link = cons & generation = 0 & distance = 1]
[sex last link = f & affinity 1st link = cons & distance = 1 & generation last link = 0]
[affinity 1st link = cons & sex = f & generation = 0 & distance = 1]
[sex last link = f & affinity 1st link = cons & sex = f & generation = 0 & generation last link = 0]
[affinity 1st link = cons & sex = f & distance = 1 & generation last link = 0]

bate
[sex last link = m & affinity 1st link = cons & generation = 0 & distance = 1]
[sex last link = m & affinity 1st link = cons & distance = 1 & generation last link = 0]
[affinity 1st link = cons & sex = m & generation = 0 & distance = 1]
[sex last link = m & affinity 1st link = cons & sex = m & generation = 0 & generation last link = 0]
[affinity 1st link = cons & sex = m & distance = 1 & generation last link = 0]

kako
[sex last link = f & affinity 1st link = cons & generation = 0 & distance = 1]
[affinity 1st link = cons & sex = f & generation = 0 & distance = 1]
[sex last link = f & affinity 1st link = cons & sex = f & generation = 0 &
  generation last link = 0]
[sex last link = f & affinity 1st link = cons & distance = 1 & generation last
  link = 0]
[affinity 1st link = cons & sex = f & distance = 1 & generation last link = 0]

bratovčede
[sex = m & generation = 0 & generation last link = −1]
[affinity 1st link = cons & sex = m & generation = 0 & distance = ≥3]
[sex = m & distance = ≥3 & generation last link = −1]

bratovčedke
[sex = f & generation = 0 & generation last link = −1]
[sex = f & generation = 0 & distance = ≥3]
[sex = f & distance = ≥3 & generation last link = −1]

sine
[sex last link = m & generation = −1 & distance = 1]
[sex last link = m & distance = 1 & generation last link = −1]
[sex = m & generation = −1 & distance = 1]
[sex = m & distance = 1 & generation last link = −1]

dăšte
[sex last link = f & generation = −1 & distance = 1]
[sex = f & generation = −1 & distance = 1]
[sex last link = f & distance = 1 & generation last link = −1]
[sex = f & distance = 1 & generation last link = −1]

plemenniko
[sex = m & distance = 2 & generation last link = −1]

plemennice
[sex = f & distance = 2 & generation last link = −1]

măžo
[sex last link = m & affinity 1st link = aff & generation = 0]
[sex last link = m & affinity 1st link = aff & generation last link = 0]
[affinity 1st link = aff & sex = m & generation = 0 & distance = 1]
[affinity 1st link = aff & sex = m & distance = 1 & generation last link = 0]

ženo
[affinity 1st link = aff & sex = f & generation = 0]
[affinity 1st link = aff & sex = f & generation last link = 0]
[sex last link = f & affinity 1st link = aff & generation = 0 & distance = 1]
[sex last link = f & affinity 1st link = aff & distance = 1 & generation last link = 0]

zetko
[sex last link = f & affinity 1st link = cons & sex = m & G ≤ 0 & generation last
  link = 0]
[sex last link = f & generation = ≤0 & distance = 2 & generation last link = 0]
[sex = m & generation = ≤0 & distance = 2 & generation last link = 0]

Table 2.8 (Continued)

badžo
[sex last link = f & affinity 1st link = aff & sex = m & generation last link = 0]
[sex last link = f & affinity 1st link = aff & sex = m & generation = 0]
[affinity 1st link = aff & distance = 3 & generation last link = 0]
[affinity 1st link = aff & generation = 0 & distance = 3]
[generation = 0 & distance = 3 & generation last link = 0]

snaho
[sex last link = m & sex = f & generation = ≤0 & generation last link = 0]
[sex last link = m & generation = ≤0 & distance = 2 & generation last link = 0]
[sex = f & generation = ≤0 & distance = 2 & generation last link = 0]

vujno
[sex last link = f & sex = f & distance = 3 & generation last link = 0]

vujno
[sex last link = f & sex = f & distance = 3 & generation last link = 0]

strino
[sex last link = m & sex = f & distance = 3 & generation last link = 0]

lelinčo
[sex last link = m & sex = m & distance = 3 & generation last link = 0]

tetinčo
[sex last link = f & affinity 1st link = cons & sex = m & distance = 3 & generation last link = 0]
[sex last link = f & sex = m & generation = 1 & distance = 3 & generation last link = 0]

Table 2.9 Norick's redundant model of Niutao kinship terms (redundant components enclosed in parentheses and empty cells in angle brackets)

	Generation (1)	Affinity (2)	Oppos.sex (3)	Sex 1st (4)	Seniority (5)	Alter Sex (6)
makupuna	1.1	(2.1)	\<e1\>	\<e2\>	5.2	\<e3\>
tupuna	1.1	(2.1)	\<e1\>	\<e2\>	5.1	\<e3\>
tamana	1.2	2.1	3.2	\<e1\>	5.1	6.1
maatua	1.2	2.1	3.2	\<e1\>	5.1	6.2
tama	1.2	2.1	3.2	\<e1\>	5.2	\<e2\>
tamatuangaane	1.2	2.1	3.1	4.2	5.2	\<e1\>
maatuatuangaane	1.2	2.1	3.1	4.2	5.1	(6.2)
tuaatina	1.2	2.1	3.1	4.1	\<e1\>	\<e2\>
fungaono	1.2	2.2	\<e1\>	\<e2\>	\<e3\>	\<e4\>
maa	1.3	2.2	3.1	\<e1\>	\<e2\>	\<e3\>
aavanga	1.3	2.2	3.2	\<e1\>	\<e2\>	\<e3\>
taina	1.3	2.1	3.2	\<e1\>	\<e2\>	\<e3\>
tuangaane	1.3	2.1	3.1	\<e1\>	\<e2\>	\<e3\>

Table 3.1 A subset of Bulgarian consanguineal kinship terms

čičo	FaBr ∨ MoBr
lelja	FaSi ∨ MoSi
bašta	Fa
majka	Mo
brat	Br
sestra	Si
sin	So
dăšterja	Da

Table 3.2 Kin types of certain American kin terms

cousin	grandson/granddaughter	nephew/niece
PaSbCh	ChCh	SbCh
PaPaChCh		SpPaChCh
PaPaSbCh		
PaPaPaSbCh		
PaSbChCh		
PaSbChChCh		
PaPaSbChCh		
PaPaPaChChCh		
PaPaPaSbChChCh		
PaPaSbChChCh		
etc.		

Abbreviations: Pa = parent, Sb = sibling, Ch = child, Sp = spouse

Table 3.3 Determining feature values of kin types

čičo	[generation = 1 & sex = m & distance = 2 & lineality = coll]
	[generation = 1 & sex = m & distance = 2 & lineality = coll]
lelja	[generation = 1 & sex = f & distance = 2 & lineality = coll]
	[generation = 1 & sex = f & distance = 2 & lineality = coll]
bašta	[generation = 1 & sex = m & distance = 1 & lineality = lin]
majka	[generation = 1 & sex = f & distance = 1 & lineality = lin]
brat	[generation = 0 & sex = m & distance = 1 & lineality = coll]
sestra	[generation = 0 & sex = f & distance = 1 & lineality = coll]
sin	[generation = −1 & sex = m & distance = 1 & lineality = lin]
dăšterja	[generation = 0 & sex = f & distance = 1 & lineality = lin]

Table 3.4 Determining kin term components

čičo	[generation = 1 & sex = m & distance = 2 & lineality = coll]
lelja	[generation = 1 & sex = f & distance = 2 & lineality = coll]
bašta	[generation = 1 & sex = m & distance = 1 & lineality = lin]
majka	[generation = 1 & sex = f & distance = 1 & lineality = lin]
brat	[generation = 0 & sex = m & distance = 1 & lineality = coll]
sestra	[generation = 0 & sex = f & distance = 1 & lineality = coll]
sin	[generation = −1 & sex = m & distance = 1 & lineality = lin]
dăšterja	[generation = 0 & sex = f & distance = 1 & lineality = lin]

Table 3.5 Contrasting features between pairs of kin terms

	čičo	*lelja*	*bašta*	*majka*	*brat*	*sestra*	*sin*	*dăšterja*
čičo		sex	dist/ lin	sex/ dist/ lin	gener/ dist	gener/ sex/ dist	gener/ dist/ lin	gener/ sex/ dist/lin
lelja	sex		sex/ dist/ lin	dist/ lin	gener/ sex/ dist	gener/ dist	gener/ sex/ dist/ lin	gener/ dist
bašta	dist/ lin	sex/ dist/ lin		sex	gener/ lin	gener/ sex/ lin	gener	gener/ sex
majka	sex/ dist/ lin	dist/ lin	sex		gener/ sex/ lin	gener/ lin	gener/ sex	gener
brat	gener/ dist	gener/ sex/ dist	gener/ dist	gener/ sex/ lin		sex	gener/ lin	gener/ sex/lin
sestra	gener/ sex/ dist	gener/ dist	gener/ sex/ lin	gener/ lin	sex		gener/ sex/ lin	gener/ lin
sin	gener/ dist/ lin	gener/ sex/ dist/ lin	gener	gener/ sex	gener/ lin	gener/ sex/ lin		sex
dăšterja	gener/ sex/ dist/ lin	gener/ dist/ lin	gener/ sex	gener	gener/ sex/ lin	gener/ lin	sex	

Note: A slash '/' stands for a logical disjunction ∨ 'or'.

Table 3.6 Contrasts with *čičo*

(sex)	/contrast with *lelja*/
(distance $\lor$ lineality)	/contrast with bašta/
(sex $\lor$ distance $\lor$ lineality)	/contrast with *majka*/
(generation $\lor$ distance)	/contrast with *brat*/
(generation $\lor$ sex $\lor$ distance)	/contrast with *sestra*/
(generation $\lor$ distance $\lor$ lineality)	/contrast with *sin*/
(generation $\lor$ sex $\lor$ distance $\lor$ lineality)	/contrast with *dǎšterja*/

Table 3.7 Simplest componential model

čičo		$sex = m$	$distance = 2$
lelja		$sex = f$	$distance = 2$
bašta	$generation = 1$	$sex = m$	$distance = 1$
majka	$generation = 1$	$sex = f$	$distance = 1$
brat	$generation = 0$	$sex = m$	
sestra	$generation = 0$	$sex = f$	
sin	$generation = -1$	$sex = m$	
dǎšterja	$generation = -1$	$sex = f$	

Table 3.8 Another simplest componential model

čičo		$sex = m$	$lineality = coll$
lelja		$sex = f$	$lineality = coll$
bašta	$generation = 1$	$sex = m$	$lineality = lin$
majka	$generation = 1$	$sex = f$	$lineality = lin$
brat	$generation = 0$	$sex = m$	
sestra	$generation = 0$	$sex = f$	
sin	$generation = -1$	$sex = m$	
dǎšterja	$generation = -1$	$sex = f$	

Table 3.9 A fully redundant componential model

čičo	$generation = 1$	$sex = m$	$distance = 2$
lelja	$generation = 1$	$sex = f$	$distance = 2$
bašta	$generation = 1$	$sex = m$	$distance = 1$
majka	$generation = 1$	$sex = f$	$distance = 1$
brat	$generation = 0$	$sex = m$	$distance = 1$
sestra	$generation = 0$	$sex = f$	$distance = 1$
sin	$generation = -1$	$sex = m$	$distance = 1$
dǎšterja	$generation = -1$	$sex = f$	$distance = 1$

138

Table 3.10 Styles of kin term definitions

čičo	<generation = 1>	sex = m	distance = 2
lelja	<generation = 1>	sex = f	distance = 2
bašta	generation = 1	sex = m	[distance = 1]
majka	generation = 1	sex = f	[distance = 1]
brat	generation = 0	sex = m	[distance = 1]
sestra	generation = 0	sex = f	[distance = 1]
sin	generation = −1	sex = m	[distance = 1]
dăšterja	generation = −1	sex = f	[distance = 1]

Note: Styles of kinship definitions: all three styles include the values not in brackets. Additionally, (1) 'fully redundant' definitions include all items in brackets; (2) 'partially redundant' include all items in angle brackets (< >) *or* in square brackets ([ ]), but not both; and (3) 'nonredundant' does not include any values in brackets.

Table 3.11 Componential scheme of Bulgarian kin terms of reference and address

pradjado
[reference = ref & sex = m & generation = 3]
[reference = ref & sex = m & distance = 3 & generation last link = 1]

prababa
[reference = ref & sex = f & generation = 3]
[reference = ref & sex = f & distance = 3 & generation last link = 1]

djado
[reference = ref & sex = m & generation = 2]
[reference = ref & affinity 1st link = cons & sex = m & distance = 2 & generation last link = 1]

baba
[reference = ref & sex = f & generation = 2]
[reference = ref & affinity 1st link = cons & sex = f & distance = 2 & generation last link = 1]

bašta
[reference = ref & sex 1st link = m & generation = 1 & distance = 1]
[reference = ref & sex 1st link = m & affinity 1st link = cons & generation = 1 & generation last link = 1]
[reference = ref & sex 1st link = m & distance = 1 & generation last link = 1]
[reference = ref & sex = m & generation = 1 & distance = 1]
[reference = ref & affinity 1st link = cons & sex = m & generation = 1 & generation last link = 1]
[reference = ref & sex = m & distance = 1 & generation last link = 1]

majka
[reference = ref & sex 1st link = f & generation = 1 & distance = 1]
[reference = ref & sex = f & generation = 1 & distance = 1]

[reference = ref & sex 1st link = f & affinity 1st link = cons & generation = 1 & generation last link = 1]

[reference = ref & affinity 1st link = cons & sex = f & generation = 1 & generation last link = 1]

[reference = ref & sex 1st link = f & distance = 1 & generation last link = 1]

[reference = ref & sex = f & distance = 1 & generation last link = 1]

vujčo

[reference = ref & sex 1st link = f & affinity 1st link = cons & sex = m & generation = 1 & distance = 2]

[reference = ref & sex 1st link = f & sex = m & generation = 1 & distance = 2 & generation last link = 0]

čičo

[reference = ref & sex 1st link = m & affinity 1st link = cons & sex = m & generation = 1 & distance = 2]

[reference = ref & sex 1st link = m & affinity 1st link = cons & sex = m & distance = 2 & generation last link = 0]

[reference = ref & sex 1st link = m & sex = m & generation = 1 & distance = 2 & generation last link = 0]

lelja

[reference = ref & sex 1st link = m & affinity 1st link = cons & sex = f & generation = 1 & distance = 2]

[reference = ref & sex 1st link = m & sex = f & generation = 1 & distance = 2 & generation last link = 0]

tetka

[reference = ref & sex 1st link = f & affinity 1st link = cons & sex = f & generation = 1 & distance = 2]

[reference = ref & sex 1st link = f & affinity 1st link = cons & sex = f & distance = 2 & generation last link = 0]

[reference = ref & sex 1st link = f & sex = f & generation = 1 & distance = 2 & generation last link = 0]

brat

[reference = ref & sex 1st link = m & affinity 1st link = cons & generation = 0 & distance = 1]

[reference = ref & sex 1st link = m & affinity 1st link = cons & distance = 1 & generation last link = 0]

[reference = ref & affinity 1st link = cons & sex = m & generation = 0 & distance = 1]

[reference = ref & sex 1st link = m & affinity 1st link = cons & sex = m & generation = 0 & generation last link = 0]

[reference = ref & affinity 1st link = cons & sex = m & distance = 1 & generation last link = 0]

sestra

[reference = ref & sex 1st link = f & affinity 1st link = cons & generation = 0 & distance = 1]

[reference = ref & sex 1st link = f & affinity 1st link = cons & distance = 1 & generation last link = 0]

Table 3.11 (Continued)

[reference = ref & affinity 1st link = cons & sex = f & generation = 0 & distance = 1]

[reference = ref & sex 1st link = f & affinity 1st link = cons & sex = f & generation = 0 & generation last link = 0]

[reference = ref & affinity 1st link = cons & sex = f & distance = 1 & generation last link = 0]

batko

[reference = ref & sex 1st link = m & affinity 1st link = cons & generation = 0 & distance = 1]

[reference = ref & sex 1st link = m & affinity 1st link = cons & distance = 1 & generation last link = 0]

[reference = ref & affinity 1st link = cons & sex = m & generation = 0 & distance = 1]

[reference = ref & sex 1st link = m & affinity 1st link = cons & sex = m & generation = 0 & generation last link = 0]

[reference = ref & affinity 1st link = cons & sex = m & distance = 1 & generation last link = 0]

kaka

[reference = ref & sex 1st link = f & affinity 1st link = cons & generation = 0 & distance = 1]

[reference = ref & affinity 1st link = cons & sex = f & generation = 0 & distance = 1]

[reference = ref & sex 1st link = f & affinity 1st link = cons & sex = f & generation = 0 & generation last link = 0]

[reference = ref & sex 1st link = f & affinity 1st link = cons & distance = 1 & generation last link = 0]

[reference = ref & affinity 1st link = cons & sex = f & distance = 1 & generation last link = 0]

bratovčed

[reference = ref & sex = m & generation = 0 & generation last link = −1]

[reference = ref & affinity 1st link = cons & sex = m & generation = 0 & distance = ≥3]

bratovčedka

[reference = ref & sex = f & generation = 0 & generation last link = −1]

[reference = ref & affinity 1st link = cons & sex = f & generation = 0 & distance = ≥3]

sin

[reference = ref & sex 1st link = m & generation = −1 & distance = 1]

[reference = ref & sex 1st link = m & distance = 1 & generation last link = −1]

[reference = ref & sex = m & generation = −1 & distance = 1]

[reference = ref & sex = m & distance = 1 & generation last link = −1]

dăšterja

[reference = ref & sex 1st link = f & generation = −1 & distance = 1]

[reference = ref & sex = f & generation = −1 & distance = 1]

[reference = ref & sex 1st link = f & distance = 1 & generation last link = −1]

[reference = ref & sex = f & distance = 1 & generation last link = −1]

plemennik
[reference = ref & sex = m & generation = −1 & distance = 2 & generation last link = −1]

plemennitsa
[reference = ref & sex = f & generation = −1 & distance = 2 & generation last link = −1]

vnuk
[sex = m & generation = −2 & generation last link = −1]

vnučka
[sex = f & generation = −2 & generation last link = −1]

pravnuk
[sex = m & generation = −3 & distance = 3]
[sex = m & generation = −3 & generation last link = −1]

pravnučka
[sex = f & generation = −3 & distance = 3]
[sex = f & generation = −3 & generation last link = −1]

măz
[reference = ref & sex 1st link = m & affinity 1st link = aff & distance = 1]
[reference = ref & affinity 1st link = aff & sex = m & distance = 1]

žena
[reference = ref & sex 1st link = f & affinity 1st link = aff & distance = 1]
[reference = ref & affinity 1st link = aff & sex = f & distance = 1]

šurej
[sex 1st link = f & affinity 1st link = aff & sex = m & generation = 0 & distance = 2]
[sex 1st link = f & affinity 1st link = aff & sex = m & distance = 2 & generation last link = 0]

šurenajka
[reference = ref & sex 1st link = f & affinity 1st link = aff & sex = f & distance = 3]
[sex 1st link = f & affinity 1st link = aff & sex = f & distance = 3 & generation last link = 0]
[sex 1st link = f & affinity 1st link = aff & sex = f & generation = 0 & distance = 3]
[sex 1st link = f & sex = f & generation = 0 & distance = 3 & generation last link = 0]

dever
[sex 1st link = m & sex = m & generation = 0 & distance = 2]
[sex 1st link = m & affinity 1st link = aff & sex = m & distance = 2 & generation last link = 0]

zet
[reference = ref & sex 1st link = f & affinity 1st link = cons & generation = ≤0 & distance = 2 & generation last link = 0]
[reference = ref & sex 1st link = f & affinity 1st link = cons & sex = m & generation = ≤0 & generation last link = 0]

Table 3.11 (Continued)

[reference = ref & affinity 1st link = cons & sex = m & generation = ≤0 & distance = 2 & generation last link = 0]

badžanak
[reference = ref & affinity 1st link = aff & sex = m & distance = 3]
[reference = ref & sex = m & generation = 0 & distance = 3 & generation last link = 0]

zălva
[sex 1st link = m & affinity 1st link = aff & sex = f & generation = 0 & distance = 2]
[sex 1st link = m & affinity 1st link = aff & sex = f & distance = 2 & generation last link = 0]

baldăza
[sex 1st link = f & sex = f & generation = 0 & distance = 2]
[sex 1st link = f & affinity 1st link = aff & sex = f & distance = 2 & generation last link = 0]

snaha
[reference = ref & sex 1st link = m & affinity 1st link = cons & sex = f & generation = ≤0 & generation last link = 0]
[reference = ref & sex 1st link = m & affinity 1st link = cons & generation = ≤0 & distance = 2 & generation last link = 0]
[reference = ref & affinity 1st link = cons & sex = f & generation = ≤0 & distance = 2 & generation last link = 0]

etărva
[reference = ref & sex 1st link = m & affinity 1st link = aff & distance = 3]
[sex 1st link = m & affinity 1st link = aff & distance = 3 & generation last link = 0]
[sex 1st link = m & affinity 1st link = aff & generation = 0 & distance = 3]
[sex 1st link = m & generation = 0 & distance = 3 & generation last link = 0]

vujna
[reference = ref & sex 1st link = f & sex = f & generation = 1 & distance = 3]
[reference = ref & sex 1st link = f & affinity 1st link = cons & sex = f & distance = 3 & generation last link = 0]

strina
[reference = ref & sex 1st link = m & sex = f & generation = 1 & distance = 3]
[reference = ref & sex 1st link = m & affinity 1st link = cons & sex = f & distance = 3 & generation last link = 0]

lelin
[reference = ref & sex 1st link = m & sex = m & generation = 1 & distance = 3]
[reference = ref & sex 1st link = m & sex = m & distance = 3 & generation last link = 0]

tetin
[reference = ref & sex 1st link = f & sex = m & generation = 1 & distance = 3]
[reference = ref & sex 1st link = f & affinity 1st link = cons & sex = m & distance = 3 & generation last link = 0]

svekăr
[reference = ref & sex 1st link = m & affinity 1st link = aff & sex = m &
  generation last link = 1]
[reference = ref & sex 1st link = m & affinity 1st link = aff & sex = m &
  generation = 1]
[reference = ref & sex 1st link = m & sex = m & generation = 1 & distance = 2 &
  generation last link = 1]

svekărva
[reference = ref & sex 1st link = m & affinity 1st link = aff & sex = f & generation
  last link = 1]
[reference = ref & sex 1st link = m & affinity 1st link = aff & sex = f &
  generation = 1]
[reference = ref & sex 1st link = m & sex = f & generation = 1 & generation last
  link = 1]

tăst
[reference = ref & sex 1st link = f & affinity 1st link = aff & sex = m & generation
  last link = 1]
[reference = ref & sex 1st link = f & affinity 1st link = aff & sex = m &
  generation = 1]
[reference = ref & sex 1st link = f & sex = m & generation = 1 & generation last
  link = 1]

tăsta
[reference = ref & sex 1st link = f & affinity 1st link = aff & sex = f & generation
  last link = 1]
[reference = ref & sex 1st link = f & affinity 1st link = aff & sex = f &
  generation = 1]
[reference = ref & sex 1st link = f & sex = f & generation = 1 & distance = 2 &
  generation last link = 1]

djado
[reference = addr & sex = m & generation = $\geq$2]

babo
[reference = addr & sex = f & generation = $\geq$2]

tatko
[reference = addr & sex = m & generation = 1 & generation last link = 1]

majko
[reference = addr & sex = f & generation = 1 & generation last link = 1]

vujčo
[reference = addr & sex 1st link = f & sex = m & generation = 1 & distance = 2 &
  generation last link = 0]

čičo
[reference = addr & sex 1st link = m & sex = m & distance = 2 & generation last
  link = 0]

leljo
[reference = addr & sex 1st link = m & sex = f & generation = 1 & distance = 2 &
  generation last link = 0]

Table 3.11 (Continued)

tetko
[reference = addr & sex 1st link = f & sex = f & distance = 2 & generation last
   link = 0]

bratko
[reference = addr & sex 1st link = m & affinity 1st link = cons & generation = 0
   & distance = 1]
[reference = addr & sex 1st link = m & affinity 1st link = cons & distance = 1 &
   generation last link = 0]
[reference = addr & affinity 1st link = cons & sex = m & generation = 0 &
   distance = 1]
[reference = addr & sex 1st link = m & affinity 1st link = cons & sex = m &
   generation = 0 & generation last link = 0]
[reference = addr & affinity 1st link = cons & sex = m & distance = 1 &
   generation last link = 0]

sestro
[reference = addr & sex 1st link = f & affinity 1st link = cons & generation = 0 &
   distance = 1]
[reference = addr & sex 1st link = f & affinity 1st link = cons & distance = 1 &
   generation last link = 0]
[reference = addr & affinity 1st link = cons & sex = f & generation = 0 &
   distance = 1]
[reference = addr & sex 1st link = f & affinity 1st link = cons & sex = f &
   generation = 0 & generation last link = 0]
[reference = addr & affinity 1st link = cons & sex = f & distance = 1 & generation
   last link = 0]

bate
[reference = addr & sex 1st link = m & affinity 1st link = cons & generation = 0
   & distance = 1]
[reference = addr & sex 1st link = m & affinity 1st link = cons & distance = 1 &
   generation last link = 0]
[reference = addr & affinity 1st link = cons & sex = m & generation = 0 &
   distance = 1]
[reference = addr & sex 1st link = m & affinity 1st link = cons & sex = m &
   generation = 0 & generation last link = 0]
[reference = addr & affinity 1st link = cons & sex = m & distance = 1 &
   generation last link = 0]

kako
[reference = addr & sex 1st link = f & affinity 1st link = cons & generation = 0 &
   distance = 1]
[reference = addr & affinity 1st link = cons & sex = f & generation = 0 &
   distance = 1]
[reference = addr & sex 1st link = f & affinity 1st link = cons & sex = f &
   generation = 0 & generation last link = 0]
[reference = addr & sex 1st link = f & affinity 1st link = cons & distance = 1 &
   generation last link = 0]

[reference = addr & affinity 1st link = cons & sex = f & distance = 1 & generation last link = 0]

bratovčede
[reference = addr & sex = m & generation = 0 & generation last link = −1]
[reference = addr & affinity 1st link = cons & sex = m & generation = 0 & distance =≥3]
[reference = addr & sex = m & distance =≥3 & generation last link = −1]

bratovčedke
[reference = addr & sex = f & generation = 0 & generation last link = −1]
[reference = addr & sex = f & generation = 0 & distance =≥3]
[reference = addr & sex = f & distance =≥3 & generation last link = −1]

sine
[reference = addr & sex 1st link = m & generation = −1 & distance = 1]
[reference = addr & sex 1st link = m & distance = 1 & generation last link = −1]
[reference = addr & sex = m & generation = −1 & distance = 1]
[reference = addr & sex = m & distance = 1 & generation last link = −1]

dǎšte
[reference = addr & sex 1st link = f & generation = −1 & distance = 1]
[reference = addr & sex = f & generation = −1 & distance = 1]
[reference = addr & sex 1st link = f & distance = 1 & generation last link = −1]
[reference = addr & sex = f & distance = 1 & generation last link = −1]

plemenniko
[reference = addr & sex = m & distance = 2 & generation last link = −1]

plemennitse
[reference = addr & sex = f & distance = 2 & generation last link = −1]

mǎzo
[reference = addr & sex 1st link = m & affinity 1st link = aff & generation = 0]
[reference = addr & sex 1st link = m & affinity 1st link = aff & generation last link = 0]
[reference = addr & affinity 1st link = aff & sex = m & generation = 0 & distance = 1]
[reference = addr & affinity 1st link = aff & sex = m & distance = 1 & generation last link = 0]

ženo
[reference = addr & affinity 1st link = aff & sex = f & generation = 0]
[reference = addr & affinity 1st link = aff & sex = f & generation last link = 0]
[reference = addr & sex 1st link = f & affinity 1st link = aff & generation = 0 & distance = 1]
[reference = addr & sex 1st link = f & affinity 1st link = aff & distance = 1 & generation last link = 0]

zetko
[reference = addr & sex 1st link = f & affinity 1st link = cons & sex = m & generation =≤0 & generation last link = 0]
[reference = addr & sex 1st link = f & generation =≤0 & distance = 2 & generation last link = 0]

146

Table 3.11 (Continued)

[reference = addr & sex = m & generation = ≤0 & distance = 2 & generation last
link = 0]

badžo
[reference = addr & sex 1st link = f & affinity 1st link = aff & sex = m &
generation last link = 0]
[reference = addr & sex 1st link = f & affinity 1st link = aff & sex = m &
generation = 0]
[reference = addr & affinity 1st link = aff & distance = 3 & generation last
link = 0]
[reference = addr & affinity 1st link = aff & generation = 0 & distance = 3]
[reference = addr & generation = 0 & distance = 3 & generation last link = 0]

snaho
[reference = addr & sex 1st link = m & sex = f & generation = ≤0 & generation
last link = 0]
[reference = addr & sex 1st link = m & generation = ≤0 & distance = 2 &
generation last link = 0]
[reference = addr & sex = f & generation = ≤0 & distance = 2 & generation last
link = 0]

vujno
[reference = addr & sex 1st link = f & sex = f & distance = 3 & generation last
link = 0]

strino
[reference = addr & sex 1st link = m & sex = f & distance = 3 & generation last
link = 0]

lelinčo
[reference = addr & sex 1st link = m & sex = m & distance = 3 & generation last
link = 0]

tetinčo
[reference = addr & sex 1st link = f & affinity 1st link = cons & sex = m &
distance = 3 & generation last link = 0]
[reference = addr & sex 1st link = f & sex = m & generation = 1 & distance = 3 &
generation last link = 0]

Table 3.12 The unique componential model of Bulgarian kin terms of reference and address

pradjado	[reference = ref & sex = m & generation = 3]
prababa	[reference = ref & sex = f & generation = 3]
djado	[reference = ref & sex = m & generation = 2]
baba	[reference = ref & sex = f & generation = 2]
bašta	[reference = ref & sex = m & generation = 1 & distance = 1]
majka	[reference = ref & sex = f & generation = 1 & distance = 1]
vujčo	[reference = ref & sex 1st link = f & sex = m & generation = 1 & distance = 2 & generation last link = 0]
čičo	[reference = ref & sex 1st link = m & sex = m & generation = 1 & distance = 2 & generation last link = 0]
lelja	[reference = ref & sex 1st link = m & sex = f & generation = 1 & distance = 2 & generation last link = 0]
tetka	[reference = ref & sex 1st link = f & sex = f & generation = 1 & distance = 2 & generation last link = 0]
brat	[reference = ref & affinity 1st link = cons & sex = m & generation = 0 & distance = 1]
sestra	[reference = ref & affinity 1st link = cons & sex = f & generation = 0 & distance = 1]
batko	[reference = ref & affinity 1st link = cons & sex = m & generation = 0 & distance = 1]
kaka	[reference = ref & affinity 1st link = cons & sex = f & generation = 0 & distance = 1]
bratovčed	[reference = ref & sex = m & generation = 0 & generation last link = −1]
bratovčedka	[reference = ref & sex = f & generation = 0 & generation last link = −1]
sin	[reference = ref & sex = m & generation = −1 & distance = 1]
dăšterja	[reference = ref & sex = f & generation = −1 & distance = 1]
plemennik	[reference = ref & sex = m & generation = −1 & distance = 2 & generation last link = −1]
plemennica	[reference = ref & sex = f & generation = −1 & distance = 2 & generation last link = −1]
vnuk	[sex = m & generation = −2 & generation last link = −1]
vnučka	[sex = f & generation = −2 & generation last link = −1]
pravnuk	[sex = m & generation = −3 & distance = 3]
pravnučka	[sex = f & generation = −3 & distance = 3]
măž	[reference = ref & affinity 1st link = aff & sex = m & distance = 1]
žena	[reference = ref & affinity 1st link = aff & sex = f & distance = 1]
šurej	[sex 1st link = f & affinity 1st link = aff & sex = m & generation = 0 & distance = 2]
šurenajka	[reference = ref & sex 1st link = f & affinity 1st link = aff & sex = f & distance = 3]
dever	[sex 1st link = m & sex = m & generation = 0 & distance = 2]
zet	[reference = ref & affinity 1st link = cons & sex = m & generation = ≤0 & distance = 2 & generation last link = 0]

148

Table 3.12 (Continued)

badžanak	[reference = ref & affinity 1st link = aff & sex = m & distance = 3]
zălva	[sex 1st link = m & affinity 1st link = aff & sex = f & generation = 0 & distance = 2]
baldăza	[sex 1st link = f & sex = f & generation = 0 & distance = 2]
snaha	[reference = ref & affinity 1st link = cons & sex = f & generation = ≤0 & distance = 2 & generation last link = 0]
etărva	[reference = ref & sex 1st link = m & affinity 1st link = aff & distance = 3]
vujna	[reference = ref & sex 1st link = f & sex = f & generation = 1 & distance = 3]
strina	[reference = ref & sex 1st link = m & sex = f & generation = 1 & distance = 3]
lelin	[reference = ref & sex 1st link = m & sex = m & generation = 1 & distance = 3]
tetin	[reference = ref & sex 1st link = f & sex = m & generation = 1 & distance = 3]
svekăr	[reference = ref & sex 1st link = m & affinity 1st link = aff & sex = m & generation = 1]
svekărva	[reference = ref & sex 1st link = m & sex = f & generation = 1 & generation last link = 1]
tăst	[reference = ref & sex 1st link = f & sex = m & generation = 1 & generation last link = 1]
tăsta	[reference = ref & sex 1st link = f & affinity 1st link = aff & sex = f & generation = 1]
djado	[reference = addr & sex = m & generation = ≥2]
babo	[reference = addr & sex = f & generation = ≥2]
tatko	[reference = addr & sex = m & generation = 1 & generation last link = 1]
majko	[reference = addr & sex = f & generation = 1 & generation last link = 1]
vujčo	[reference = addr & sex 1st link = f & sex = m & generation = 1 & distance = 2 & generation last link = 0]
čičo	[reference = addr & sex 1st link = m & sex = m & distance = 2 & generation last link = 0]
leljo	[reference = addr & sex 1st link = m & sex = f & generation = 1 & distance = 2 & generation last link = 0]
tetko	[reference = addr & sex 1st link = f & sex = f & distance = 2 & generation last link = 0]
bratko	[reference = addr & affinity 1st link = cons & sex = m & generation = 0 & distance = 1]
sestro	[reference = addr & affinity 1st link = cons & sex = f & generation = 0 & distance = 1]
bate	[reference = addr & affinity 1st link = cons & sex = m & generation = 0 & distance = 1]
kako	[reference = addr & affinity 1st link = cons & sex = f & generation = 0 & distance = 1]
bratovčede	[reference = addr & sex = m & distance = ≥3 & generation last link = −1]

bratovčedke	[reference = addr & sex = f & generation = 0 & distance = ≥ 3]
sine	[reference = addr & sex = m & generation = -1 & distance = 1]
dăšte	[reference = addr & sex = f & generation = -1 & distance = 1]
plemenniko	[reference = addr & sex = m & distance = 2 & generation last link = -1]
plemennice	[reference = addr & sex = f & distance = 2 & generation last link = -1]
măžo	[reference = addr & sex 1st link = m & affinity 1st link = aff & generation = 0]
ženo	[reference = addr & affinity 1st link = aff & sex = f & generation = 0]
zetko	[reference = addr & sex = m & generation = ≤ 0 & distance = 2 & generation last link = 0]
badžo	[reference = addr & generation = 0 & distance = 3 & generation last link = 0]
snaho	[reference = addr & sex = f & generation = ≤ 0 & distance = 2 & generation last link = 0]
vujno	[reference = addr & sex 1st link = f & sex = f & distance = 3 & generation last link = 0]
strino	[reference = addr & sex 1st link = m & sex = f & distance = 3 & generation last link = 0]
lelinčo	[reference = addr & sex 1st link = m & sex = m & distance = 3 & generation last link = 0]
tetinčo	[reference = addr & sex 1st link = f & sex = m & generation = 1 & distance = 3 & generation last link = 0]

Table 4.1 Simplest componential analysis of American English

great-grandfather	[sex = m & generation = 3]
great-grandmother	[sex = f & generation = 3]
great-uncle	[sex = m & generation = 2 & distance = 3]
great-aunt	[sex = f & generation = 2 & distance = 3]
grandfather	[sex = m & generation = 2 & distance = 2]
grandmother	[sex = f & generation = 2 & distance = 2]
uncle	[sex = m & generation last link = 0 & generation = 1]
aunt	[sex = f & generation last link = 0 & generation = 1]
father	[sex = m & generation = 1 & distance = 1]
mother	[sex = f & generation = 1 & distance = 1]
son	[sex = m & generation = -1 & distance = 1]
daughter	[sex = f & generation = -1 & distance = 1]
brother	[sex = m & generation last link = 0 & generation = 0 & affinity = cons]
sister	[sex = f & generation last link = 0 & generation = 0 & affinity = cons]
cousin	[generation 1st link = 1 & generation last link = -1]
nephew	[generation 1st link = 0 & sex = m & generation last link = -1]

150

Table 4.1 (Continued)

niece	[generation 1st link = 0 & sex = f & generation last link = −1]
grandson	[sex = m & generation = −2 & distance = 2]
grandaughter	[sex = f & generation = −2 & distance = 2]
great-grandson	[generation 1st link = −1 & sex = m & generation = −3]
great-granddaughter	[generation 1st link = −1 & sex = f & generation = −3]
husband	[sex = m & distance = 1 & affinity = aff]
wife	[sex = f & distance = 1 & affinity = aff]
father-in-law	[generation 1st link = 0 & sex = m & generation = 1 & str equiv = non-eq]
mother-in-law	[generation 1st link = 0 & sex = f & generation = 1 & str equiv = non-eq]
son-in-law	[sex = m & generation last link = 0 & generation = −1 & str equiv = non-eq]
daughter-in-law	[sex = f & generation last link = 0 & generation = −1 & str equiv = non-eq]
brother-in-law	[sex = m & generation = 0 & distance =≥ 2 & affinity = aff & str equiv = non-eq]
sister-in-law	[sex = f & generation = 0 & distance =≥ 2 & affinity = aff & str equiv = non-eq]
step-father	[sex = m & generation = 1 & str equiv = eq]
step-mother	[sex = f & generation = 1 & str equiv = eq]
step-son	[sex = m & generation = −1 & str equiv = eq]
step-daughter	[sex = f & generation = −1 & str equiv = eq]
step-brother	[sex = m & generation = 0 & affinity = aff & str equiv = eq]
step-brother	[sex = m & distance = 3 & affinity = aff & str equiv = eq]
step-sister	[sex = f & generation = 0 & affinity = aff & str equiv = eq]

Table 4.2 Simplest componential analysis of Swedish (alternative 1)

fader	[sex 1st link = m & generation = 1 & distance = 1]
moder	[sex 1st link = f & generation = 1 & distance = 1]
farfar	[sex 1st link = m & sex 2nd link = m & generation = 2]
morfar	[sex 1st link = f & sex 2nd link = m & generation = 2]
farmor	[sex 1st link = m & sex 2nd link = f & generation = 2]
mormor	[sex 1st link = f & sex 2nd link = f & generation = 2]
son	[sex 1st link = m & generation = −1 & distance = 1]
dotter	[sex 1st link = f & generation = −1 & distance = 1]
broder	[sex 1st link = m & generation = 0 & distance = 1]
syster	[sex 1st link = f & generation = 0 & distance = 1]
farbror	[sex 1st link = m & sex 2nd link = m & generation = 1 & distance = 2]
morbror	[sex 1st link = f & sex 2nd link = m & generation = 1 & distance = 2]
faster	[sex 1st link = m & sex 2nd link = f & generation = 1 & distance = 2]
moster	[sex 1st link = f & sex 2nd link = f & generation = 1 & distance = 2]
sonson	[sex 1st link = m & sex 2nd link = m & generation = −2]

dotterson	[sex 1st link = f & sex 2nd link = m & generation = −2]
sondotter	[sex 1st link = m & sex 2nd link = f & generation = −2]
dotterdotter	[sex 1st link = f & sex 2nd link = f & generation = −2]
brorson	[sex 1st link = m & sex 2nd link = m & generation = −1 & distance = 2]
systerson	[sex 1st link = f & sex 2nd link = m & generation = −1 & distance = 2]
brordotter	[sex 1st link = m & sex 2nd link = f & generation = −1 & distance = 2]
systerdotter	[sex 1st link = f & sex 2nd link = f & generation = −1 & distance = 2]
kusin	[distance = 3]

Table 4.3 Simplest componential analysis of Swedish (alternative 2)

fader	[sex = m & generation = 1 & distance = 1]
moder	[sex = f & generation = 1 & distance = 1]
farfar	[sex 1st link = m & sex = m & generation = 2]
morfar	[sex 1st link = f & sex = m & generation = 2]
farmor	[sex 1st link = m & sex = f & generation = 2]
mormor	[sex 1st link = f & sex = f & generation = 2]
son	[sex = m & generation = −1 & distance = 1]
dotter	[sex = f & generation = −1 & distance = 1]
broder	[sex = m & generation = 0 & distance = 1]
syster	[sex = f & generation = 0 & distance = 1]
farbror	[sex 1st link = m & sex = m & generation = 1 & distance = 2]
morbror	[sex 1st link = f & sex = m & generation = 1]
faster	[sex 1st link = m & sex = f & generation = 1]
moster	[sex 1st link = f & sex = f & generation = 1 & distance = 2]
sonson	[sex 1st link = m & sex = m & generation = −2]
dotterson	[sex 1st link = f & sex = m & generation = −2]
sondotter	[sex 1st link = m & sex = f & generation = −2]
dotterdotter	[sex 1st link = f & sex = f & generation = −2]
brorson	[sex 1st link = m & sex = m & generation = −1 & distance = 2]
systerson	[sex 1st link = f & sex = m & generation = −1]
brordotter	[sex 1st link = m & sex = f & generation = −1]
systerdotter	[sex 1st link = f & sex = f & generation = −1 & distance = 2]
kusin	[distance = 3]

Table 4.4 Simplest componential analysis of Irish

mathair	[sex = f & generation = 1 & distance = 1]
athair	[sex = m & generation = 1 & distance = 1]
mac	[sex = m & generation = −1 & distance = 1]
inion	[sex = f & generation = −1 & distance = 1]
deanthair	[sex = m & generation = 0 & distance = 1]
deirfiur	[sex = f & generation = 0 & distance = 1]
aintin	[sex = f & generation = 1 & distance =$\geq$ 2]
uncail	[sex = m & generation = 1 & distance =$\geq$ 2]
nia	[sex = m & generation = −1 & distance = 2]
neacht	[sex = f & generation = −1 & distance = 2]
seanmhathair	[sex = f & generation = 2]
seanathair	[sex = m & generation = 2]
garmhac	[sex = m & generation = −2]
garinion	[sex = f & generation = −2]
col gaolta	[generation = 0 & distance = 3]

Table 4.5 Simplest componential analysis of Spanish

bizabuelo	[sex = m & generation = 3]
bizabuela	[sex = f & generation = 3]
abuelo	[sex = m & generation = 2 & distance = 2]
abuela	[sex = f & generation = 2 & distance = 2]
tio-abuelo	[sex = m & generation = 2 & distance = 3]
tia-abuela	[sex = f & generation = 2 & distance = 3]
tio	[sex = m & generation = 1 & distance = 2 & affinity = cons]
tia	[sex = f & generation = 1 & distance = 2 & affinity = cons]
madre	[sex = f & generation = 1 & distance = 1]
padre	[sex = m & generation = 1 & distance = 1]
hermana	[sex = f & generation = 0 & distance = 1 & affinity = cons]
hermano	[sex = m & generation = 0 & distance = 1 & affinity = cons]
prima	[sex = f & generation = 0 & distance = ge(3)]
primo	[sex = m & generation = 0 & distance = ge(3)]
hijo	[sex = m & generation = −1 & distance = 1]
hija	[sex = f & generation = −1 & distance = 1]
sobrino	[sex = m & generation = −1 & distance = 2 & affinity = cons]
sobrina	[sex = f & generation = −1 & distance = 2 & affinity = cons]
nieto	[sex = m & generation = −2]
nieta	[sex = f & generation = −2]
biznieto	[sex = m & generation = −3]
biznieta	[sex = f & generation = −3]
marido	[sex = m & distance = 1 & affinity = aff]
esposa	[sex = f & distance = 1 & affinity = aff]
suegra	[sex = f & generation = 1 & affinity = aff]
suegro	[sex = m & generation = 1 & affinity = aff]
yerno	[sex = m & generation = −1 & affinity = aff]
nuera	[sex = f & generation = −1 & affinity = aff]
cunado	[sex = m & generation = 0 & distance = 2]
cunada	[sex = f & generation = 0 & distance = 2]

Table 4.6 Simplest componential analysis of Polish (alternative 1)

pradziad	[sex = m & generation = 3]
prababka	[sex = f & generation = 3]
dziad	[sex = m & generation = 2]
babka	[sex = f & generation = 2]
ojciec	[sex 1st link = m & generation = 1 & distance = 1]
matka	[sex 1st link = f & generation = 1 & distance = 1]
wuj	[sex 1st link = f & affinity 1st link = cons & sex 2nd link = m & generation = 1 & distance = 2]
stryj	[sex 1st link = m & affinity 1st link = cons & sex = m & generation = 1 & distance = 2]
ciotka	[affinity 1st link = cons & sex = f & generation = 1 & distance = 2]
syn	[sex 1st link = m & generation = −1 & distance = 1]
córka	[sex 1st link = f & generation = −1 & distance = 1]
siostra	[sex 1st link = f & affinity 1st link = cons & generation = 0 & distance = 1]
brat	[sex 1st link = m & affinity 1st link = cons & generation = 0 & distance = 1]
siostra-stryjeczna	[sex 1st link = m & sex 2nd link = m & sex = f & generation = 0]
siostra-cioteczna	[sex 2nd link = f & sex = f & generation = 0 & distance = 3]
siostra-wujeczna	[sex 1st link = f & sex 2nd link = m & sex = f & generation = 0 & distance = 3]
brat-stryjeczna	[sex 1st link = m & sex 2nd link = m & sex = m & generation = 0 & distance = 3]
brat-cioteczna	[sex 2nd link = f & sex = m & generation = 0 & distance = 3]
brat-wujeczna	[sex 1st link = f & affinity 1st link = cons & sex 2nd link = m & sex = m & generation = 0]
brat-wujeczna	[sex 1st link = f & sex 2nd link = m & sex = m & generation = 0 & distance = 3]
bratanek	[sex 1st link = m & sex = m & generation = −1 & distance = 2]
siostrzeniec	[sex 1st link = f & sex 2nd link = m & generation = −1 & distance = 2]
bratanica	[sex 1st link = m & sex 2nd link = f & generation = −1 & distance = 2]
siostrzenica	[sex 1st link = f & sex = f & generation = −1 & distance = 2]
wnuk	[sex = m & generation = −2]
wnuczka	[sex = f & generation = −2]
prawnuk	[sex = m & generation = −3]
prawnuczka	[sex = f & generation = −3]
maż	[sex 1st link = m & affinity 1st link = aff & distance = 1]
żona	[sex 1st link = f & affinity 1st link = aff & sex = f & generation = 0]
swiekr	[sex 1st link = m & affinity 1st link = aff & sex = m & generation = 1]
teść	[sex 1st link = f & affinity 1st link = aff & sex = m & generation = 1]
swiekra	[sex 1st link = m & affinity 1st link = aff & sex = f & generation = 1]
teściowa	[sex 1st link = f & affinity 1st link = aff & sex = f & generation = 1]
szwagier	[sex = m & generation = 0 & distance = 2]
szwagrowa	[sex 1st link = m & affinity 1st link = aff & sex = f & generation = 0]

154

Table 4.7 Simplest componential analysis of Polish (alternative 2)

pradziad	[sex = m & generation = 3]
prababka	[sex = f & generation = 3]
dziad	[sex = m & generation = 2]
babka	[sex = f & generation = 2]
ojciec	[sex 1st link = m & generation = 1 & distance = 1]
matka	[sex 1st link = f & generation = 1 & distance = 1]
wuj	[sex 1st link = f & sex 2nd link = m & generation = 1 & distance = 2 & affinity = cons]
stryj	[sex 1st link = m & sex = m & generation = 1 & distance = 2 & affinity = cons]
ciotka	[sex = f & generation = 1 & distance = 2 & affinity = cons]
syn	[sex 1st link = m & generation = −1 & distance = 1]
córka	[sex 1st link = f & generation = −1 & distance = 1]
siostra	[sex 1st link = f & generation = 0 & distance = 1 & affinity = cons]
brat	[sex 1st link = m & generation = 0 & distance = 1 & affinity = cons]
siostra-stryjeczna	[sex 1st link = m & sex 2nd link = m & sex = f & generation = 0]
siostra-cioteczna	[sex 2nd link = f & sex = f & generation = 0 & distance = 3]
siostra-wujeczna	[sex 1st link = f & sex 2nd link = m & sex = f & generation = 0 & distance = 3]
brat-stryjeczna	[sex 1st link = m & sex 2nd link = m & sex = m & generation = 0 & distance = 3]
brat-cioteczna	[sex 2nd link = f & sex = m & generation = 0 & distance = 3]
brat-wujeczna	[sex 1st link = f & sex 2nd link = m & sex = m & generation = 0 & affinity = cons]
brat-wujeczna	[sex 1st link = f & sex 2nd link = m & sex = m & generation = 0 & distance = 3]
bratanek	[sex 1st link = m & sex = m & generation = −1 & distance = 2]
siostrzeniec	[sex 1st link = f & sex 2nd link = m & generation = −1 & distance = 2]
bratanica	[sex 1st link = m & sex 2nd link = f & generation = −1 & distance = 2]
siostzenica	[sex 1st link = f & sex = f & generation = −1 & distance = 2]
wnuk	[sex = m & generation = −2]
wnuczka	[sex = f & generation = −2]
prawnuk	[sex = m & generation = −3]
prawnuczka	[sex = f & generation = −3]
maż	[sex 1st link = m & distance = 1 & affinity = aff]
żona	[sex 1st link = f & sex = f & generation = 0 & affinity = aff]
swiekr	[sex 1st link = m & sex = m & generation = 1 & affinity = aff]
teść	[sex 1st link = f & sex = m & generation = 1 & affinity = aff]
swiekra	[sex 1st link = m & sex = f & generation = 1 & affinity = aff]
teściowa	[sex 1st link = f & sex = f & generation = 1 & affinity = aff]
szwagier	[sex = m & generation = 0 & distance = 2]
szwagrowa	[sex 1st link = m & sex = f & generation = 0 & affinity = aff]

Table 4.8 Simplest componential analysis of Czech

děd	[sex = m & generation = 2]
babička	[sex = f & generation = 2]
strčc	[sex = m & generation = 1 & distance = 2 & affinity = cons]
teta	[sex = f & generation = 1 & distance = 2 & affinity = cons]
matka	[sex = f & generation = 1 & distance = 1]
otec	[sex = m & generation = 1 & distance = 1]
sestra	[sex = f & generation = 0 & distance = 1 & affinity = cons]
bratr	[sex = m & generation = 0 & affinity = cons]
syn	[sex = m & generation = −1 & distance = 1]
dcera	[sex = f & generation = −1 & distance = 1]
bratanec	[distance = 3]
synovec	[sex = m & generation = −1 & distance = 2 & affinity = cons]
neteč	[sex = f & generation = −1 & distance = 2 & affinity = cons]
vnuk	[sex = m & generation = −2]
vnučka	[sex = f & generation = −2]
muž	[sex = m & distance = 1 & affinity = aff]
žena	[sex = f & distance = 1 & affinity = aff]
tchčn	[sex = m & generation = 1 & affinity = aff]
tchynč	[sex = f & generation = 1 & affinity = aff]
zet'	[sex = m & generation = −1 & affinity = aff]
snacha	[sex = f & generation = −1 & affinity = aff]
švagr	[sex = m & generation = 0 & distance = 2]
švragrovaì	[sex = f & generation = 0 & distance = 2]

Table 4.9 Simplest componential analysis of Persian

mādar	[sex = f & generation = 1 & distance = 1]
pedar	[sex = m & generation = 1 & distance = 1]
pesar	[sex = m & generation = −1]
doxtar	[sex = f & generation = −1]
amu	[sex 1st link = m & sex = m & generation = 1 & distance = 2]
dāi	[sex 1st link = f & sex = m & generation = 1]
amme	[sex 1st link = m & sex = f & generation = 1]
xāle	[sex 1st link = f & sex = f & generation = 1 & distance = 2]
barādar	[sex = m & generation = 0 & distance = 1]
xāhar	[sex = f & generation = 0 & distance = 1]
mādar-bozorg	[sex = f & generation = 2]
pedar-bozorg	[sex = m & generation = 2]
nave/nabire	[generation = −2]
pedar-jad	[sex = m & generation = 3]
mādar-jad	[sex = f & generation = 3]
bājenāq	[sex = m & generation = 0 & distance = 2]
xāhar-zan	[sex 1st link = f & sex = f & generation = 0 & distance = 2]
xāhar-šowhar	[sex 1st link = m & sex = f & generation = 0]

156

Table 4.10 Simplest componential analysis of Albanian (alternative 1)

nene/mami	[sex = f & generation last link = 1 & distance = 1]
ate	[sex = m & generation last link = 1 & distance = 1]
bir/djale	[sex = m & generation last link = −1 & distance = 1]
vajze/bije	[sex = f & generation last link = −1 & distance = 1]
vellai	[sex = m & generation last link = 0 & distance = 1]
vellackoja	[sex = m & generation last link = 0 & distance = 1]
moter	[sex = f & generation last link = 0 & distance = 1]
moterz	[sex = f & generation last link = 0 & distance = 1]
nip	[generation 1st link = −1 & sex = m & distance = 3]
mbese	[generation 1st link = se(0) & sex = f & generation last link = −1 & distance = ge(2)]
gjyshe	[generation 1st link = 1 & sex = f & generation last link = 1 & distance = 2]
gjysh	[generation 1st link = 1 & sex = m & generation last link = 1 & distance = 2]
daje	[generation 1st link = 1 & sex = m & generation last link = 0]
teze	[generation 1st link = 1 & sex = f & generation last link = 0]
kusherire	[generation 1st link = 1 & sex = f & distance = ge(3)]
kusheri	[generation 1st link = 1 & sex = m & distance = ge(3)]
nipi	[sex = m & generation last link = −1 & distance = 2]
vjeherra	[generation 1st link = 0 & sex = f & generation last link = 1]
vjeherr	[generation 1st link = 0 & sex = m & generation last link = 1]
dhender	[generation 1st link = −1 & sex = m & distance = 2]
nuse	[generation 1st link = −1 & sex = f & generation last link = 0]

Table 4.11 Simplest componential analysis of Albanian (alternative 2)

nene/mami	[sex = f & generation = 1 & distance = 1]
ate	[sex = m & generation = 1 & distance = 1]
bir/djale	[sex = m & generation = −1 & distance = 1]
vajze/bije	[sex = f & generation = −1 & distance = 1]
vellai	[sex = m & generation = 0 & distance = 1]
moter	[sex = f & generation = 0 & distance = 1]
moterz	[sex = f & generation = 0 & distance = 1]
nip	[sex = m & generation = −3]
mbese	[sex = f & generation last link = −1 & generation = ≤ −1 & distance = ≥ 2]
gjyshe	[sex = f & generation = 2]
gjysh	[sex = m & generation = 2]
daje	[sex = m & generation last link = 0 & generation = 1]
teze	[sex = f & generation last link = 0 & generation = 1]
kusherire	[sex = f & generation = 0 & distance = ≥ 3]
kusheri	[sex = m & generation = 0 & distance = ≥ 3]
nipi	[sex = m & generation last link = −1 & distance = 2]
vjeherra	[sex = f & generation last link = 1 & generation = 1 & distance = 2]
vjeherr	[sex = m & generation last link = 1 & generation = 1 & distance = 2]
dhender	[sex = m & generation last link = 0 & generation = −1]
nuse	[sex = f & generation last link = 0 & generation = −1]

Table 4.12 Componential analysis of Albanian (alternative 3)

nene/mami	[sex = f & generation = 1 & distance = 1]
ate	[sex = m & generation = 1 & distance = 1]
bir/djale	[sex = m & generation = −1 & distance = 1]
vajze/bije	[sex = f & generation = −1 & distance = 1]
vellai	[sex = m & generation = 0 & distance = 1]
vellackoja	[sex = m & generation = 0 & distance = 1]
moter	[sex = f & generation = 0 & distance = 1]
moterz	[sex = f & generation = 0 & distance = 1]
nip	[sex = m & generation = −3]
mbese	[sex = f & generation = ≤ −1 & distance = ≥ 2 & affinity = cons]
gjyshe	[sex = f & generation = 2]
gjysh	[sex = m & generation = 2]
daje	[sex = m & generation = 1 & distance = 2 & affinity = cons]
teze	[sex = f & generation = 1 & distance = 2 & affinity = cons]
kusherire	[sex = f & generation = 0 & distance = ≥ 3]
kusheri	[sex = m & generation = 0 & distance = ≥ 3]
nipi	[sex = m & generation = −1 & distance = 2 & affinity = cons]
vjeherra	[sex = f & generation = 1 & affinity = aff]
vjeherr	[sex = m & generation = 1 & affinity = aff]
dhender	[sex = m & generation = −1 & affinity = aff]
nuse	[sex = f & generation = −1 & affinity = aff]

Table 4.13 Simplest componential analysis of Armenian

hayr	[sex 1st link = m & generation = 1 & distance = 1]
mayr	[sex 1st link = f & generation = 1 & distance = 1]
pap	[generation = 2]
tat	[generation = 3]
ordi	[generation = −1 & distance = 1]
ełbayr	[sex 1st link = m & generation = 0 & distance = 1 & affinity = cons]
k'uyr	[sex 1st link = f & generation = 0 & distance = 1 & affinity = cons]
t'orŕ(nik)	[generation = −2]
horełbayr	[sex 1st link = m & sex 2nd link = m & generation = 1 & distance = 2 & affinity = cons]
k'erŕi	[sex 1st link = f & sex 2nd link = m & generation = 1 & distance = 2 & affinity = cons]
horak'uyr	[sex 1st link = m & sex 2nd link = f & generation = 1 & distance = 2 & affinity = cons]
morak'uyr	[sex 1st link = f & sex 2nd link = f & generation = 1 & distance = 2 & affinity = cons]
ełborordi	[sex 1st link = m & sex 2nd link = m & generation = −1 & distance = 2]
k'erŕordi	[sex 1st link = f & sex 2nd link = m & generation = −1 & affinity = cons]

158

Table 4.13 (Continued)

ełbor alǰik	[sex 1st link = m & sex 2nd link = f & generation = −1 & distance = 2 & affinity = cons]
k'roǰ ałǰik	[sex 1st link = f & sex 2nd link = f & generation = −1]
morak'roǰ tła/ałǰik	[sex 1st link = f & sex 2nd link = f & generation = 0 & distance = 3 & affinity = cons]
horak'roǰ tła/ałǰik	[sex 1st link = m & sex 2nd link = f & generation = 0 & distance = 3]
k'erŕu tła/ałǰik	[sex 1st link = f & sex 2nd link = m & generation = 0 & distance = 3]
horełbor tła/ałǰik	[sex 1st link = m & sex 2nd link = m & generation = 0 & distance = 3 & affinity = cons]
hars	[sex 1st link = m & generation = −1 & affinity = aff]
p'esa	[sex 1st link = f & generation = −1 & affinity = aff]
amusing	[sex 1st link = m & distance = 1 & affinity = aff]
kin	[sex 1st link = f & distance = 1 & affinity = aff]
skesrayr	[sex 1st link = m & sex 2nd link = m & generation = 1 & affinity = aff]
skesur	[sex 1st link = m & sex 2nd link = f & generation = 1 & affinity = aff]
tagr/tegr	[sex 1st link = m & sex 2nd link = m & generation = 0 & distance = 2]
tagerakin	[sex 1st link = m & distance = 3 & affinity = aff]
tal	[sex 1st link = m & sex 2nd link = f & generation = 0 & distance = 2]
aner	[sex 1st link = f & sex 2nd link = m & generation = 1 & distance = 2 & affinity = aff]
zok'anč'	[sex 1st link = f & sex 2nd link = f & generation = 1 & affinity = aff]
anerjag	[sex 1st link = f & sex 2nd link = m & generation = 0 & distance = 2]
k'eni	[sex 1st link = f & sex 2nd link = f & generation = 0 & distance = 2]
baǰanał	[sex 2nd link = f & distance = 3 & affinity = aff]
k'erŕakin/k'erŕekin	[generation = 1 & distance = 3]

Table 4.14 Simplest componential analysis of Turkish (alternative 1)

büyük baba	[sex = m & affinity last link = cons & generation = 2]
babaanne	[parallelity = cross & sex = f & affinity last link = cons & generation = 2]
anneanne	[parallelity = par & sex = f & affinity last link = cons & generation = 2]
baba	[sex = m & generation = 1 & distance = 1]
ana	[sex = f & generation = 1 & distance = 1]
oğul	[sex = m & generation = −1 & distance = 1]
kız	[sex = f & generation = −1 & distance = 1]
teyze kızı	[parallelity = par & sex 1st link = f & sex = f & affinity last link = cons & distance = 3]
dayı kızı	[parallelity = cross & sex 1st link = f & sex = f & affinity last link = cons & distance = 3]
hala kızı	[parallelity = cross & sex 1st link = m & affinity 1st link = cons & sex = f & affinity last link = cons & generation = 0]
amca kızı	[parallelity = par & sex 1st link = m & affinity 1st link = cons & sex = f & affinity last link = cons & generation = 0]
teyze oğlu	[parallelity = par & sex 1st link = f & sex = m & affinity last link = cons & generation = 0 & distance = 3]
dayı oğlu	[parallelity = cross & sex 1st link = f & sex = m & affinity last link = cons & generation = 0 & distance = 3]
hala oğlu	[parallelity = cross & sex 1st link = m & sex = m & affinity last link = cons & generation = 0 & distance = 3]
amca oğlu	[parallelity = par & sex 1st link = m & sex = m & affinity last link = cons & generation = 0 & distance = 3]
dayı	[parallelity = cross & affinity 1st link = cons & sex = m & affinity last link = cons & generation = 1]
amca	[parallelity = par & affinity 1st link = cons & sex = m & affinity last link = cons & generation = 1 & distance = 2]
teyze	[parallelity = par & affinity 1st link = cons & sex = f & affinity last link = cons & generation = 1 & distance = 2]
hala	[sex = m & affinity last link = cons & generation = −1 & distance = 2]
kız yeğen	[sex = f & affinity last link = cons & generation = −1 & distance = 2]
büyük dede	[affinity last link = cons & generation = 3]
torun	[sex = m & generation = −2]
kız torun	[sex = f & generation = −2]
kardeş	[affinity 1st link = cons & sex = m & generation = 0 & distance = 1]
kız dardes	[affinity 1st link = cons & sex = f & generation = 0 & distance = 1]
koca	[affinity 1st link = aff & sex = m & distance = 1]
karı	[affinity 1st link = aff & sex = f & distance = 1]
kayınpeder	[affinity 1st link = aff & sex = m & generation = 1]
kaynana	[affinity 1st link = aff & sex = f & generation = 1]

160

Table 4.14 (Continued)

kayın	[affinity 1st link = aff & sex = m & generation = 0 & distance = 2]
baldız	[sex 1st link = f & affinity 1st link = aff & sex = f & generation = 0 & distance = 2]
görümce	[sex 1st link = m & affinity 1st link = aff & sex = f & generation = 0 & distance = 2]
bacanak	[affinity 1st link = aff & sex = m & distance = 3]
elti	[affinity 1st link = aff & sex = f & distance = 3]
yenge	[affinity 1st link = cons & sex = f & affinity last link = aff & generation =≥ 0]
enişte	[affinity 1st link = cons & sex = m & affinity last link = aff & generation =≥ 0]
damat	[sex = m & affinity last link = aff & generation = −1]
gelin	[sex 1st link = m & affinity last link = aff & generation = −1]

Table 4.15 Simplest componential analysis of Turkish (alternative 2)

büyük baba	[sex = m & affinity last link = cons & generation = 2]
babaanne	[sex 1st link = m & sex = f & affinity last link = cons & generation = 2]
anneanne	[sex 1st link = f & sex = f & affinity last link = cons & generation = 2]
baba	[sex = m & generation = 1 & distance = 1]
ana	[sex = f & generation = 1 & distance = 1]
oğul	[sex = m & generation = −1 & distance = 1]
kız	[sex = f & generation = −1 & distance = 1]
teyze kızı	[sex 1st link = f & sex 2nd link = f & sex = f & affinity last link = cons & distance = 3]
dayı kızı	[sex 1st link = f & sex 2nd link = m & sex = f & affinity last link = cons & distance = 3]
hala kızı	[sex 1st link = m & affinity 1st link = cons & sex 2nd link = f & sex = f & affinity last link = cons & generation = 0]
teyze oğlu	[sex 1st link = f & sex 2nd link = f & sex = m & affinity last link = cons & generation = 0]
dayı oğlu	[sex 1st link = f & sex 2nd link = m & sex = m & affinity last link = cons & generation = 0 & distance = 3]
hala oğlu	[sex 1st link = m & sex 2nd link = f & sex = m & affinity last link = cons & generation = 0 & distance = 3]
amca oğlu	[sex 1st link = m & sex 2nd link = m & sex = m & affinity last link = cons & generation = 0 & distance = 3]
dayı	[sex 1st link = f & affinity 1st link = cons & sex 2nd link = m & affinity last link = cons & generation = 1 & distance = 2]
amca	[sex 1st link = m & affinity 1st link = cons & sex = m & affinity last link = cons & generation = 1 & distance = 2]
teyze	[sex 1st link = f & affinity 1st link = cons & sex = f & affinity last link = cons & generation = 1 & distance = 2]

hala	[sex 1st link = m & affinity 1st link = cons & sex 2nd link = f & affinity last link = cons & generation = 1 & distance = 2]
yeğen	[sex = m & affinity last link = cons & generation = −1 & distance = 2]
kız yeğen	[sex = f & affinity last link = cons & generation = −1 & distance = 2]
büyük dede	[affinity last link = cons & generation = 3]
torun	[sex = m & generation = −2]
kız torun	[sex = f & generation = −2]
kardeş	[affinity 1st link = cons & sex = m & generation = 0 & distance = 1]
kız dardes	[affinity 1st link = cons & sex = f & generation = 0 & distance = 1]
koca	[affinity 1st link = aff & sex = m & distance = 1]
karı	[affinity 1st link = aff & sex = f & distance = 1]
kayınpeder	[affinity 1st link = aff & sex = m & generation = 1]
kaynana	[affinity 1st link = aff & sex = f & generation = 1]
kayın	[affinity 1st link = aff & sex = m & generation = 0 & distance = 2]
baldız	[sex 1st link = f & affinity 1st link = aff & sex = f & generation = 0 & distance = 2]
görümce	[sex 1st link = m & affinity 1st link = aff & sex = f & generation = 0 & distance = 2]
bacanak	[affinity 1st link = aff & sex = m & distance = 3]
elti	[affinity 1st link = aff & sex = f & distance = 3]
yenge	[affinity 1st link = cons & sex = f & affinity last link = aff & generation => 0]
enişte	[affinity 1st link = cons & sex = m & affinity last link = aff & generation => 0]
damat	[sex = m & affinity last link = aff & generation = −1]
gelin	[sex = f & affinity last link = aff & generation = −1]

Table 4.16 Simplest componential analysis of Turkish (alternative 3)

büyük baba	[sex = m & generation = 2 & affinity = cons]
babaanne	[parallelity = cross & sex = f & generation = 2 & affinity = cons]
anneanne	[parallelity = par & sex = f & generation = 2 & affinity = cons]
baba	[sex = m & generation = 1 & distance = 1]
ana	[sex = f & generation = 1 & distance = 1]
oğul	[sex = m & generation = −1 & distance = 1]
kız	[sex = f & generation = −1 & distance = 1]
teyze kızı	[parallelity = par & sex 1st link = f & sex = f & distance = 3 & affinity = cons]

162

Table 4.16   (Continued)

dayı kızı	[parallelity = cross & sex 1st link = f & sex = f & affinity = cons]
hala kızı	[parallelity = cross & sex 1st link = m & sex = f & generation = 0 & affinity = cons]
amca kızı	[parallelity = par & sex 1st link = m & sex = f & generation = 0 & affinity = cons]
teyze oğlu	[parallelity = par & sex 1st link = f & sex = m & generation = 0 & affinity = cons]
dayı oğlu	[parallelity = cross & sex 1st link = f & sex = m & generation = 0 & affinity = cons]
hala oğlu	[parallelity = cross & sex 1st link = m & sex = m & generation = 0 & affinity = cons]
amca oğlu	[parallelity = par & sex 1st link = m & sex = m & generation = 0 & distance = 3 & affinity = cons]
dayı	[parallelity = cross & sex = m & generation = 1 & affinity = cons]
amca	[parallelity = par & sex = m & generation = 1 & distance = 2 & affinity = cons]
teyze	[parallelity = par & sex = f & generation = 1 & distance = 2 & affinity = cons]
hala	[parallelity = cross & sex = f & generation = 1 & affinity = cons]
yeğen	[sex = m & generation = −1 & distance = 2 & affinity = cons]
kız yeğen	[sex = f & generation = −1 & distance = 2 & affinity = cons]
büyük dede	[generation = 3 & affinity = cons]
torun	[sex = m & generation = −2]
kız torun	[sex = f & generation = −2]
kardeş	[sex = m & generation = 0 & distance = 1 & affinity = cons]
kız dardes	[sex = f & generation = 0 & distance = 1 & affinity = cons]
koca	[sex = m & distance = 1 & affinity = aff]
karı	[sex = f & distance = 1 & affinity = aff]
kayınpeder	[affinity 1st link = aff & sex = m & generation = 1]
kaynana	[affinity 1st link = aff & sex = f & generation = 1]
kayın	[affinity 1st link = aff & sex = m & generation = 0 & distance = 2]
baldız	[sex 1st link = f & affinity 1st link = aff & sex = f & generation = 0 & distance = 2]
görümce	[sex 1st link = m & affinity 1st link = aff & sex = f & generation = 0 & distance = 2]
bacanak	[affinity 1st link = aff & sex = m & distance = 3]
elti	[affinity 1st link = aff & sex = f & distance = 3]
yenge	[affinity 1st link = cons & sex = f & generation =≥ 0 & affinity = aff]
enişte	[affinity 1st link = cons & sex = m & generation =≥ 0 & affinity = aff]
damat	[sex = m & generation = −1 & affinity = aff]
gelin	[sex = f & generation = −1 & affinity = aff]

Table 4.17 Simplest componential analysis of Turkish (alternative 4)

büyük baba	[sex = m & generation = 2 & affinity = cons]
babaanne	[sex 1st link = m & sex = f & generation = 2 & affinity = cons]
anneanne	[sex 1st link = f & sex = f & generation = 2 & affinity = cons]
baba	[sex = m & generation = 1 & distance = 1]
ana	[sex = f & generation = 1 & distance = 1]
oğul	[sex = m & generation = −1 & distance = 1]
kız	[sex = f & generation = −1 & distance = 1]
teyze kızı	[sex 1st link = f & sex 2nd link = f & sex = f & distance = 3 & affinity = cons]
dayı kızı	[sex 1st link = f & sex 2nd link = m & sex = f & distance = 3 & affinity = cons]
hala kızı	[sex 1st link = m & sex 2nd link = f & sex = f & generation = 0 & affinity = cons]
amca kızı	[sex 1st link = m & sex 2nd link = m & sex = f & affinity = cons]
teyze oğlu	[sex 1st link = f & sex 2nd link = f & sex = m & generation = 0 & affinity = cons]
dayı oğlu	[sex 1st link = f & sex 2nd link = m & sex = m & generation = 0 & affinity = cons]
hala oğlu	[sex 1st link = m & sex 2nd link = f & sex = m & generation = 0 & distance = 3 & affinity = cons]
amca oğlu	[sex 1st link = m & sex 2nd link = m & sex = m & generation = 0 & distance = 3 & affinity = cons]
dayı	[sex 1st link = f & sex 2nd link = m & generation = 1 & distance = 2 & affinity = cons]
amca	[sex 1st link = m & sex = m & generation = 1 & distance = 2 & affinity = cons]
teyze	[sex 1st link = f & sex = f & generation = 1 & distance = 2 & affinity = cons]
hala	[sex 1st link = m & sex 2nd link = f & generation = 1 & distance = 2 & affinity = cons]
yeğen	[sex = m & generation = −1 & distance = 2 & affinity = cons]
kız yeğen	[sex = f & generation = −1 & distance = 2 & affinity = cons]
büyük dede	[generation = 3 & affinity = cons]
torun	[sex = m & generation = −2]
kız torun	[sex = f & generation = −2]
kardeş	[sex = m & generation = 0 & distance = 1 & affinity = cons]
kız dardes	[sex = f & generation = 0 & distance = 1 & affinity = cons]
koca	[sex = m & distance = 1 & affinity = aff]
karı	[sex = f & distance = 1 & affinity = aff]
kayınpeder	[affinity 1st link = aff & sex = m & generation = 1]
kaynana	[affinity 1st link = aff & sex = f & generation = 1]
kayın	[affinity 1st link = aff & sex = m & generation = 0 & distance = 2]
baldız	[sex 1st link = f & affinity 1st link = aff & sex = f & generation = 0 & distance = 2]

164

Table 4.17 (Continued)

görümce	[sex 1st link = m & affinity 1st link = aff & sex = f & generation = 0 & distance = 2]
bacanak	[affinity 1st link = aff & sex = m & distance = 3]
elti	[affinity 1st link = aff & sex = f & distance = 3]
yenge	[affinity 1st link = cons & sex = f & generation =≥ 0 & affinity = aff]
enişte	[affinity 1st link = cons & sex = m & generation =≥ 0 & affinity = aff]
damat	[sex = m & generation = −1 & affinity = aff]
gelin	[sex = f & generation = −1 & affinity = aff]

Table 4.18 Componential analysis of Seneca

ha²nih	[parallelity = par & sex = m & generation = 1]
no²yēh	[parallelity = par & sex = f & generation = 1]
hakhno²sēh	[parallelity = cross & sex = m & generation = 1]
ake:hak	[parallelity = cross & sex = f & generation = 1]
hahtsi²	[parallelity = par & seniority = y & sex = m & generation = 0]
he²kē:²	[parallelity = par & seniority = e & sex = m & generation = 0]
ahtsi²	[parallelity = par & seniority = y & sex = f & generation = 0]
khe²kē:²	[parallelity = par & seniority = e & sex = f & generation = 0]
akyā:²se:²	[parallelity = cross & generation = 0]
he:awak (ms)	[parallelity = par & sex speaker = m & sex = m & generation = −1]
he:awak (fs)	[parallelity = par & sex speaker = f & sex = m & generation = −1]
khe:awak (ms)	[parallelity = par & sex speaker = m & sex = f & generation = −1]
khe:awak (fs)	[parallelity = par & sex speaker = f & sex = f & generation = −1]
heyē:wõ:tē²	[parallelity = cross & sex speaker = m & sex = m & generation = −1]
hehsõ²neh	[parallelity = cross & sex speaker = f & sex = m & generation = −1]
kheyē:wõ:t~e²	[parallelity = cross & sex speaker = m & sex = f & generation = −1]
khehsõ²neh	[parallelity = cross & sex speaker = f & sex = f & generation = −1]

Table 4.19 Simplest componential analysis of Zapotec

šoza$^?$gul	[sex = m & generation = 2 & distance = 2]
šna$^?$agul	[sex = f & generation = 2 & distance = 2]
šoza$^?$	[sex = m & generation = 1 & distance = 1]
šna$^?$	[sex = f & generation = 1 & distance = 1]
buľča$^?$	[sex = m & generation = 0 & distance = 1 & <sex sp - iff - sex rel> = par]
rjila$^?$	[sex = f & generation = 0 & distance = 1 & <sex sp - iff - sex rel> = par]
zana$^?$	[generation = 0 & distance = 1& <sex sp - iff - sex rel> = cross]
rji$^?$na$^?$	[generation = −1 & distance = 1]
rsna$^?$	[generation = −2]
tio	[sex = m & generation = 1 & distance = 2]
tia	[sex = f & generation = 1 & distance = 2]
primo kiu$^?$	[distance =≥ 3]
sobrinukin$^?$	[generation = −1 & distance = 2]

Table 4.20 Simplest componential analysis of Popoloca (alternative 1)

tači$^?$na	[sex = m & generation = 2]
nači$^?$na	[sex = f & generation = 2]
$^?$apanaa	[sex = m & generation last link = 1 & generation = 1]
$^?$amanaa	[sex = f & generation last link = 1 & generation = 1]
s$^?$onaa	[sex = m & generation last link = 0 & generation = 0]
thakhoonaa	[sex = f & generation last link = 0 & generation = 0]
ča$^?$na	[generation 1st link = −1 & generation = −1]
čand$^?$inaa	[generation 1st link = −1 & generation = −2]
či$^?$ninaa	[sex = m & generation last link = 0 & generation = 1]
khva$^?$naa	[sex = f & generation last link = 0 & generation = 1]
čauv$^?$e	[generation 1st link =≥ 0 & generation last link = −1]

Table 4.21 Simplest componential analysis of Popoloca (alternative 2)

tači$^?$na	[sex = m & generation = 2]
nači$^?$na	[sex = f & generation = 2]
$^?$apanaa1	[sex = m & generation last link = 1 & generation = 1]
$^?$qapanaa2	[sex = m & generation = 1 & lineality = lin]
$^?$amanaa1	[sex = f & generation last link = 1 & generation = 1]
$^?$amanaa2	[sex = f & generation = 1 & lineality = lin]
s$^?$onaa	[sex = m & generation last link = 0 & generation = 0]
thakhoonaa	[sex = f & generation last link = 0 & generation = 0]
ča$^?$na	[generation = −1 & lineality = lin]
čand$^?$inaa	[generation = −2 & lineality = lin]
ci$^?$ninaa1	[sex = m & generation last link = 0 & generation = 1]
ci$^?$ninaa2	[sex = m & generation = 1 & lineality = coll]
khva$^?$naa1	[sex = f & generation last link = 0 & generation = 1]
khva$^?$naa2	[sex = f & generation = 1 & lineality = coll]
čauv$^?$e	[generation last link = −1 & lineality = coll]

166

Table 4.22 Simplest componential analysis of Popoloca (alternative 3)

tači²na	[sex = m & generation last link = 1 & distance = 2]
nači²na	[sex = f & generation last link = 1 & distance = 2]
²apanaa	[sex = m & generation last link = 1 & distance = 1]
²amanaa	[sex = f & generation last link = 1 & distance = 1]
s²onaa	[sex = m & generation last link = 0 & distance = 1]
thakhoonaa	[sex = f & generation last link = 0 & distance = 1]
ča²na	[generation last link = −1 & distance = 1]
čand²inaa	[generation 1st link = −1 & distance = 2]
či²ninaa	[sex = m & generation last link = 0 & distance = 2]
khva²naa	[sex = f & generation last link = 0 & distance = 2]
čauv²e	[generation 1st link =≥ 0 & generation last link = −1]

Table 4.23 Simplest componential analysis of Popoloca (alternative 4)

tači²na	[sex = m & generation = 2]
nači²na	[sex = f & generation = 2]
²apanaa	[sex = m & generation = 1 & distance = 1]
²amanaa	[sex = f & generation = 1 & distance = 1]
s²onaa	[sex = m & generation = 0 & distance = 1]
thakhoonaa	[sex = f & generation = 0 & distance = 1]
ča²na	[generation = −1 & distance = 1]
čand²inaa	[generation 1st link = −1 & generation = −2]
či²ninaa	[sex = m & generation = 1 & distance = 2]
khva²naa	[sex = f & generation = 1 & distance = 2]
čauv²e	[generation 1st link =≥ 0 & generation =≤ 0 & distance =≥ 2]

Table 4.24 Simplest componential analysis of Popoloca (alternative 5)

tači²na	[sex = m & generation last link = 1 & distance = 2]
nači²na	[sex = f & generation last link = 1 & distance = 2]
²apanaa	[sex = m & generation last link = 1 & distance = 1]
²amanaa	[sex = f & generation last link = 1 & distance = 1]
s²onaa	[sex = m & generation last link = 0 & distance = 1]
thakhoonaa	[sex = f & generation last link = 0 & distance = 1]
ča²na	[generation last link = −1 & distance = 1]
čand²inaa	[generation last link = −1 & distance = 2 & lineality = lin]
či²ninaa	[sex = m & generation last link = 0 & distance = 2]
khva²naa	[sex = f & generation last link = 0 & distance = 2]
čauv²e	[generation last link = −1 & lineality = coll]

Table 4.25 Simplest componential analysis of Popoloca (alternative 6)

tači$^?$na	[sex = m & generation = 2]
nači$^?$na	[sex = f & generation = 2]
$^?$apanaa	[sex = m & generation = 1 & lineality = lin]
$^?$amanaa	[sex = f & generation = 1 & lineality = lin]
s$^?$onaa	[sex = m & distance = 1 & lineality = coll]
thakhoonaa	[sex = f & distance = 1 & lineality = coll]
ča$^?$na	[generation = -1 & lineality = lin]
čand$^?$inaa	[generation = -2 & lineality = lin]
či$^?$ninaa	[sex = m & generation = 1 & lineality = coll]
khva$^?$naa	[sex = f & generation = 1 & lineality = coll]
čauv$^?$e	[generation = ≤ 0 & distance = ≥ 2 & lineality = coll]

Table 4.26 Simplest componential analysis of Huave (alternative 1)

šéèč	[affinity 1st link = cons & sex 2nd link = m & generation last link = 1 & distance = 2]
nčéy	[affinity 1st link = cons & sex 2nd link = f & generation last link = 1 & distance = 2]
téàt	[sex 1st link = m & generation last link = 1 & distance = 1]
mí m	[sex 1st link = f & generation last link = 1 & distance = 1]
kóh	[seniority = y & affinity 1st link = cons & generation last link = 0 & distance = 1]
čîg	[seniority = e & affinity 1st link = cons & generation last link = 0 & distance = 1]
kwál	[generation last link = -1]
ntáh	[sex 1st link = f & affinity 1st link = aff & distance = 1]
òkwáàc	[sex 1st link = f & affinity 1st link = aff & generation last link = 1]
nòh	[sex 1st link = m & affinity 1st link = aff & distance = 1]
píw	[sex 1st link = m & affinity 1st link = aff & generation last link = 1]
kùnyádà	[generation last link = 0 & distance = 2]
híy	[distance = 3]

Table 4.27 Simplest componential analysis of Huave (alternative 2)

šéèč	[affinity 1st link = cons & sex = m & generation last link = 1 & distance = 2]
nčéy	[affinity 1st link = cons & sex = f & generation last link = 1 & distance = 2]
téàt	[sex = m & generation last link = 1 & distance = 1]
mí m	[sex = f & generation last link = 1 & distance = 1]
kóh	[seniority = y & affinity 1st link = cons & generation last link = 0 & distance = 1]
čîg	[seniority = e & affinity 1st link = cons & generation last link = 0 & distance = 1]
kwál	[generation last link = -1]
ntáh	[affinity 1st link = aff & sex = f & distance = 1]
òkwáàc	[sex 1st link = f & affinity 1st link = aff & generation last link = 1]
nòh	[affinity 1st link = aff & sex = m & distance = 1]
píw	[sex 1st link = m & affinity 1st link = aff & generation last link = 1]
kùnyádà	[generation last link = 0 & distance = 2]
híy	[distance = 3]

168

Table 4.28　Simplest componential analysis of Huave (alternative 3)

šéèč	[sex 2nd link = m & generation = 2]
nčéy	[sex 2nd link = f & generation = 2]
téàt	[sex 1st link = m & generation = 1 & distance = 1]
mí m	[sex 1st link = f & generation = 1 & distance = 1]
kóh	[seniority = y & affinity 1st link = cons & generation = 0 & distance = 1]
čîg	[seniority = e & affinity 1st link = cons & generation = 0 & distance = 1]
kwál	[generation = − 1]
ntáh	[sex 1st link = f & affinity 1st link = aff & distance = 1]
òkwáàc	[sex 1st link = f & generation = 1 & distance = 2]
nòh	[sex 1st link = m & affinity 1st link = aff & distance = 1]
píw	[sex 1st link = m & generation = 1 & distance = 2]
kùnyádà	[generation = 0 & distance = 2]
híy	[distance = 3]

Table 4.29　Simplest componential analysis of Huave (alternative 4)

šéèč	[sex = m & generation = 2]
nčéy	[sex = f & generation = 2]
téàt	[sex = m & generation = 1 & distance = 1]
mí m	[sex = f & generation = 1 & distance = 1]
kóh	[seniority = y & affinity 1st link = cons & generation = 0 & distance = 1]
číìg	[seniority = e & affinity 1st link = cons & generation = 0 & distance = 1]
kwál	[generation = − 1]
ntáh	[affinity 1st link = aff & sex = f & distance = 1]
òkwáàc	[sex 1st link = f & generation = 1 & distance = 2]
nòh	[affinity 1st link = aff & sex = m & distance = 1]
píw	[sex 1st link = m & generation = 1 & distance = 2]
kùnyádà	[generation = 0 & distance = 2]
híy	[distance = 3]

Table 4.30　Simplest componential analysis of Huave (alternative 5)

šéèč	[sex 2nd link = m & generation = 2]
nčéy	[sex 2nd link = f & generation = 2]
téàt	[sex 1st link = m & generation = 1 & distance = 1]
mí m	[sex 1st link = f & generation = 1 & distance = 1]
kóh	[seniority = y & affinity last link = cons & generation = 0 & distance = 1]
čîg	[seniority = e & affinity last link = cons & generation = 0 & distance = 1]
kwál	[generation = − 1]
ntáh	[sex 1st link = f & affinity last link = aff & distance = 1]
òkwáàc	[sex 1st link = f & generation = 1 & distance = 2]
nòh	[sex 1st link = m & affinity last link = aff & distance = 1]
píw	[sex 1st link = m & generation = 1 & distance = 2]
kùnyádà	[generation = 0 & distance = 2]
híy	[distance = 3]

Table 4.31 Simplest componential analysis of Huave (alternative 6)

šéèč	[sex = m & generation = 2]
nčéy	[sex = f & generation = 2]
téàt	[sex = m & generation = 1 & distance = 1]
mí m	[sex = f & generation = 1 & distance = 1]
kóh	[seniority = y & affinity last link = cons & generation = 0 & distance = 1]
čîg	[seniority = e & affinity last link = cons & generation = 0 & distance = 1]
kwál	[generation = − 1]
ntáh	[sex = f & affinity last link = aff & distance = 1]
òkwáàc	[sex 1st link = f & generation = 1 & distance = 2]
nòh	[sex = m & affinity last link = aff & distance = 1]
píw	[sex 1st link = m & generation = 1 & distance = 2]
kùnyádà	[generation = 0 & distance = 2]
híy	[distance = 3]

Table 4.32 Simplest componential analysis of Huave (alternative 7)

šéèč	[sex 2nd link = m & distance = 2 & affinity = cons]
nčéy	[sex 2nd link = f & distance = 2 & affinity = cons]
téàt	[sex 1st link = m & generation last link = 1 & distance = 1]
mí m	[sex 1st link = f & generation last link = 1 & distance = 1]
kóh	[seniority = y & generation last link = 0 & affinity = cons]
čîg	[seniority = e & generation last link = 0 & affinity = cons]
kwál	[generation last link = − 1]
ntáh	[sex 1st link = f & distance = 1 & affinity = aff]
òkwáàc	[sex 1st link = f & generation last link = 1 & distance = 2 & affinity = aff]
nòh	[sex 1st link = m & distance = 1 & affinity = aff]
píw	[sex 1st link = m & generation last link = 1 & distance = 2 & affinity = aff]
kùnyádà	[generation last link = 0 & distance = 2]
híy	[distance = 3]

Table 4.33 Simplest componential analysis of Huave (alternative 8)

šéèč	[sex = m & distance = 2 & affinity = cons]
nčéy	[sex = f & distance = 2 & affinity = cons]
téàt	[sex = m & generation last link = 1 & distance = 1]
mí m	[sex = f & generation last link = 1 & distance = 1]
kóh	[seniority = y & generation last link = 0 & affinity = cons]
čîìg	[seniority = e & generation last link = 0 & affinity = cons]
kwál	[generation last link = − 1]
ntáh	[sex = f & distance = 1 & affinity = aff]
òkwáàc	[sex 1st link = f & generation last link = 1 & distance = 2 & affinity = aff]
nòh	[sex = m & distance = 1 & affinity = aff]
píw	[sex 1st link = m & generation last link = 1 & distance = 2 & affinity = aff]
kùnyádà	[generation last link = 0 & distance = 2]
híy	[distance = 3]

Table 4.34 Simplest componential analysis of Huave (alternative 9)

šéèč	[sex 2nd link = m & generation = 2]
nčéy	[sex 2nd link = f & generation = 2]
téàt	[sex 1st link = m & generation = 1 & affinity = cons]
mí m	[sex 1st link = f & generation = 1 & affinity = cons]
kóh	[seniority = y & generation = 0 & affinity = cons]
čîg	[seniority = e & generation = 0 & affinity = cons]
kwál	[generation = − 1]
ntáh	[sex 1st link = f & distance = 1 & affinity = aff]
òkwáàc	[sex 1st link = f & generation = 1 & affinity = aff]
nòh	[sex 1st link = m & distance = 1 & affinity = aff]
píw	[sex 1st link = m & generation = 1 & affinity = aff]
kùnyádà	[generation = 0 & distance = 2]
híy	[distance = 3]

Table 4.35 Simplest componential analysis of Huave (alternative 10)

šéèč	[sex = m & generation = 2]
nčéy	[sex = f & generation = 2]
téàt	[sex = m & generation = 1 & affinity = cons]
mí m	[sex = f & generation = 1 & affinity = cons]
kóh	[seniority = y & generation = 0 & affinity = cons]
čîg	[seniority = e & generation = 0 & affinity = cons]
kwál	[generation = − 1]
ntáh	[sex = f & distance = 1 & affinity = aff]
òkwáàc	[sex 1st link = f & generation = 1 & affinity = aff]
nòh	[sex = m & distance = 1 & affinity = aff]
píw	[sex 1st link = m & generation = 1 & affinity = aff]
kùnyádà	[generation = 0 & distance = 2]
híy	[distance = 3]

Table 4.36 Analysed languages and number of their alternative dimension sets and componential models

Language	No. of dimension sets	No. of simplest dimension sets	No. of simplest componential models
English	1	1	1
Swedish	14	2	2
Irish	4	1	1
Spanish	18	1	1
Polish	15	2	2
Czech	18	1	1
Persian	6	1	1
Albanian	6	3	3
Armenian	36	1	1
Turkish	14	4	4
Seneca	1	1	1
Zapotec	8	1	1
Popoloca	12	6	6
Huave	14	10	10
Bulgarian	4	1	1

Bibliography

Assiter, A. (1984) 'Althusser and structuralism'. *The British Journal of Sociology*, 35: 272–96.

Barbolova, Z. (2000) 'Nazvanija za 'zălva' i 'dever' v bălgarskite dialekti'. In *Za dumite i rečnicite. Leksikografski i leksikoložki četenija'98*, pp. 391–9 (Sofia).

Bălgarski tălkoven rečnik (1973) (Sofia: Izdatelstvo Nauka i izkustvo).

Bernard, H. R. (2011) *Research Methods in Anthropology*, 4th edition (Lanham, MD: AltaMira Press).

Bhargava, M. and J. Lambek (1992) 'A production grammar for Sanskrit kinship terminology'. *Theoretical Linguistics*, 18: 45–60.

Bhargava, M. and J. Lambek (1995) 'A rewrite system of the Western Pacific: Lounsbury's analysis of Trobriand kinship terminology'. *Theoretical Linguistics*, 21: 241–53.

Blust, R. (1994) 'Austronesian sibling terms and culture history'. In A. Pawley and M. D. Ross (eds.) *Austronesian Terminologies: Continuity and Change*, pp. 31–72 (Pacific Linguistics, Canberra: Australian National University Press).

Boyd, J. P., J. H. Haehl and L. D. Seiler (1972) 'Kinship systems and inverse semigroups'. *The Journal of Mathematical Sociology*, 2: 37–61.

Burling, R. (1964) 'Cognition and componential analysis: God's truth or hocus-pocus?' *American Anthropologist*, 66: 20–8.

Burling, R. (1965) 'Burmese kinship terminology'. *American Anthropologist*, 67, Part 2: 106–17.

Chang, Ch.-L. and R. Ch.-T. Lee (1973) *Symbolic Logic and Mechanical Theorem Proving* (New York: Academic Press).

Cherry, C., M. Halle and R. Jakobson (1953) 'Toward the logical description of languages in their phonemic aspect'. *Language*, 29: 34–47.

Choi, G.-J. (1997) 'Viewpoint shifting in Korean and Bulgarian: the use of kinship terms'. *Pragmatics*, 7: 389–95.

Comrie, B. and G. Corbett (eds.) (1993) *The Slavonic Languages* (London and New York: Routledge).

Epling, P. J., J. Kirk and J. P. Boyd (1973) 'Genetic relations of Polynesian sibling terminologies'. *American Anthropologist*, 75: 1596–1625.

Fox, J. J. (1994) 'Who's who in ego's generation: probing the semantics of Malayo-Polynesian kinship classification'. In A. Pawley and M. D. Ross (eds.) *Austronesian Terminologies: Continuity and Change*, pp. 127–40 (Pacific Linguistics, Canberra: Australian National University Press).

Frake, C. O. (1962) 'Cultural ecology and ethnography'. *American Anthropologist*, 64: 53–9.

Frake, C. O. (1964) 'Further discussion of Burling'. *American Anthropologist*, 66: 119.

Frisch, J. A. and N. W. Schutz, Jr. (1967) 'Componential analysis and semantic reconstruction: the Proto Central Yuman kinship system'. *Ethnology*, 6: 272–93.

Gălăbov, I. (1986) 'Za proizhoda na grupa nazvanija ot bălgarskata narodna terminologija'. In *Izbrani trudove po ezikoznanie*, pp. 472–83 (Sofia: Nauka i izkustvo).

Geeraerts, D. (2010) *Theories of Lexical Semantics* (Oxford: Oxford University Press).

Gerov, N. (1897) *Rečnik na bălgarskii ezik*, vol.2 (Plovdiv).

Goodenough, W. H. (1956) 'Componential analysis and the study of meaning'. *Language*, 32: 195–216.

Goodenough, W. H. (1964) 'Componential analysis of Könkämä Lapp kinship terminology'. In W. H. Goodenough (ed.) *Explorations in Cultural Anthropology*, pp. 221–38 (New York: McGraw-Hill).

Goodenough, W. H. (1965) 'Yankee kinship terminology: a problem in componential analysis'. *American Anthropologist*, 67, Part 2: 259–87.

Goodenough, W. H. (1967) 'Componential analysis'. *Science*, 156: 1203–9.

Greenberg, J. H. (1949) 'The logical analysis of kinship'. *Philosophy of Science*, 16: 58–94.

Greenberg, J. H. (1966) *Language Universals (with Special Reference to Feature Hierarchies)* (The Hague: Mouton & Co).

Greenberg, J. H. (1980) 'Universals of kinship terminology'. In J. Maquet (ed.) *On Linguistic Anthropology: Essays in Honor of Harry Hoijer*, pp. 9–32 (Malibu: Udena Publications).

Hammel, E. A. (1964) 'Further comment on componential analysis'. *American Anthropologist*, 66: 1167–71.

Hammel, E. A. (ed.) (1965) *Formal Semantic Analysis*. Special Issue of *American Anthropologist*, 67, Part 2.

Hymes, D. (1964) 'Discussion of Burling's paper ('Cognition and componential analysis: God's truth or hocus-pocus?'). *American Anthropologist*, 66: 116–19.

Kay, P. (1974) 'On the form of dictionary rules: English kinship semantics'. In C.-J. N. Bailey and R. Shuy (eds.) *Toward Tomorrow's Linguistics*, pp. 120–38 (Washington DC: Georgetown University Press).

Kay, P. (1975) 'The generative analysis of kinship semantics: a reanalysis of the Seneca data'. *Foundations of Language*, 13: 201–14.

Kroeber, A. L. (1909) 'Classificatory systems of relationship'. *Journal of the Royal Anthropological Institute*, 39: 77–84.

Kronenfeld, D. B. (1974) 'Sibling terminology: beyond Nerlove and Romney'. *American Ethnologist*, 30: 263–7.

Kronenfeld, D. B. (1976) 'Computer analysis of skewed kinship terminologies'. *Language*, 52: 891–918.

Leech, G. (1974) *Semantics* (Harmondsworth: Penguin).

Lounsbury, F. G. (1956) 'A semantic analysis of the Pawnee kinship usage'. *Language*, 32: 158–94.

Lounsbury, F. G. (1964) 'The structural analysis of kinship semantics'. In H. Lunt (ed.) *Proceedings of the 9th International Congress of Linguists*, pp. 1073–90 (The Hague: Mouton).

Lounsbury, F. G. (1965) 'Another view of the Trobriand kinship categories'. In E. A. Hammel (ed.) *Formal Semantic Analysis*, Special Issue of *American Anthropologist*, 67, Part 2: 142–85.

Malinowski, B. (1929) *The Sexual Life of Savages* (New York: Harcourt, Brace and World).

Marinov, D. (1892) *Živa starina. Etnografsko (folklorno) izučavane na Vidinsko, Kulsko, Belogradčiško, Lomsko, Berkovsko, Orjahovsko i Vidinsko* (Russe).

McGregor, W. (1996) 'Dyadic and polyadic kin terms in Gooniyandi'. *Anthropological Linguistics*, 38: 216–47.

Mladenov, St. (1979[1929]) *Geschichte der bulgarischen Sprache* (Berlin und Leipzig: Walter de Gruyter & Co.) [Translated by I. Duridanov, *Istorija na bălgarskija ezik*. Sofia: Izdatelstvo na bălgarskata akademija na naukite.]

Morgan, L. H. (1871) *Systems of Consanguinity and Affinity of the Human Family* (Washington: Smithsonian Institution).

Murdock, G. P. (1949) *Social Structure* (New York: Macmillan).

Nakao, K. and A. K. Romney (1984) 'A method for testing alternative theories: an example from English'. *American Anthropologist*, 86: 668–73.

Neisser, U. (1967) *Cognitive Psychology* (New York: Appleton, Century Crofts).

Nerlove, S. and A. K. Romney (1967) 'Sibling terminology and cross-sex behavior'. *American Anthropologist*, 69: 179–87.

Nida, E. (1969) 'Science of translation'. *Language*, 45: 483–98.

Nogle, L. (1974) *Method and Theory in Semantics and Cognition of Kinship Terminology* (The Hague: Mouton).

Noricks, J. S. (1987) 'Testing for cognitive validity: componential analysis and the question of extensions'. *American Anthropologist*, 89: 424–38.

Pericliev, V. (2010) *Machine-Aided Linguistic Discovery: An Introduction and Some Examples* (London and Oakville: Equinox).

Pericliev, V. and R. Valdés-Pérez (1998) 'Automatic componential analysis of kinship semantics with a proposed structural solution to the problem of multiple models'. *Anthropological Linguistics*, 40: 272–317.

Read, W. D. (1984) 'An algebraic account of the American kinship terminology'. *Current Anthropology*, 25: 417–50.

Read, W. D. (2000) 'Formal analysis of kinship terminologies and its relationship to what constitutes kinship' (Complete text), *Mathematical Anthropology and Cultural Theory*, http://www.sbbay.com.

Read, W. D. and C. A. Behrens (1990a) 'KAES: an expert system for the algebraic analysis of kinship terminologies'. *Journal of Quantitative Anthropology*, 2: 353–93.

Read, W. D. and C. A. Behrens (1990b) 'Computer representation of cultural constructs: new research tools of the study of kinship systems'. In M. Boone and J. Wood (eds.) *Computer Applications in Anthropology*, pp. 228–50 (Belmont, CA: Wadsworth Publishing Company).

Romney, A. K. (1967) 'Kinship and family'. In R. Wauchope (ed.) *Handbook of Middle American Indians: vol. VI, Social Anthropology* (Austin: University of Texas).

Romney, A. K. and R. G. D'Andrade (1964) 'Cognitive aspects of English kin terms'. *American Anthropologist*, 66: 146–70.

Rose, M. D. and A. K. Romney (1979) 'Cognitive pluralism or individual differences: a comparison of alternative models of American English kin terms'. *American Ethnologist*, 6: 752–62.

de Saussure, F. (1996[1916]) *Course in General Linguistics*, edited by Ch. Bally and A. Sechehaye, with the collaboration of Albert Riedlinger, translated and annotated by Roy Harris (Chicago and La Salle, ILL: Open Court).

Schneider, D. M. (1965) 'American kin terms and terms for kinsmen: a critique of Goodenough's componential analysis of Yankee kinship terminology'. In E. A. Hammel (ed.) *Formal Semantic Analysis*, Special Issue of *American Anthropologist*, 67: 288–306.

Sheffler, H. and Lounsbury, F. G. (1971) *A Study of Structural Semantics: The Siriono Kinship System* (Englewood Cliffs, NJ: Prentice-Hall).

Spencer, A. (1996) *Phonology: Theory and Description* (Oxford: Blackwell Publishers).

Stoeva, A. (1972) 'Njakoi semantični osobenosti pri rodninskite nazvanija'. *Bălgariski ezik*, 22: 73–6.

Stojkov, St. (1993[1962]) *Bălgariska dialektologija* (Sofia: Izdatelstvo na Bălgariskata akademija na naukite).

Dum-Tragut, J. (2009) *Armenian: Modern Eastern Armenian* (Amsterdam: John Benjamins).

Wallace, A. F. C. (1965) 'The problem of psychological validity of componential analyses'. In E. A. Hammel (ed.) *Formal Semantic Analysis*, Special Issue of *American Anthropologist*, 67: 231–48.

Wallace, A. F. C. (1970) 'A relational analysis of American kinship terminology'. *American Anthropologist*, 72: 841–5.

Wallace, A. F. C. and J. Atkins (1960) 'The meaning of kinship terms'. *American Anthropologist*, 62: 58–80.

Wexler, K. N. and A. K. Romney (1972) 'Individual variation in cognitive structures'. In A. K. Romney, A. Shepard and S. Nerlove (eds.) *Multidimensional Scaling: Theory and Applications in the Behavioral Sciences*, vol. 2, pp. 73–92 (New York: Seminar Press).

Wierzbicka, A. (1991) 'Kinship semantics: lexical universals as a key to psychological reality'. *Anthropological Linguistics*, 29:131–56.

Wierzbicka, A. (1992) *Semantics, Culture and Cognition: Universal Human Concepts in Culture-Specific Configurations* (New York and Oxford: Oxford University Press).

Woolford, E. (1984) 'Universals and rule options in kinship terminology: a synthesis of three formal approaches'. *American Ethnologist*, 11: 771–90.

Wordick, F. J. (1973) 'Another view of American kinship'. *American Anthropologist*, 31: 1634–56.

Index